mother on fire

Also by Sandra Tsing Loh

A Year in Van Nuys

If You Lived Here, You'd Be Home by Now

Depth Takes a Holiday

Aliens in America

mother on fire

A True Motherf%#$@ Story
About Parenting!

Sandra Tsing Loh

Crown Publishers
New York

CROWN and the Crown colophon are registered trademarks of
Random House, Inc.

Library of Congress Cataloging-in-Publication Data

Loh, Sandra Tsing.
Mother on fire / Sandra Tsing Loh.—1st ed.
p. cm.
1. Loh, Sandra Tsing.   2. Authors, American—20th century—Biography.
3. Authors, American—21st century—Biography.   4. Middle-aged women—
United States—Biography.   5. Middle-aged mothers—United States—
Biography.   6. Midlife crisis—Humor.   I. Title.

PS3562.O459Z46 2008
818'.6—dc22   2008000496
[B]

ISBN 978-0-609-60813-5

Printed in the United States of America

DESIGN BY ELINA D. NUDELMAN

10 9 8 7 6 5 4 3

First Edition

For my mother, whose belly — for various reasons — always burned

Author's Note

This is a true story, in the sense that the major plot points—the ones that seem almost too absurd to have happened—actually happened. To protect the privacy of the innocent, however, I have changed the names and certain details about some of the characters and places featured in my tale, and in some cases created character composites based on two or more real people. Although my story is real, I have in some cases embellished the dialogue by approximating what was said to me; in other cases, I made up the dialogue to facilitate the telling of my story. I have also taken some liberties with things like Joy Behar's sarongwear and the exact details of John Steinbeck's daily writing schedule but feel quite sure people like Mr. Steinbeck, at this point anyway, will not mind. If the guilty feel composites have been invented that are uncomfortably close to real life, seeming to somehow "finger" them, well oi for the punx! And enjoy.

Contents

contents

Mother on fire

1

The War Room

This is a story about the year I exploded into flames.

Which turns out to be more common than you'd think, among forty-something humans. Yea, we can hold it together in our thirties, with a raft of hair products and semi-tall nonfat half-caf beverages and much brisk walking to a lot of interesting appointments.

Come the forties, though, cracks begin to appear. One staggers suddenly along life's path; gourmet coffee splats; the wig slips askew.

In other words, my friends, THE WHEELS COME OFF. Whatever vehicle you were so confidently hurtling along in in Act One of your life, that sped you to age twenty-six, thirty-four, thirty-nine . . . even forty-two? Yea, that buggy will skitter sideways into a ditch, flip over, burst into flames; firemen will have to use the Jaws of Life to get you out. And if you do not find another car to climb into, well . . .

"Look at Anna Karenina!" I remember exhorting my female writing students at Marymount College, spreading my arms wide, and expansively. The Rebecca A. Mirman Chair of Creative Writing— this was my Second Act, the sudden forgiving windfall of a plum teaching job, complete with a year's worth of truly excellent health insurance, and I played it to the hilt, never mind that I was sweating a lot. Even trying to figure out the faculty parking made me sweat. Anyway, I'd been trying to describe the difference between metaphor and metonymy, how Anna Karenina's little red handbag sitting by the side of the train tracks does not "symbolize" her but actually "is" her, which is to say it STANDS for her, in the manner of a linguistic SIGN . . .

When all at once I heard myself veer off into a tangent about how depressed I am that over and over I read that novel, year after year, and things never turn out better for Anna. By my count, the last time Anna is happy is on page seventy-six out of a five-hundred-page tome. She peaks at the ball, where she dances with Count Vronsky— and it's not even during the WHOLE ball—it's not during the waltz, the gavotte, the schottische, or the fox-trot but in particular during . . . the MAZURKA.

That's how it was for women in those days, it was all about the MAZURKA—

And then, inevitably, the MAZURKA ends and now come four hundred pages of falling action, of dragging tediously around Europe with Vronsky, consuming all those carbs together, putting on weight, particularly around the neck (with a potato-based diet, all the weight for those Russians would certainly fly to the neck). It's all about overpriced English baby prams and go-nowhere piazza remodeling projects in Italy (It is! Reread it! Feel free to skip the endless Levin/wheat farming parts, I always do), modern plots for women in the post–Jane Austen/*Pride and Prejudice*/Elizabeth Bennet era boiling down to just four words:

NO MORE MR. DARCY

Indeed—with sudden inspiration, I turned and wrote, in giant letters on the board:

MR.
DARCY

And then I drew a circle AROUND and a diagonal slash THROUGH Mr. Darcy, as one might on a verboten NO FUMAR sign at the train station of life.

"Portrait of the narrative in the postfeminist age?"

And I felt my Marymount College girls actually shrink, and gasp.

"But that's what true liberation of the soul means!" I cried out, smacking my chalk triumphantly on the board, like a teeny tiny épée. "It's not like you put on your 'Save Darfur' T-shirt, march ... and then go home to Mr. Darcy ..."

At which point we entered a brief conversational *snorl* in which one of the girls argued that HER Mr. Darcy might well encourage her to march, as long as she went home every night to Mr. Darcy's estate at Pemberley, which she felt she could live with. Another imagined she could share a tent with HER Mr. Darcy in Darfur, perhaps Mr. Darcy was even the co-organizer of the Save Darfur effort . . . And now imagining the safari wear, the eco-carbon credits, and the tangle of yellow rubber Lance Armstrong bracelets, I was struck with a distinct, dismal Jane-Austen-novel-remade-as-a-summer-cable-TV-movie-starring-Matthew-McConaughey feeling. No!

"What I'm saying is, no matter what you do, at age forty . . . THE WHEELS COME OFF!

A pierced-nose student in a Frida Kahlo muscle T clarified it for her more flighty, foolish sisters: "She means for women, at forty, the TRAINING WHEELS come off—"

"No!" I yelled. My upper lip was beaded with moisture, the room felt so hot. "THE WHEELS OF YOUR CAR! THEY SIMPLY! COME! OFF!"

The tragedy for Anna Karenina, of course, is that she lived in St. Petersburg in the 1870s rather than America in the 2000s. One no longer has to hurl oneself under a train upon turning forty—there is medication for that. No, nowadays forty and all the ages like forty (which apparently can range up to fifty-two or even sixty-one) are a mystical opportunity to begin an inward journey of fabulous *wisdoming*. (On the back of a tea packet I saw it recently, used as a verb: "Wisdoming." Even the prose of our herbal tea nowadays is amazing!) No, with proper hormonal and nutritional supplements, and a full tasting menu of Pfizer antidepressants, it's no longer necessarily a bad thing, this bursting-into-flames, this midlife "transition," this second adolescence—

(Well, perhaps for the men it is bad, particularly for those who've already managed to live THEIR ENTIRE ADULT LIVES in a state of adolescence, and here I am thinking not of Count Vronsky of Russia but of my ex-boyfriend of Culver City, Count Bruce.)

Forty-something women, though—this kicking off of their calcified/thirty-something/Gail Sheehy/*Passages* lobster shells is the golden time. By God, they've EARNED their raucous "You go, girl!"s, their giddy high-fives with somewhat flabby upper arms (upon which shudder bold temporary tattoos), their raspberry-flavored tequila shots, their "Woo woo!"s gaily Dopplering out the back of the speeding-off Mustang. Lord love 'em, they deserve escape, these sparkle-eyed, plus-aged women, and makeovers, and perhaps a fashion spree, or at least a mad, buffalo-sized wicker basket of wildflower soaps, raffia twine tumbling everywhere amid a crazy menagerie of rose petals and tiny mad bottles of lotion . . . AROMATHERAPY LITERALLY UNBOUND.

Yea, these women deserve it all, so long have they plowed in the arid fields of their marriages, with dull oxen husbands, in that ceaseless drumbeat of domestic tedium. Divorce is tragic . . . but becomes a bold new start as, wiping tears, our heroine manages to pack just the one overnight bag and grab the red-eye to Portugal or Bali to live in a thatched-roof beach hut and feel the sand in her toes and wear a sarong and drink sangria and have a hot affair with a poetry-writing swordfisherman named Paolo who helps her shed her puritanical type A ways and teaches her about the tides. Come midnight, they tear off her bra and BURN it, howling, like wine-drunk Santa Fe coyotes, up at the stars!

Or at least that was how the forties were being rapturously described in the book I fell asleep on, my face smashed into the spine, on the night my year of fire began.

The book in question was the lush midlife literary romance *28 Beads*. It was an Oprah pick, and supposedly ideal book-to-fall-asleep-by—all the female hosts on all the morning shows were reading it. *28 Beads* had inspired new lines of scents, tropical marinades, wraparound sarongs (I had never seen Joy Behar in a sarong—it was quite a revelation). I had been so swept away by the fantasy, I myself had just placed twin swordfish filets on the grill, squeezed on a rhapsodic amount of lemon, hiked up my white caftan pants, and in fact was just preparing to wade into the ocean, Paolo waving at me from beyond, under a giant blue cyclorama with puffy white clouds— (And that should have been the tip-off—that sky was much too blue . . .)

When my eyes popped robotically open in my familiar stiflingly close bedroom, much like Linda Blair's in *The Exorcist*. The time: 2:07 A.M. Damn! Where was MY fab world-traveling divorce? I thought. I have the miles (coach)! But no. Here I was, once again, waking up in the middle of my life . . . adventure-impaired.

Adventure? Me? In my forties? Where would I even start?

I sat up in the darkness, took a sip of warmish, even brackish, water out of a cartoon jelly glass.

I could start with feverishly burning my bra, sure. But that heady act of womyn's liberation was so much easier in yon freewheelin' Joni Mitchell days of olde, wasn't it? For me personally, a braflagration . . . that would take a full week because by now I have so damned many of them. Look at that unsorted pile of laundry, heaped like a dark hunchback on my dresser. Over the years, in a haze of Condé Nast confusion, I've bought—what?—"angel bras," "T-shirt bras," "Wonderbras," "Miracle Bras" . . . I have such a flotilla, I could make my own giant bra ball. The triumphant Carole King music would screech to a halt as I literally struggled to rope the bras together.

(I'm also not sure if the Miracle Bra would actually burn—bought in 1998, the Miracle has since disintegrated into a lone plastic strap upon which hang two lumpen cups of strange discolored polymer. It's Victoria's most poorly kept Secret.)

Of course, a bigger gravitational force holding me prisoner of un-Unspontaneity in un-Adventure land (a new un-Ride in un-Disneyland) are my two daughters. They are disproportionately young, ages two and four, because in the wacky postmodern jumble of things, I've happened to birth relatively late, like one of those *National Geographic* turtles who washes up gasping on the beach with her last leathery eggs. At my advanced age, it is all I can do to keep track of all the teeny-tiny slightly unmatched socks that flow past, along with all the pint-sized children with their teeny-tiny unmatched names (Colin, Cole, Corey, Coley, Colby). Which is why I refer to all children now as "Honey." I even refer to socks as "Honey."

Adding to that gravitational pull (ciao, Paolo!) is my partner for the past eighteen years—a nice man who is even, unfortunately, soulful. Mike plays guitar, grows tomatoes, bakes bread, and can chat about the tides all day long. A musician, the father of my children has failed to have the sort of heartless if bracingly lucrative career (corporate law, international banking, periodontal surgery) that would now fund defiant whirlwind travels for me in full flaming *Condé Nast Traveler* style. Picture the *soul* of Mr. Darcy with the *income* of Mr. Collins. (If you recall, Mr. Collins's wealth was in third place, behind Mr. Darcy and Mr. Bingley and even behind Mr. Collins's patroness, the insufferable Lady Catherine de Bourgh.)

In a way, though, these things are all a moot point. I can't run away to a tropical island, I'm very much needed right where I am, because . . .

Well . . . ?

Okay. Has it ever seemed to you like this planet we live on is a hairsbreadth from utterly exploding out of control? Has it? What's interesting is, you're right! And it turns out that hairsbreadth of restraint, that one lone figure with that one saving finger in the dike . . . is me.

And in the dead of night, when everyone else is asleep, that's when I personally check and re-check that all the burners are off on the world's stove.

It's similar to air travel. When I'm on a two-hour flight, I open my airline magazine to our route map and, usually up in the clear space around Alaska? I draw two circles, divide each pie into twelve slices, and carefully shade in each new slice every time another five minutes has gone by. See?

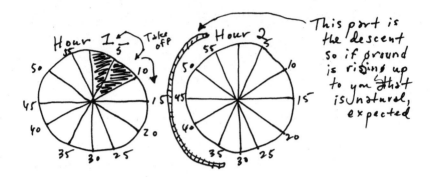

In this way, instead of helplessly "riding along" on the flight, I am actively, energetically "completing" the flight. I also make evenly spaced hash marks along our route and shade those in as well. (If it is available, I listen in to what our pilots are talking about in the cockpit, to ensure that they're "getting it.")

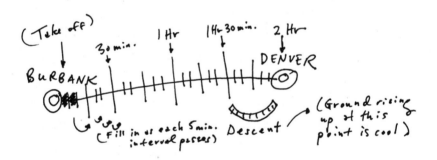

On arrival, I carefully replace the magazine in the seat pocket, so the next passenger can fly into a panic, realizing he is flying across the country with crazy people.

So—checking the current state of the entire world—let's get to it. I put my water glass down, swing my legs out of the bed, and go to work.

If he were awake, of course, Mike would get up and bar my path. Unlike myself, a nervous denizen of the city, Mike, from South Dakota, holds the quaint agrarian belief that the night hours are for sleeping, not angsting. It is Mike who proferred the idea that falling-asleep books should be calming, comforting . . . And, indeed, on his nightstand, which I'm passing right now, the happy moonlight (I picture a Man in the Moon playing a banjo) reveals a veritable boatload of Tom Sawyer–ish cheer. You have books about whaling adventures, bass fishing, how to cook meat, and of course, *Popular Mechanics*. Have you ever looked inside *Popular Mechanics*? (I have, in the bathroom—where it belongs.) *Popular Mechanics* will have a whole article on how an outdoor barbecue works, complete with fussy computer diagrams. Here is a steak! How does it heat? Grill? Convect? What IS convection? Does BACON convect?

That's why Mike himself bought me the *28 Beads* (which I've started referring to as *28 Beads and No Pants,* what with all the Tantric sex), on sale at Costco. He laid the book down before me and slowly backed away from it, with his hands up, saying: "Apparently it's a very popular women's book. For women." On the word *women,* he waggled his fingers, as though saying: "These are tampons. It's a women's thing. It's for women." (Or alternatively: "It's an Oprah book. Doctors recommend you insert this inspiring-female-journey-from-darkness-to-light into a medicated bath puff. Smear with aloe vera. It's a women's thing. For women.")

Mike wasn't bothered by the book being an escapist divorce romantic fantasy. Indeed, I can just picture my husband in my pulsing Caribbean dream, under that too-blue cinematic sky, a bit farther down the beach, in shorts and a baseball cap, cheerfully throwing a line into the water. (Like Paolo, Mike is an avid fisherman, although, from the Midwest, Mike likes to catch trout.) Yea, I can see Mike airily waving us on: "Sandra, Paolo, have fun this weekend! Read poetry to each other! Learn the macarena! Compare scents of different massage oils! Do all those girly vacation things you enjoy! While you're away, I'll turn these swordfish filets over for you. Although in my opinion, Sandra, you may have over-lemoned. But never mind, it's your dream—lemon these fish the way you like. However, whatever

ELSE you do in bed at two A.M.—" Here Mike's normally sunny snub-nosed face would darken: "Do not let me find you lying awake ANGSTING!"

Too bad for Mike, though. Look at him on his side of the bed, snoring contentedly away under his Qantas sleep mask. The man sleeps like a stone. So, in fact, he has no idea WHAT I do in the dead of night unless I snap on every light in the house, stand over his side of the bed, and shriek, "FUUUUUUUCK . . . YOUUUUUU!!!" Which I apparently used to do at four A.M. during the first year I was nursing, which, to be honest, I cannot remember. This is why, with the assistance of my therapist, Ruth, and my sister, Kaitlin, in a group intervention—essentially at Marital Gunpoint—Mike and I hammered out a Marital New Deal. A central tenet of the deal is that I, the mother, can be awake at two and I can be awake at five, but I am never to be awake at both two AND five. I am never to be awake while crossing the Delaware of four.

Anyway, so here I am wide awake at—what is it now?—2:17 A.M. Plenty of time! Mike's plaintive attempt to lobotomize me before bed with the *28 Beads* and some herbal tea (chamomile! "wisdoming!") has failed.

But Mike needn't have troubled himself. I am up at night alone, yes, but this is not angsting. Who could call this angsting?

Look at me here in the bathroom, serenely splashing water on my face . . . Which in the bad old days itself might have triggered its own queasy spiral. Hunched over the sink, looking at my reflection, I might have started to worry about my forehead worry lines. Or my eye bags. Or—?

No longer. That was in my angst-filled thirties.

Since turning fabulous forty, one of MY stipulations in our Marital New Deal was that Mike put dimmers on every light in the house. Not only is our house magically cleaner—it could be me or one of those Japanese bathtub harpies from *The Grudge* in that mirror—but I really can't tell.

More to the point, in my thirty-sixth year, tormented by my hound-dog eye bags, one day I just . . . whipped out that VISA and lazed them home. It was so guiltless, drive-thru quick, and (what with the Valium) enjoyable. Good Lord—why had I even waited? All those wasted years, why had I creamed, and lotioned, and—and angsted . . . ? Indeed, when the haze wore off, I stood right here before this bathroom counter . . . That busy, self-important cityscape of Clinique and Lancôme and Nivea, all those moisturizers, revital-izers, exfoliators, scrubs, washes, serums . . . And I suddenly saw it for what it was—an utter sham! With one sweep of my arm, I razed that drab, dusty shantytown down—I threw those jars and bottles and tubes into the trash, every single one!

Further, how good am I supposed to look at forty-two, anyway? Yes, I may look a bit wilted for the inner twenty-eight-year-old I always magically envision myself to be. Then again, do the math, you think: For almost fifty, hey, I look pretty good!

And anyway, who knows what sort of fantastical procedure the boomers will have pushed surgeons to invent by the year 2025? (Meg Ryan alone! She won't go so quietly!) Maybe I'll just sit this self-creaming rat race out for twenty years, take a "moisturizer and toner" sabbatical. Pick the baton up again when I'm sixty-five, when modern science will have invented some kind of zapper or peeler or stunner that can spray on an entirely new face, perhaps that of the young Cher! Or even Sonny! I got YOU, babe!

And the madness of owning a bathroom scale . . . Heavens to Pete, what was that all about? I can't believe it took me thirty years of step-ping on scales before it dawned on me that *even if I tried stepping on them for another thirty years, I was never going to get a good number.* No matter how gingerly I approach scales—how gently I try to waft over them, like a hummingbird, how much I, essentially, try not to wake these irritable digital beasts from their troubled slumbers—they always wake up and scream, "OW!"

And then at age thirty-seven, after a life of gingerly balancing, I became pregnant. I started gobbling Carl's Jr. burgers and orange-glazed pound cake. In my second trimester, intriguingly enough, I began channeling a squat Bavarian person (while I'm Chinese on my father's side, I'm German on my mother's) and hence was forced to consume ropes of knackwursts washed down by oom-pah-pah foods like Havarti and liverwurst on pumpernickel with cornichon pickles. You'd think I might try to start AVOIDING the scale, shielding the eyes, but no, a slave of habit, I kept mounting the scale like a breathless sailor ever higher atop a crow's nest, and thus began glimpsing exotic, never-before-seen lands in the already sensational world of Sandra Poundage, with amazing, surreal new numbers like 174, 186, 191! What was I doing? Where was this all heading? I would literally start JUMPING on the scale, like the fat lady in a sideshow, sort of CANNONBALLING onto it!

And people would STILL say, "Wow! You look great! So radiant!"

And the fact is, what with the forty-watt dimmers, the lazed-out eye bags, and the sensational poundage . . . and then a HoneyBaked Ham's worth of weight dropping off with the placenta (I ask you, in passing, what was THAT?)—

Well, I realize I have no idea what I look like anymore. And what does it matter? I'm no longer a nervous Young Ingenue in my twenties, or thirties (or even forties—we have forty-something ingenues nowadays, we do). No, I'm a Mother of Small Children, which is a great thing to be in this day and age. We M.O.S.C.'s are waved to the front of airport lines; we're pardoned from jury duty; we will boldly *wear anything* while we muscularly gas up our minivans at Shell. Wrinkled old T-shirts, our husband's sweatpants, flip-flops, scrunchies, a yellow Dora Band-Aid across our nose . . . sometimes all at the same time.

And society . . . condones this. It basically does. Look at this pair of black drawstring pants I'm wearing. Ten dollars. Target. These are ten-dollar black Target pants that balance perilously on culture's very mother-who-works-from-home fulcrum. Are they running pants? Exercise pants? Pajama pants? How could they be when, look, what is this here up the side? It's a racing stripe. A stripe that suggests at any moment I might burst into a jog! I haven't in years, but who knows?

And who is to blame for these ten-dollar Target drawstring pants? I believe that it is no less than Isaac Mizrahi. Yea, I'll have you know I yanked these ten-dollar black drawstring pants off a shiny red-and-silver Target rack underneath a giant poster of Isaac Mizrahi throwing back his head in a literal SHOUT of laughter. Isaac Mizrahi seemed tickled that some of us are chubby within, some of us are chubby without, and some of us mix and match our inner and outer chubbiness in cheery, colorful stripe-and-polka-dot combinations! I love Target!

Anyway! Thoroughly refreshed now, I'm ready to lie back in bed on TOP of the comforter (because even though the AC is cranked down to seventy-two, I'm schvitzing) . . .

And now that it is 2:42 A.M.—

I am now ready to do my relaxing, lull-myself-back-to-sleep visualization. Not the one my therapist, Ruth, always suggests, making slow circles with her large, turquoise-beringed hands, where you picture an orb with gentle waves of light pulsing off it—red, orange, yellow, gold, white—then the white deepens into sapphire and emerald and periwinkle, and just thinking about it, I get a throbbing headache. Or the one of sheep jumping over the fence Mike favors. No, the thing that has helped most was when Mike used to pat my hand and say, "Relax—you don't control the universe"—and I found that notion so UN-relaxing . . . I reversed it! Far easier to imagine I *do* control the universe, to imagine every night it is I and I alone who's responsible for tucking the world in. Because if I myself do it, I know the job will *get done*.

And watch how, using this calming visualization, I easily fall back asleep.

Which is to say, still lying on the comforter, I imagine myself now lifting the TV remote and aiming it not at our dusty television but toward THE CENTER OF THE HOUSE—which by weird feng shui ends up being a cramped little hallway. I squeeze Play, and out of the wooden floor a trapdoor drops open. *Shoom!* Stairs *click, click, click* open down to a cool, echoing, underground James Bond–style bunker, where we find . . .

My War Room.

Picture a vast circular U.N.-style table ringed by twenty leather swivel chairs, squeaking slightly in the breeze of the central air that is constantly humming to keep all the computer banks at their ideal cool temperatures. Each chair faces its own pitcher of water, yellow tablet, and neat row of black Razor Point pens.

Just beyond is the Big Grid, a map of the entire world, topped by clocks showing what time it is in all the different time zones.

And on the one hand, yes, some might feel it IS this utter marvel—madness even—that CONTROL OF THE ENTIRE WORLD has been placed into the hands of me, a forty-two-year-old teacher/mother/midlist book writer/public radio commentator/one-woman show purveyor/essentially literary jill-of-all-trades who can barely lift the two-inch-thick binder that supposedly describes our family's twelve-part PPO health insurance plan. But the truth is, at forty-two, I am old and clever and crafty. I have delegated quite a bit of this . . . Running of the World.

That's my secret: crafty delegation.

You see all those various foreign lands, whose signs on the wall perplexingly read "Kabul," "Malawi," "British Guinea"? Or is it "British Ghiana." "British Ghanea"? Damn. I saw some country with some name like that in the opening ceremony of the Athens Olympics and it has haunted me since. Fudge! It was a tiny land with just three ninety-pound athletes, in gold MC Hammer pants and toreador hats. Leaping over a javelin. Or curling. Closely followed by "Virgin Ghiana." Or is that an airline? A cocktail? I get so lost in this detail. Some mornings I'm so overwhelmed with detail, I can't even start the car. "British Guineah." (I'm still upset over the whole brand-new-pronunciation-of Beijing thing. "Bay jhingg . . . Bay jhingg . . ." Why?)

Anyway, regarding that whole sweep of foreign lands, knowing I'm bad with detail and geography, I've delegated all the foreign lands to NPR. In particular, to a raft of NPR correspondents who crisscross the globe with their constant murmurings. Somehow, in their inscrutable NPR way, they are getting the "foreign land" business done, or at least "maintaining" the chaos, because let's face it, the continent of Africa is never going to BE done.

I call them "my NPR contingent." I have Sylvia Pojole on it—she runs the meetings of NPR and its subsidiaries, which include the Peace Corps. And also the Gates Foundation. Gates money is involved. And Maria Shriver also has a mysterious hand in it. Via the United Way, Maria Shriver is always flying around the globe, fomenting a web of corporate/community partnership–type . . . thingies. It's a very bipartisan . . . watchamadoodle.

Next we have America, which is clearly chock-full o' problems, and . . .

I know it's an odd choice. But for the moment, I've delegated the worrying about America exclusively . . . to my ex-boyfriend-who-after-seven-years-was-still-not-quite-ready-to-commit-to-a-long-term-relationship, Bruce.

Which is to say Bruce has lots of free time to agonize over the horrible state of America because he's single. A child of the sixties, Bruce never wanted to encumber himself—to chain himself down to "The Grid"—by committing such conventional acts as actually owning, say, a bed. Of course, then one morning you wake up and realize YOU'RE FIFTY AND YOU DON'T HAVE AN ACTUAL BED. And who wants to sleep with you? No one. Not even crazy, divorced fifty-seven-year-old hippie chicks with four methamphetamine-lab-employee teenaged sons want to sleep with Bruce anymore. There was fish in a barrel, there was the bottom of the barrel, now there is no barrel.

And where does one go when there is no barrel? Where Bruce told me he went last week. To his monthly meeting, in Culver City, of Vegetarian Singles. (I mean, Vegetarian Singles. The whole idea. Where is the romance? "Listen, I hear that you . . . don't eat meat. How intriguing. What else don't you eat?" What kind of pickup lines does this suggest? "Meat has NOT been inside your body since WHO was president?")

With such exacting standards, Bruce is able to stay the way he says he wants to be: Free, Free, Free!

Well! Bruce may think he's single, but he does have a tortured, passionate, unrequited, lifelong relationship with . . . the Republicans. Bruce is obsessed with their evil, tracking it tirelessly, 24/7. Amateurs merely watch Jon Stewart, Stephen Colbert, and Keith Olbermann while continually monitoring all the blogs—Arianna Huffington, the Daily Kos, truthdig.com. But Bruce has been at it for decades. Do you know how far back his files stretch? The man has one hundred hours of old Iran Contra hearings . . . on Beta! That's how free he is!

Never mind that—like some unnamed prom queen of yore—the Republican Party seems completely unaware of Bruce's very existence. I don't believe a day goes by when Dick Cheney thinks about Bruce at all. But the rest of us have Bruce on our minds continually. How could we not, given his relentless Unabomber-like mass e-mails raving about how Bush stole ALL the elections—via the Electoral College . . . from Nader. ("Have you figured out how to unsubscribe?" "I can't—I try to hit Unsubscribe and then I get RE-subscribed three more times!") Still Bruce's e-mails come, as though it is we who yearn for them, thinking: "What I find frustrating about my quality of life is a worrisome lack of rabid political punditry. Thank heavens I got another five e-mails today from BRUCE!"

Or alternatively, "Never mind all the experts—let's see what

BRUCE has to say! Normally I'm not that interested in gerrymandering—except when my unemployed friend BRUCE, with absolutely no training in the law WHATSOEVER, e-mails me about it!"

GERRYMANDERING!

Oh no!

Now I have a crow.

If my Zen mind is a smooth white bluff, a Worry . . . a nagging Worry . . . That is what I think of as a black crow.

It's 2:59—dammit—and . . .

Well, I can't help it. Now I have a crow.

There is nothing for it but to slip the rubber off this particular FOLDER of worry, angst through it, get the worry DONE, slip the rubber band back around the folder . . . and I can probably still make it back to sleep by 3:30 . . . 3:40 at the latest, 3:50—

Which is to say:

I am now flashing back to dinner earlier this evening with my old Caltech dormmate—and current JPL engineer—Jonathan Lindberg. Jonathan and his rarely seen wife, Aimee. Half-Japanese. Pharmaceutical executive. Who is always away at a conference. Or, on the rare occasion that she is actually among you, is always listening to a remote conversation on an earpiece and tapping away on her BlackBerry.

First, let me say that I have long been aware that we appear to be living in a time of a modern epidemic. An epidemic . . . of frighteningly gifted children.

Everywhere I go, there is always some parent complaining that their four-year-old is gifted. Scary gifted. So gifted that, at his small Montessori preschool, the entire community has built an enormous two-hundred-foot flaming pyre for him, in the belief that his moods determine the weather (as mysteriously related to electrical systems and barometric pressure in the upper thermosphere).

All right. So no surprise that Jonathan and Aimee were confessing to us that while they love parenting, they find it exhausting.

The problem is not their long work hours (due to a precisely choreographed fleet of terrific babysitters), but the fact that their two sons, Seth and Ben, are gifted. Highly gifted. Seth and Ben were reading by two, multiplying by four . . . In regular classrooms, among children of average IQ, there was chafing, twisting—at one point Jonathan feared it might become biting. The third child psychologist Aimee took Seth to tested him in the top .5 percent of the population. Dr. Viswanathan felt Seth's true score might even be higher (possibly even closer to .1 percent), except that Seth, like many extremely gifted children, is moody, and the test does not account for moodiness. Meanwhile, Ben has such musical talent, the violin practically explodes into flames in his arms. Aimee has to drive the kid practically to Ventura to study with the one teacher who will even dare see him—

(Thank God we were meeting at a restaurant. How much I loathe going to the Lindberg residence, and having to sit frozen for seemingly hours at a time in front of Ben and his Mozart violin scrapings, his ceaseless virtuosic scrapery.)

Look, I'm not saying my own two daughters aren't gifted. It's just that many of us do not demonstrate our gifts through manipulation of blocks and cubes, standardized IQ tests, or even knowing remotely what we want to do with our lives come graduation time. I myself didn't get my big career "break" until the age of thirty-four. (And I had been plotting my fame since the age of eleven.)

And anyway, Jonathan and Aimee have clearly long stoked and fueled their own gifted nightmare. In college, Jonathan and Aimee were endearingly geeky, but since spawning, they have disappeared into this vanilla-hued gated community of the mind, an enigmatic Townsville that houses a whirlwind of food allergies and pediatric orthodontia and much frantic driving. (Most recently, they have discovered that Ben has a talent for fencing. His private fencing coach says that with proper training three days a week, come adolescence

Ben will be ready to try out for the Olympics. Anything less than that and Ben will lose that Olympic chance. Still, one wonders, how MANY American children actually fence? Or have that kind of time? Or that level of personal transportation? You just pray Ben doesn't one day accidentally trip over a luge.)

You know, Jonathan and Aimee are those insane types of parents who played Mozart in the womb, festooned their baby cribs with black and white mobiles, and forced their sons from the age of six months into strange yuppie art forms like Shakespearobics and Kindertanz and—and—and . . . *tumbling jazzerbastics.*

I suppose I am grateful that, unlike the Lindbergs, ours is probably not a dangerously gifted family.

And then Jonathan asked us if we had started thinking about schools.

I had not, as . . . School is Mike's department. Another linchpin of our Marital New Deal, aside from trying to use the night for actually sleeping, is that of improved . . . Delegation. Delegation . . . and Trust.

As we discovered in therapy, during that first parental Year of Hell . . . My notes indicate that Sandra often does not Trust Mike, as a Co-Parent, to Successfully Complete Certain Parental Tasks. Whereas in fact, as Mike and his (mysteriously sympathetic/consistently partisan!) witnesses Ruth and Kaitlin would point out, the problem is not that Mike Is Not Completing His Half of the Parenting but that he is Not Doing So in the Exact Same Way That Sandra Herself Would Do It. Okay! While seeing it there on the page, I admit it doesn't ring a bell for me, but that's what my notes say.

So far in our great parenting Voyage in Los Angeles, I have located the pediatrician, the day care, and the preschool. Kindergarten, we agreed, would fall to Mike. A project he reports he has been making great strides on. I'm vaguely aware that Mike has a manila folder titled "SCHOOL" on his volcanic computer pile. A folder which, by the terms of our agreement, I would never look into. Because of the Delegation . . . and the Trust.

So when Jonathan asked us at dinner if we had "started thinking about schools" . . .

Well, in that first instant, I felt no worry at all. I felt only, if you will, a sudden lift, at the thought of my little Hannah going off to kindergarten.

Not to blow our own horn, but Hannah is clever with a pencil and looks fetching in a jumper. Her favorite game, aside from bathing her stuffed unicorns and "rescuing" wounded insects, IS school, which she actually plays with her little sister, at twin toy desks, in a highly and charmingly theatrical manner.

But what would be the perfect school for Hannah? One that matched her perfect happy heart. I saw, I don't know . . .

Green lawns, white picket fence, a clanging old school bell. Beyond, dappled maple trees, Montessori-type . . . yarn making. I guess I was basically picturing a small village in Vermont where there is much cheese making.

For the chaotic years of middle school—and this goes for both girls—appropriate, I think, would be a literal ivory tower, nuns paddling boats around in a moat, patrolling, with more nuns standing watch up above in gun towers. That's the ticket—nuns with guns.

And college? Would it be like—oh, God—those many California state colleges that look like Czechoslovakian bunkers, with lowering seventies buildings of gray cement blocks, foreign engineering students with pockmarked skin, crumpled under knapsacks, their glasses dourly reflected in vending machines full of Cheetos?

And while dazed in this reverie, I hear Mike say, "Oh yeah. No worries."

Aimee puts down her BlackBerry.

"What's your school district?" she asks, in a weirdly light, unconcerned voice.

And Mike replies, "Well, I don't know. City of Los Angeles? I guess, what, that makes us L.A. Unified?"

And now here is what happens.

Both Jonathan and Aimee imperceptibly freeze.

Aimee makes almost no sound, except for this small, telltale intake of breath that sounds like "Whoa." She doesn't say anything more than that, nor does her expression change. But she does give this small, involuntary "Whoa."

And then Jonathan jumps in, a shade too quickly.

"I'm sure it'll be just fine!" he says. He has that oddly high-pitched tone friends use when insisting, too loudly, "Of COURSE your mole isn't cancer!" Jonathan waves his wineglass in boisterous encouragement. "What with all the new charters and magnets and re-districting and . . ." Here he says a bunch of other words I can't follow—I want to say "permits with transportation" and, of course, that circling crow "GERRYMANDERING." It is a whole list of frantic and, to my mind, impossibly complex contingencies.

Mike, in the manner of unflappable Midwestern men, accepts on face value Jonathan's proffered—probably absurd—wavelength on the hope/fear spectrum. Mike accepts and cashes the blithe "Of course it isn't cancer" voucher.

"Yes, magnet schools . . ." Mike says. "All my musician friends sent their kids through magnets. Said they were great. Bob Someone and Chuck Someone Else . . ."

And he says names that surprise me. I was unaware that these mangy, pushing-sixty, divorced Harley-driving former Iron Butterfly drummers and Vanilla Fudge electric-bongo players even HAD children.

Mike even names his chain-smoking cartage guy, Ricky. The last time I saw Ricky was thirteen years ago, when we rode to Ensenada in the back of his van, whose wildly listing "backseat" was an old couch bungee-corded to the floor. Mike, Ricky, and I drank tequila mixed with frozen limeade, popped hallucinogenic mushrooms, and ate octopus hand-scooped out of murky lukewarm water by toothless Mexican octogenarians pushing battered unrefrigerated wooden carts. *What could go wrong?*

But apparently even Ricky is now part of this dubious network of rheumy L.A. Unified arteries. Now even Ricky's surly tattooed teen daughter, Reyna, is doggedly studying modern dance in some brave little performing arts magnet in Pacoima.

Aimee, however, sits, skinny arms crossed, unmoving.

And it is safe to say the klieg lights on my mental "big board" have snapped on. The supercharged lights have suddenly come up, at midnight, on a previously dark football field. Linda Blair's eyes have popped open.

I am like a giant mother-to-mother satellite dish, turned on Aimee, who is notably . . . silent. The "Of course it isn't cancer" canape plate is being passed around and Aimee is conspicuously saying "No thank you"—she isn't having any.

I can sense humming, vibrating . . . this is a door I shouldn't open.

But the thing is, I already have a problem with insomnia. So I don't want Aimee's narrow face rising up at me tonight at 2:07 as I wonder what informational cards she was holding.

Because yes . . . I have a vague suspicion that we do not live in a good school district. Because typically, if fellow parents aren't roundly congratulating you about your FANTASTIC school district, you probably don't live in a good one.

And it's true that the names of good school districts have a certain ring:

Maybe not exactly Harvard. Yale. Princeton. St. Albans.

But at least Briarcliff. Westerland. Heathersford or Heatherstone.

Often the good public schools are named after some pleasing form of geography—a little copse, glen, wood, or grove where one might like to live. Like . . .

"Greenbelt Forest Heights."

"West Montclair Meadows."

Any titles with "Aspen," "Laurel," "Mulberry," "Walnut," "Willows," or "Birches" in them . . . For California, nonnative foliage is good. East Coasty foliage. Not so good are more native plant items such as "Cactus," "Palms," "Yucca," "Jalapeño."

Sometimes good public-school names are simply mellifluous. At one point, Mike dreamed of buying a house in Carmel Valley because he found it so leafy and idyllic. "And it's just forty minutes from the Monterey airport! You could be anywhere in California in about three hours!" This from a musician whose skin explodes into hives when a drive to a session takes more than twelve minutes. (And yet, year after year, Mike goes on summer vacation and real estate–fantasizes. "Why don't we live HERE?" he exclaims, flinging his arms open before the Bear Tooth Mountains. Which, as my sister, Kaitlin, puts it, can be filed under "Conversation #703.")

But Carmel Valley charmed even me. To this day, I can't even utter the words "Carmel Valley" without going into my husky Sally Kellerman "Hidden Valley Ranch dressing" voice. And, as you might expect, it was also home to (cue Sally Kellerman voice) "Carmel Valley Elementary," which looked, as we drove by it, cute, bucolic, absolutely adorable. Unfortunately, houses were also, like, a zillion trillion billion dollars. They all were, in all the charmingly named Carmels—Carmel Valley, Carmel Village, Carmel Heights, Carmel Woods, Carmel-by-the-Sea. Probably more affordable would have been homes in Carmel Buttes, Carmel Badlands, or Carmel Stinkpots, but . . . Carmel doesn't have those.

It is true we live in braying-voiced "Van Nuys," as opposed to the tonier "Sherman Oaks." However, I've sensed recently that the area is gentrifying. It must be. For God's sake, according to the *L.A. Times,* houses in our zip code are going for over $700,000. And who knows how long we're even going to be in "Van Nuys"? The west of The Nuys has fallen off and become "Lake Balboa." The south has become "Valley Village," the east has become "Valley Glen" . . .

Surely "Valley Heights" can't be far behind . . . even though, geolog-ically, that makes no sense. But that hasn't stopped Angelenos before. "Toluca WOODS?" Hello! We live in a desert!

But perhaps the schools are NOT gentrifying.

I put my hand on the forbidden, humming door and give it a lit-tle shove.

I say, "I notice Aimee . . . is a bit hesitant."

And Aimee says, in the quietest voice you can imagine, practically a whisper: "L.A. Unified . . . the horror, the horror."

"That's why we moved to La Cañada Flintridge," Jonathan says apologetically, politely regretful over the fact that they do NOT have cancer.

"But really," I shrill, taking another giant swallow of wine, "what IS it about the Los Angeles Unified School District?"

Aimee makes another sound, like an "ach." It is similar to the sound one might make if someone breezily asked, "So . . . the Mid-dle East? Things aren't so perky, are they?"

And Aimee finally says, tersely, "It's just big. Very big."

"Big?" I say.

Aimee spreads her arms out, to indicate impossible size.

"Seth and Ben would get lost. Utterly lost."

Jonathan leans in, drops his voice as though he might be overhead, possibly by spies under the employ of pro–school district government officials. "Elementary's not so bad. But the high schools . . . If we'd stayed where we were in LAUSD, our high school would have been—?"

Aimee utters the words: "Grant! Ulysses . . . S. . . . Grant!"

She spits out the president's name as though it were "Nixon!" As if to say: "Our children would have had to attend that filthy high school on Sepulveda behind Costco . . . NIXON!" But what about middle school? "AGNEW!"

"So La Cañada doesn't have those problems of . . . size?" Mike asks.

Aimee puts her hands up.

Jonathan takes a deep, weighty breath, then admits: "Of course, the irony is that as excellent as the La Cañada schools are . . ."

"Because Seth tested so highly gifted," Aimee adds, tearing apart a tiny crust of bread.

"In the top point-five percent . . ."

"Probably point-one percent," Aimee amends, sharply.

Here Jonathan pushes back, just a little.

"We don't know that for sure. In the end we have to go with the number Dr. Viswanathan gave us . . ."

Aimee flashes out, bitter, with the wound of it: "It's very HARD for gifted children!"

And here Jonathan and Aimee entered a brief marital *snorl* over the fact that while they are lucky enough to live in La Cañada Flintridge, and in fact are paying through the nose for it, La Cañada schools being ones the entire world including Taiwan would kill for . . . Well, even amid all this academic excellence, because of their freakish, off-the-charts giftedness, their sons have to be sequestered for EVEN MORE money in a secret private academy in Pasadena for frighteningly gifted children called The Coleman School, or simply, Coleman. Now on top of their astronomical mortgage (which includes the second-story remodel) they are paying dual full tuitions. And fund-raising!

And Aimee isn't even that wild about The Coleman School (or simply, Coleman).

"Developmentally speaking, the ideal school in Los Angeles for HG's is Wonder Canyon, but it's so exclusive, even GETTING A TOUR is impossible. They won't even release me a brochure. You have to sleep with David Geffen or something."

"Isn't he gay?" Jonathan asks, momentarily sidetracked.

"If David Geffen had test-tube babies, THEY would go to Wonder Canyon," Aimee declares, flatly. "All the experimental Hollywood children go there. If Diane Keaton married I. M. Pei . . . The code is impossible to crack."

"But I'm sure YOUR children will be fine," Jonathan concludes, a little madly. It is as if all at once he has realized how awkward the whole conversation has become . . . The implication being that, as opposed to his and Aimee's, Mike's and mine are such stupid children, any old rotten HUGE school district would be fine for them, even if it fell to our daughters to go to a disease-ridden HBO *Oz* prison-like high school with a name like "Millard Fillmore" ("Where will they matriculate to, after fifth grade?" "Warren Harding!" Or even worse, for middle school? "Ike Turner!") . . .

So to ease the sting of it, Jonathan leans forward wincing, as though it is actually THEY who have cancer. Voice dropped, Jonathan shakily throws us a bone:

"The thing is . . . Seth may have Asperger's."

"What's your local elementary?" Aimee can't help herself from asking.

And Mike says, "Our corner school? It's . . . I can't recall, this elementary has a funny name . . . Sort of like some obscure Ecuadorian melon. Oh, I remember . . ."

He brightens in the act of remembering it:

"Guavatorina!"

2
Into the Vortex
of the Snorl

What I know, at age forty-two, is that maintaining Emotional Seren-ity is important.

Angst is a state of mind—an act—that you select. Angst is not a thing that "happens" to you. External phenomena occur, and you have a choice. Given a troubling development, you may choose calm . . . or you may choose angst.

This is what Motherhood has taught me. Because Motherhood itself is Promethean—well, let's call her "Mrs. Prometheus." Which is to say, yes, you bring fire to humanity, but you also end up being chained to a rock and having your liver pecked out over and over again, every day, with ever-fresh, dive-bombing black crows of Worry.

Further, Motherhood today is unbelievably complicated, and has never been more scary. For instance, in the twenty-first century, babies now apparently swallow everything . . . And what's worse is, these are typically going to be things so small you can't see them. So your world is a minefield. ("Oh no! What's that on the coffee table! Beads! Little beads! Teeny tiny beads!") I found that the only way to get through those early years without actually descending into gibbering madness was to maintain a certain middle-focus glaze. One time, in the splattersville of my younger one's diaper, I found the small tooth of a purple comb, a comb I hadn't seen since college. Imagine if I'd seen it go in! So I was spared one—that was one folder of worry, in the middle of the night, I never had to mentally take the rubber band off of.

And now, somehow, Child #2 has made it to toddler graduation and is finally joining her big sister in preschool. Off she goes to preschool . . .

The first day of which can be hard. Hard hard hard . . .

I bend gently down to our baby, Isabel . . . whose name has never fit her. Not even today. "Isabel" is too grown up, implies too many sophisticated language skills, a Good Driver discount, an aversion to shellfish, and perhaps a mutual fund. Perhaps when she is thirty-eight years old her name will fit her. Until then, #2 is our Squidlet, our Shrimp, our Poopsadella. I smooth out the folds of her little red Kittykat skirt, cup her pointy chin in my hand.

"Don't be scared, sweetie," I murmur, in honeyed tones. "Mommy will be sitting RIGHT HERE in the hallway, all morning, with her computer. She is going to plug her laptop right there into that wall. Your mommy is not going to BUDGE, sweetie. Your mommy will be writing her radio commentary *right outside this window.* If you feel lonely, or sad, or have anything at all you want to share with Mommy—"

WHOOOMP!

I am almost knocked over by the force of my two-and-a-half-year-old tearing away from me. There are practically tire marks, and a little wisp of smoke, where she once stood.

"Sweetie!" I cry out in alarm. "Don't forget your lunch box! Here's your lunch box!"

Frantic to join the others, like a small scrabbling animal, she pushes open the bright green classroom door . . . which through sheer force, ricochets shut behind her.

BAM!

I fly like a bird to the glass window, tap at it, *tap, tap, tap.*

"Sweetie! Your lunch!"

The door opens again. The teacher, in a blue apron—and is that a slightly pitying expression?—takes the lunch box, closes the door again.

I had reserved the whole morning to be here, to stand faithfully by in case of tears, collapse, hysteria, but . . .

Well!

Mike and I sit at Nat's Early Bite in The Nuys, looking over our menus.

We haven't breakfasted out together, just the two of us, in—what is it? FIVE YEARS?

It's strange to have a whole morning suddenly open.

But there you have it. Both girls are suddenly in preschool. They bolted into their classrooms and the Red Sea has closed up behind them. And the cell phone is not chirping. Is the ringer even on? Yes. Okay!

Okay. Back to the menu. A menu! Wow! Look at this! Look at all the things a person might eat, just for the asking! Bagel. Whitefish. Eggs . . .

"I'm going to have the cheese, sprout, and avocado omelet," I declare boldly.

"Corned beef hash . . ." Mike muses.

"When did you last have corned beef hash?" I exult.

"Never!" he says.

"Have it!"

We continue looking at our menus.

"Coffee?" the waitress asks.

"I think I'm coffee'ed out," I say.

"Me too," he says. "Maybe just some water."

"With ice?" she asks.

"Yes!" I agree. "Me too! Ice!"

She goes away.

A beat.

"You want a section of the paper?" Mike says.

"Sure," I say.

"Front page?" he says.

" 'Kay," I say.

We open our papers. And here we sit.

Here my beloved and I sit on a Monday morning at 9:30 A.M., eighteen years in.

I hear a burst of muffled laughter, then "Shhh!" I turn. Several booths down is a young, pimply rock-and-roll couple with black skinny jeans and green hair. They lean forward across their shiny diner table, gripping hands, their voices low, urgent with excitement.

And in the mirrored wall, a few booths down, by contrast, I can see us—two lifted newspapers.

I turn back.

"Oh my God," I say. "We've become one of those couples!"

"What couples?" Mike says, eyes still on the paper.

"You know—those couples you see in restaurants . . . On the dripping eleventh shoal of marriage . . . who have absolutely nothing left to say to each other anymore."

He lowers his paper, thinks about it.

"Well . . . I just . . . feel like when I share my thoughts, half the time I'm repeating myself."

"Try me!" I challenge.

"For instance, as you know, I'm not working very much right now. There's Don's album project and those two possible cable things MAYBE, but overall work has been a bit, shall we say, thin. I used to panic when I hit a dry spell. But as you know, I've decided not to obsess about it anymore. But nor am I going to belabor it. Best left undiscussed."

I see my husband's point, all too well. I was asleep by the second sentence. Mike's Not Working—as Kaitlin would say, that is Conversation #409. In the eighteen years I've known him, as a musician in Los Angeles, Mike always DOESN'T work for a while, and then he always DOES. Then he has no work. Then he has too much work. (You've heard the joke: "How do you get a musician to complain? Hire him.")

Mike's working and NOT working. It's . . . what do you call it? Oh yes! A cycle.

I suddenly notice, on the back of his Calendar section, a sudoku puzzle . . .

But, trained in therapy, he dutifully lobs the "Let's check in with each other" ball right back at me.

"And how are you?" he asks, a bit dubiously.

Oh, Lord. If I thought his inner life was tedious . . .

"Oh hey! I'm fine," I reply lamely.

"How's teaching?"

"Fine."

"Radio commentaries?"

"Cool."

"Any new book ideas?"

"Not really. But it's okay. I'm enjoying a creative sabbatical. Good Lord, sometimes what sounds really tempting is to take five years off just to . . . sleep."

He puts down his paper, now fully engaged.

"I've been . . . worried about you."

Well, this is a turn for the worse. This breakfasting out, in restaurants, among people—I'm so out of practice . . . !

"Me?"

"It not that you seem depressed exactly. But I've noticed that—Maybe it's since the kids have come but—" He releases the cat out of its bag, it hesitates—he gives it a little extra push. "You don't seem to have women anymore. Friends who are women. Women friends. You know . . ." Here he lifts his hands, makes that uncertain waggling motion with his fingers, as though afraid to touch exposed live wires. "Women."

"I have women!" I retort, stung.

"But you don't hang out with them. When I'm depressed I go fish. I think your women . . . are like my fish."

I think about it. It is true all the women friends I had in my twenties and thirties . . . ? What did I do with them? In which Rubbermaid bins did I store all those girlfriends, to make room, when that mountain of baby gear started arriving?

My husband, now, he's on a mini-aria:

"I think you need more women around you. Women. Whatever happened to your women? Of course, I know what happened to . . . you know . . . her—"

"Don't even say her name."

"Okay. Forget her. But what about, um . . ." He reaches into the attic of his memory, pulls out a dusty box. Aha! "What about that—that women's book group you used to go to?"

I groan.

My women's book group has been together fifteen years, aka fourteen years too long. By now we've gone through our vampire phase, our geisha phase, and our *Bridges of Madison County* phase. Most recently, we'd waded into this frantic *Perils of Pauline* phase filled with nonfiction books about how working mothers are BLOWING EVERYTHING. The titles were all in HUGE BLOCK LET-

TERS . . . "CRUSH! You're Working Too Much!" "SMUSH! You're Mothering Too Much!" "SQUASH! Your Obese Bipolar Children Pine for You!" "CRASH: Even in the Simple Act of Reaching for That Coffee, You're Hemorrhaging Future Retirement Benefits, Not Just Social Security But Tax-Free Funds That Should Have Been Placed in an IRA Yesterday!" All the covers had women in business suits, collapsed weeping over steering wheels while all around them a tsunami of frantic sippy cups tumbled.

This was the very Tower of Literary Pain Mike cleared off my nightstand and replaced with what he thought would be a much more restful . . . *28 Beads.*

"Do you really want me to tell you the details of WHY my women's book group became so tedious?"

"No," he replies abruptly, thinking better of that. "But how about . . . Oh, what's her name, from USC . . . Nikki?"

"As a matter of fact, Nikki called recently," I say, smartly. "Apparently she has finally met her dream man. Again. But this time he is so not like all the others. Again. They spent seventy-two hours straight together laughing. Again. Within two months something will go terribly wrong, so they'll be crying, they'll go into therapy, she'll be curled into a fetal position, he'll move to Portland . . . Then Nikki will rise again with her new mission, a line of jewelry or— Oh, the last time? Here was her plan . . . New head shots! Nikki is forty-seven and has literally never enjoyed paid employment as an actress. As Kaitlin would say, 'New head shots? Conversation number 331.' "

"What about— Why don't you just, ah, set her up with your ex-boyfriend Bruce?"

"'Cause HE doesn't do yoga and SHE isn't a vegetarian."

"What's the difference?"

"I don't even know."

Mike shoots a surreptitious glance down at his paper. I feel him, too, eyeing the sudoku, the deliciously blank sudoku.

But now the floodgates are open. He wanted to talk! I'll talk!

"Yes, my friends! My tiresome friends!" I say. "Then we move to the category of unbearable couples. On the one hand, as you saw last night, Jonathan and Aimee, the neurotic über-parents, have become intolerable. However, their polar opposite, Kent and Maria? Just as intolerable—"

"Uh—I've changed my mind," Mike says to the passing waitress, resignedly. "I guess I WILL have some coffee."

"As opposed to Jonathan and Aimee, Kent and Maria seem unaware that, within the past five years, we have even HAD children. They're always calling on Friday for a spontaneous Saturday eight-thirty P.M. dinner party. I believe Kent and Maria are literally the latest-dining people on the planet. They're basically on Barcelona time. They're always going, 'Things will really get rolling at ten! Supper begins at eleven! We've got some great ARCHITECTS coming over—you'll love them! In case you ever need an architect!' At some point, with Kent and Maria, I want to ask them, 'Really, is there ANYTHING AT ALL you remember about us?'

"So once, I think two years ago when you were on the road, I hied myself off to one of these dinners. I'm introduced to all the other couples—their names are, like, Carl and Sumiko, John and Jon . . . They're all childless, which means, as Maria puts her hand on my arm and hilariously announces, 'NO PARENT TALK, Sandra! PARENT TALK IS NOT ALLOWED. We know you're a parent . . . But there are no other PARENTS here. NO PARENT TALK.'

"And the point is—I think—made, but Maria keeps running with it. 'And you know WHY no Parent Talk? Because PARENTAL CONVERSATION IS SO BORING. What is more boring than the conversation of PARENTS? Take my cousin Dara! I'm on the phone with her the other day, and it's all blah blah blah Kyle, blah blah blah FOOD allergy, blah blah blah PEANUT allergy, blah blah blah WHEAT allergy, blah blah blah PEDIATRICIAN . . .'"

Mike is openly reading his paper by this point. The waitress is putting down our breakfasts, so I conclude my monologue . . . to her.

"And Maria goes, 'But what haunted me about Dara's tale, many hours later—if I can even call it a tale, given there was no beginning, middle, or end, only this phlegmy gray middle that hung on and hung on, as though the tale itself were a kind of allergy—' "

"Ketchup?" the waitress asks, reaching in her pocket.

"Please," I reply. "And do you have Tabasco? Thanks. Anyway, and Maria says, 'What haunts me about Dara's tale is what I call the Illogical Piece. Dara had said her pediatrician suspected Kyle might have a wheat allergy because Kyle has blood type O. But I ask you: Is O not the most common blood type on the planet, and is wheat not one of our commoner grains? Does that mean the majority of the human race—your Basques, Tutsis, Hmong, your Bedouins—are naturally allergic to bread, croutons, pita, halvah?' "

"And . . . Tabasco," the waitress says. "Be right back."

"But get this, Mike," I say. Bolstered by the first few bites of corned beef hash, color flooding back to his face, he manages an assenting grunt. I press on: "NOW Sumiko's phone beeps. It is a call from, you guessed, their dog sitter. Because Carl and Sumiko have—of course—three pugs. 'Oh my God,' exclaims Jon, 'you have pugs, too?' John and Jon have five pugs . . . and a greyhound. All four NOW tear off onto parallel monologues about all their little dogs, which include sleep habits, walking habits, pooping habits, and yes, there were photos. Even Kent and Maria produce a photo of Bailey, their giant, leaping, slathering dog, remember him—"

"Urgh."

"—that I may well take a rifle to one day. My entire left rib cage is bruised from, over the years, having practically been RAPED by their dog. Him jumping on me. Every single time I walk into the house. While they do nothing. So let us review: I am not allowed to bring my children to Kent and Maria's, to discuss them, and I have never so much as proferred a photo. But now I am looking at wallet photo after wallet photo . . . of dogs. And I now suddenly realize how long I have been abused by these PEOPLE, my childless couple friends, and . . . their DOGS!"

I lift my fork.

"And it has become clear to me that humans, as a species, have simply become intolerable to one another. In 1900 the average person could expect to live to thirty-eight. Now people live until eighty-nine and you have to be friends with them for ninety-seven years!"

"Yep, it's a drag," Mike says, shaking ketchup onto his hash browns. "And marriages last two centuries."

"Ha-ha," I say, "good one. But I don't think single people have it much easier. Apparently even meeting NEW people is overrated. I think about what my girlfriend Rachel said. After four years on JDate, she finally canceled her subscription thingy, saying, 'Heterosexual and Jewish? It's not enough anymore. I'd rather stay in with a nice bottle of merlot and sort my mail.' "

"What happened to Rachel?" he says.

"Moved to France," I say.

The waitress returns with a flourish.

"And . . . Tabasco!"

Having nothing else to do this morning, now that I have officially been fired as a mother by my two-and-a-half-year-old, I now celebrate our graduation from the State of Having Two VERY Small Children by doing something else unheard of . . .

Cleaning out the minivan. When did I last do this? Has it been . . . FIVE YEARS?

Our Toyota minivan has become like a rolling mildewed chariot of typhus. Even our own children have attempted to stage revolts over the interior of the minivan. Hannah has complained it smells too bad to actually ride in. Another time, it was our little Squid who howled—there were ants in her car seat. Reasonable protests, I agree, but not until this morning have I had the time to actually get down on my knees and hack through the layers of crust.

I begin with what I call my "office," which is to say the front passenger seat, a nest containing all the flotsam and jetsam of collected paper, sedimentary layers of history.

We have, for instance, from the hospital, a twenty-page pamphlet on breast-feeding. Why is getting babe to breast so complicated? Let me summarize for you, in a sketch:

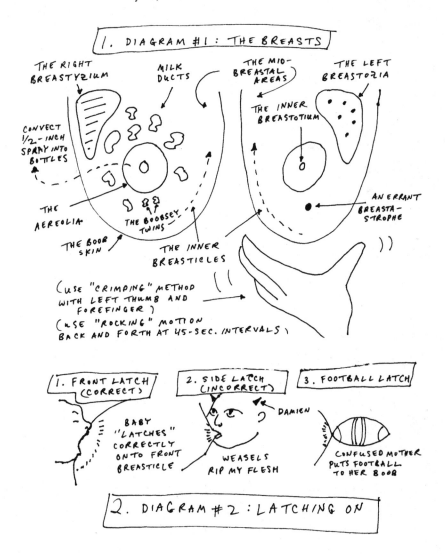

1. DIAGRAM #1 : THE BREASTS

THE RIGHT BREASTYZIUM

MILK DUCTS

THE MID-BREASTAL AREAS

THE LEFT BREASTOZIA

THE INNER BREASTOTIUM

CONVECT 1/2-INCH SPRAY INTO BOTTLES

AN ERRANT BREASTA-STROPHE

THE AEREOLIA

THE BOOBSEY TWINS

THE BOOB SKIN

THE INNER BREASTICLES

(USE "CRIMPING" METHOD WITH LEFT THUMB AND FOREFINGER)
(USE "ROCKING" MOTION BACK AND FORTH AT 45-SEC. INTERVALS)

1. FRONT LATCH (CORRECT)

2. SIDE LATCH (INCORRECT)

3. FOOTBALL LATCH

BABY "LATCHES" CORRECTLY ON TO FRONT BREASTICLE

DAMIEN

WEASELS RIP MY FLESH

CONFUSED MOTHER PUTS FOOTBALL TO HER BOOB

2. DIAGRAM #2 : LATCHING ON

As we move on to solid foods, here's a crumpled sample one-year-old's lunch menu from Dr. Glauberman, our overprotective pediatrician:

> ½ C green vegetables
>
> ¼ C yellow vegetables
>
> 3 tsp. organic 1% milk
>
> ½ whole grain rice cake w/ ⅔ tsp. almond butter

I particularly love the painstaking distinction between the two colors of vegetables. That really makes me laugh.

And look, here are the many lost to-do lists of yore. I ponder one made on the back of a Wells Fargo deposit envelope. It reads:

> Wash. Mut.
>
> Frst cupcks.
>
> LA WEEKLY ART.
>
> CIOFFI!!!
>
> Restaurant reservations for 4, call accountant, collect tax receipts, 2003???
>
> Acc. #1034324332
>
> Frsdrggb???
>
> ♦♎♐♦♏●❑🙰♍♦♏❑♦♐♦♎🙰♐♋♍♦♎♐♦♑♑♑

How interesting! At some point it appears I was making to-do lists in cuneiform, literally channeling Armenian. Boy, when I don't sleep!

And here's a coffee-stained mini-parachute from Gymboree. Gymboree! How I came to hate that parachute.

I remember the time when Hannah was fifteen months old and I was eight months pregnant with Number Two. Even though I was pushing my usual 185 pounds, I was feeling unusually lithe and feline that day in the hip black maternity tent and leggings a (childless) girlfriend had given me. It was the NEW maternity wear: Just because you're almost 200 pounds and have four chins doesn't mean you should feel, God forbid . . . fat!

And lo and behold, standing next to me that day in Gymboree class was Cute Baseball Cap Dad. I'm enjoying chatting with him as we parents gather in a circle and begin whooshing the parachute up and down over our screaming children, up and down. The song involves quite a bit of squatting and rising. I remind you I am 185 pounds, sweating a bit in my black maternity tent. I've been trying to eat a lot of kale this second pregnancy, and quite frankly . . .

I fart.

It is almost . . . silent, but in fact, very deadly. Let's put it this way: It is kale-y.

In alarm, I flap the parachute airily, breezily, a little more vigorously than usual, attempting to casually flap away the odor. And it looks like I have succeeded. No children are actually falling over dead under the parachute.

But my scheme has clearly backfired, or sidefired . . . because a wave of kale fart now hits, to my right, Cute Baseball Cap Dad. He starts, first in surprise, then horror, then even amazement, exclaiming:

"Whoa! They're gettin' *busy* in there!"

And I betray the children. I sell them out, saying, "Boy, are they!"

Ha-ha-ha! All my pregnancies . . . good times. Good times.

But now look at this.

Here is a green flier from our preschool, Valley Co-Op, announcing a program for confused Los Angeles parents called "Into Kindergarten": ALL YOUR QUESTIONS ABOUT LOS ANGELES SCHOOLS ANSWERED, OPTIONS DISCUSSED. Whoa. The fact that this flier is still on the front passenger seat, actually kind of stuck to it, is sure indication that this is not on my husband's radar. The sign-up deadline was of course one month ago, NO EXCEPTIONS, the seminar is tonight, and the organizer is Valley Co-Op Preschool über-mom Joan Archer.

Okay! Joan.

I know who Joan is.

Checks go to Joan. Canned food goes to Joan. Joan's name is at the top of every committee list. Joan is at the trunk of every phone tree: All the leaves and branches spread out from Joan.

Which is to say, in our household, phone calls from Joan have tended to go . . . unreturned. Why? Because like an ever-renewable resource, Joan will simply call again, two, three times. She'll leave a reminder note in your child's cubby, which you will ignore. The next morning, Joan will literally pin a note to your child. At long last, Joan will simply throw up her hands and PAY the $1.75 for the fire station field trip, and you will see the amount added to your monthly bill with a note, "Please reimburse!" Smiley face. "Thank you, Joan."

But now the tables have turned and I am seeking *her*. Joan will be delighted.

I arrive early, at the preschool, to pick up The Squid and Hannah.

And as usual, Joan is easy to locate. She is sitting right here in the front hallway, with her chestnut pageboy haircut and cheerful, slightly funky denim dress, behind a card table bearing the banner SPRING FUND-RAISING JAMBOREE.

Which may or may not have anything to do with many tiny little jams. For years I have successfully blocked any Spring Fund-Raising Jamboree details from my mind. I'm the sort of mother who will flee a "Jamboree"-infected area, preferring to simply fling a check out the window of my speeding-away car. Of course, you miss a lot of pertinent kindergarten information that way—which I now see.

Before Joan Archer, there is a line. It is not about the Spring Fund-Raising Jamboree.

Accosting Joan now is a blond springy-haired mother whose torso seems literally caved over in anxiety.

"But our moms' group, the Booby Club, in Sherman Oaks . . . We HAVE to get in to 'Into Kindergarten' tonight!"

She goes into a cresting, keening monologue. Something about the Magnolia K–8 charter span school having not made its funding goals, so it will not open until the following year, leaving the entire Sherman Oaks Booby Club up a creek without a paddle!

While Joan listens, herself in a bit of a glaze, she tears tickets and drops them into a basket. I notice that her hands are constantly in motion, like two hummingbirds building a nest.

Joan finally gets a tired word in.

"It's just that we're so overbooked. There's a waiting list of seventeen. The room only holds thirty. And now you say there are TWELVE OF YOU??????"

Okay. It's clear I can't just rip the Band-Aid off and invite myself to "Into Kindergarten." To get into the workshop tonight, I'm going to have to move to Plan B—to bend Joan backward, lift her denim dress up, and blow her in the back of her Honda minivan.

But no. Even better idea. Crafty me, I notice the Spring Fund-Raising Jamboree committee meeting is at six-thirty and "Into Kindergarten" is at seven-thirty . . . in the very same room.

I wait out the other hysterical mothers very patiently, with extreme good humor, and when I get to the front, I say, with a big smile:

"Hey, Joan! I'm just leaving twenty dollars for our two Spring Fund-Raising Jamboree tickets and— Hey, is there still room to volunteer on the committee? The fund-raising committee! Love to be on that!"

"YOU want to be on the committee?" Joan's glazed look turns into one of incredulity.

Feeling a little stung to be found out, here I actually attempt to rewrite—or at least re-interpret—my conspicuously non-committee-volunteering-mother history, all in one mangled run-on sentence. I fabricate something about a big writing deadline I have had, for several years, which all at once I am abruptly clear of, and so of course now will return to my original plan of TOTAL CO-OP

PRESCHOOL INVOLVEMENT. I also make a mental note that if the whole time commitment thing gets too out of control, my youngest can always develop a sudden ear infection. That's the beauty of the shape-shifting work/mother balance. (Is that a running pant? Is that a pajama pant? Who knows?)

"You sure you don't have twelve people you want to get into 'Into Kindergarten'?" Joan asks, weary, wry.

"Absolutely not!" I trill. "Kindergarten—we're good! And Joan? Can I help you clip those tickets? Do you need a hand?"

"You know what? I do. Here . . ." she adds, turning.

And as she bends over behind the table, I see two matching blue Tupperwares labeled "Into Kindergarten" holding perfect accordions of manila folders whose colored tabs read "Elementary School," "Middle School," "High School," "Charters," "Magnets," and is that . . . the UC System? UCLA? She can foresee all the way up to UCLA?

Unlike the volcano that is my husband's computer pile, Joan's files are beautifully, stunningly organized.

I want to attach myself, like a pilot fish, to the side of Joan.

Maybe she needs a new best friend? Who knows?

"If you don't mind unboxing these knitting kits . . ." she says.

"Unboxing? I'll buy one!" I exclaim.

"They're pretty great," Joan says. "And the proceeds go to a good cause. It's for the Literacy Project. They provide Caldecott Medal–winning books for poor children—"

I don't know from literacy projects, and I've never knit in my life.

"I'll buy two!"

At 6:30 P.M., a dozen mothers gather in the nursery on small child chairs with powder-blue seat cushions. On four walls around us is red-and-white-striped wallpaper covered with bears. There is one stay-at-home dad named Brad who hovers for a few minutes, sort of jogging, from heel to heel, while bouncing his crumple-faced baby in a plaid BabyBjörn carrier. But what with the powder blue and the bears and the women and the baby, I feel anxious for Brad, as if there, right in front of us, his manhood might actually fall off. Fortunately, his phone cheeps and off he jogs.

Joan opens the Spring Jamboree meeting, "Shall we get started?" My job is to take notes.

There are announcements of deadlines, calls for gift baskets, solicitations of items for the teddy bear raffle . . .

And then Joan gives the floor over to a mother named Elise. Clearly, it's a huge symbolic moment.

"Elise worked very hard at the fund-raiser LAST year," Joan says. "And she very much wanted to organize it this year? So we thought, this year, she should be ALLOWED to do it?" Joan's tone is both questioning and firm, as though forestalling any . . . argument about the matter? "We think she has some great ideas? Elise?"

Elise stands. She has a tight brown ponytail, slick in front, then exploding into frizz down her back. She wears a sleeveless white blouse. She is bouncing what appears to be a miniature Dwight D. Eisenhower in a flowered pink baby sling.

"All right, people," she says, shifting from foot to foot with an odd heightened excitement. "Listen up!"

She points to an easel.

"I've split up the planning of the Spring Jamboree evening into four categories," which she reads aloud as she taps:

Food
Beverages
Theme
Decorations

As soon as I see the list, it strikes me that there is a problem with this order. I believe a better order would be:

Theme

Decorations

Food

Beverages

Or even:

Theme

Food

Decorations

Beverages

Really, any of these would do, as long as Theme GOES FIRST.

"Elise?" Joan asks. She is now stuffing envelopes for yet another mysterious ongoing project. "What IS the theme?"

"The theme is Cinco de Mayo," Elise replies flatly.

"Cinco de Mayo!" exclaims another mom, whose name I'm pretty sure is Sharon. "We should get it catered from Puerto Vallarta!"

"What is Puerto Vallarta?" Elise asks.

"It's this great Mexican restaurant near our house!"

"It's a very tight budget," Elise says. "I think like last year? Keep it simple. I'm thinking platters from Costco."

"Costco platters!" Joan exclaims cheerfully. "Those were just fine!"

"Aw!" Sharon sighs, in sharp disappointment. "It's just that Puerto Vallerta is really, really great and really, really cheap."

"Well," Joan says again, "maybe you can get us some numbers. Elise? Would you like her to get you some numbers?"

For Sharon, this is beside the point. She shakes her head with surprising energy, like a horse champing at the bit.

"OKAY! Maybe it's a few more dollars, but the point is—"

"You know what?" Elise retorts, her vocal pitch titching up just a notch. "I just think, 'Keep it simple.' Keep the food simple. Because then we can bump up the decorations. Target has these cute little one-dollar cactus pots—"

"I just think if you HAVE a Mexican theme, you should HAVE good Mexican food!" persists Sharon. "Was there a theme LAST year? I don't remember a theme. Why do we even HAVE a theme?"

I now notice what appears to be dried pink strawberry Danimal on Sharon's white blouse, and it occurs to me that, mothers of small children, we are all just very, very tired. I myself feel as though I'm falling into a stupor, writing slower and slower and slower in my notepad . . .

In fact, looking down, it appears that instead of "beverage," I have written "begerave" . . . and next to it something that looks like

Frsdrggb???

•⚏⛿⤴&•●℮⊤•ⅿ◻•ⅿ◻•ⅿⅿ◻◻◻◻◻◻◻

Oh no! There's that cuneiform again!

"Maybe we should move on," suggests Joan. "And we'll keep Puerto Vallarta on the table. Thanks for that suggestion, Colleen," she says, patting Sharon on the hand.

Why is she calling Sharon "Colleen"? Then suddenly I realize Sharon's name may actually *be* Colleen. And I was so sure Colleen's name was Sharon. Crap! Now I have to go back and relabel that whole passage of notes. I should just go back to my fail-safe practice of calling everybody "Honey."

"I just want to decide on the stationery," Elise shrills, verging on hysteria. "Tonight! I just . . . want . . . to decide . . . on the stationery!"

"Okay . . ." Joan says.

Although, in fact, what Elise means is not exactly STATIONERY but merely one of three possible BORDERS of stationery upon which we are going to print INVITATIONS . . . for the Spring Fund-Raising Jamboree raffle . . . which we will actually be stuffing INTO the labeled cubbies . . . of one another.

Which you'd think would be simple but somehow . . . The very teeny tininess of this task . . . I mean, look at this:

∼···†≑♭∓⁎∗√ ‴ ↗∼‴ ✕⁎∗∼♥Ď◡‴⌐◡♥∼◡

∼♥†◡≑‴ ∓ ⁎∗m⁎∗Ǹ3✕⁎∗↗∼ · ∼♥◡↗♭†♭····

∼3♥◡†‴ ✕↗√⁎∗ ∓⁎∗⌐ ♥Ǹ3‴ ↗✕m⁎∗∗∗∼◡♥

For the life of me, I can't tell the difference. IS there a difference?

But no, now I and the twelve other sleep-deprived mothers seem to be going into a kind of decisionary paralysis. I can actually feel our brain chemicals slowing down. It's like if certain types of birds or lemmings see themselves in a mirror and they get so confused they suddenly hopelessly lose their sense of direction and plunge into the sea.

"What was the theme again?" another mother stabs out suddenly, in panic.

"Do I have to feed my parking meter after six?" wails another.

"Is Jamboree really spelled with two *e*'s?" cries a third.

It's not just a Snorl, it's the literal . . .

VORTEX OF THE SNORL.

We are now interrupted—awakened—by singles, pairs, and trios of hysterical parents starting to crowd into the nursery. It is a parade of goatees, crocs, baby strollers, baby slings, the odd Ramones T-shirt, a little tie-dye, canvas Trader Joe's bags . . .

Who keep coming. And coming.

If Guavatorina was my own circling crow . . . The anxieties of my fellow Los Angeles parents—they're not just a few crows, they are a murder of crows . . . like *The Birds*! It's like a Worry blizzard straight out of Hitchcock!

"Where is 'Into Kindergarten'?" "Is this 'Into Kindergarten'?" "What's YOUR home school?" "What's YOUR home school?" None of the news is good. These are Valley public schools, Van Nuys public schools, frightening unknown elementaries no one had ever heard of . . . their names a gutteral blend of contemporary Mexican and historical Dutch! The grotesque syllables came out like horn blats.

"Cramplin!"

"Guavatorina!"

"Meldonblag!"

"Oaxacateptl!"

"Van Triscuit!"

"Tijuanaville!"

"Cocopo!"

"Hufflepuff!"

"I don't even KNOW what our school is," weeps one mother, in a batik skirt. "All I know is we can't go there! Eighty percent free and reduced lunch! The scores are frightening!"

It is soon clear that the nursery can't hold all the incoming parents. Joan's husband, Walt, a short, blond 'fro-haired, slightly perspiring man who looks a bit like a kindly ferret, shouts: "Joan! We need to move into the lunchroom!"

"All right!" she cries out.

New doors are opened. Folding chairs clatter apart. Tables are lifted, pushed—

It's like a scene from *Dr. Zhivago,* of madding crowds at a breadline.

"Do you want me to continue taking notes, Joan?" I yell over to her. "I see you're kind of overwhelmed here!"

"Fine!" she says, barely hearing me, madly gathering her materials, her Tupperwares, her clipboards, her paperwork. "Fine!"

Waving a clipboard like a semaphore above him, Walt urges us into the bigger room. We form a large ragged semicircle against a double-stacked crush of child-sized blue lunch tables, their metal legs poking every which way. Surrounded on every side, Walt seems to need to talk fast to keep from being stoned.

"Let's begin with just a quick data dump of some of the general kindergarten questions and concerns you have!" Walt yells, over the hubbub.

And now, instead of Aimee's vague accusation of "bigness," "Los Angeles Unified"—a noxious term I can't hear now without feeling a tight choking sensation in my chest, followed by a slight burning acid reflux . . . The dragon that is our large urban school district, the giant dark hydra, is shown to me, with all its hideous heads, tongues, arms, claws, wings . . .

I scribble down the notes, and scribble and scribble. I'm writing as fast as I can and can still barely keep up . . .

URBAN PUBLIC SCHOOL WORRY LIST

Republicans have caused U.S. public education to become complete, unsolvable travesty

Fifty children packed into classrooms designed for twelve

Thanks to No Child Left Behind, giant lowering "Mao Tse-Tung"–like oil paintings of George W. Bush hanging everywhere

It's all testing!

High-stakes testing!

Students are tested every single minute of every single hour of every single day

Even on bathroom breaks students retrace the letter *A* over and over again while drunk, angry teacher beats ruler until students crumple forward to their knees weeping

Thanks to teachers' union, teachers insist on getting huge benefits, teaching short hours, and having lots of vacations

Teachers who smile, love children, and get excited about anything are barred by the union

McDonald's transfats are required, sold everywhere in vending machines

Due to strange corporation arrangement with Wal-Mart (to make up for all the budget cuts), only music by Kenny G or Kenny Loggins—only the Kennys—is allowed

What about magnet schools? Dead grass, filthy, odds are one in 2,400 of getting in, funding iffy

Middle schools are continually in *Oz*-style lockdowns

Mountain lion virus outbreak

Thanks to hormone-filled milk, teen girls mature four years earlier than ever before and are like crazy Britney Spears animals now

Boys' pants are all down around their ankles now—it's all about the butt

Gold teeth seen in butt

Have you heard of this new thing called "pantsing"?

Because due to budget cuts there are no custodians, middle-school bathrooms are flooded ankle deep in water; Hurricane Katrina-like, girls can only get out of the bathroom if they submit to "pantsing"

And then for high school . . . "Cheney!" Everyone has to go to "Cheney High School!" which feeds straight into the military!

There is so much bureaucracy, not even one idea can make it through

GIANT benefits for teachers, and the kids don't even have a pencil—typical teachers will waggle vacation photos from Cancun over the children and say: "Hah! You don't even have a pencil!"

Teachers fill up their bank accounts by calling in sick

Bureaus upon bureaus upon bureaus, the LAUSD takes up forty city blocks, extensions that literally go nowhere, it's exactly like Terry Gilliam's movie *Brazil*, corpses found in stairwells dating back to the pre-1960s

There are some pockets of safety in Los Angeles, but those are few and far between.

A map of Los Angeles reveals very few "safe spots" . . .

REAL GOOGLE MAP OF LOS ANGELES ("LAIR OF THE LAWNIFIED DRAGON")

SAFE HAVEN

CALA-BASAS

ONLY 3 SAFE HAVENS IN ENTIRE CITY (+ IVANHOE + CARPENTER — LIE ABOUT YOUR GAS BILL, IT'S THE ONLY WAY!)

SOME VAGUE HILLS HERE

OOH, LOOK AT US!

WE'RE SANTA MONICA (JUST ENJOYING OUR COOL OCEAN BREEZES AND SELF-ENCLOSED SCHOOL DISTRICTS)

PACIFIC OCEAN

VENICE ACK, WHAT HAPPENED?) SHI----;;;

CRAP, IT'S RESEDA

STINKPOTS OF VAN NUYS

405

101

CARPENTER (TENNIS MOM MAFIA?) 134

WEST HOLLY-WOOD (NO-ONE HAS CHILDREN, ONLY PUGS)

LYCÉE FOR PUGS IS PROBABLE

10

I DON'T ACTUALLY KNOW WHAT THIS AREA IS CALLED, DOESN'T BODE WELL

SAFE HAVEN

LA CANADA

"PASADENA" (UNCOMFORTABLE SILENCE)

2 LA "NOT QUITE CANADA" CRESCENTA

FETID SHOALS o BURBANK

210

170

Fx o!! IT'S NORTH HOLLYWOOD!

GLENDALE ("BAJA LAGNADA")

HOLLYWOOD (BAD)

ECHO PARK (BADER)

HIGHLAND PARK (BADDEST)

"MIRACLE MILE"? PROBABLE NOT REALLY!

IVANHOE (WHERE ALTERNATIVE WEEKLY JOURNALISTS LIE ABOUT THEIR GAS BILLS)

BOYLE HEIGHTS

"LA RAZA!" (AND GOOD LUCK WITH THAT)

60

GOD HAVE MERCY ON SOUTH CENTRAL!

FIRST AME CHURCH

SAFE HAVEN

SOUTH PASADENA

GOD HAVE MERCY ON WHOEVER LIVES OUT HERE

IS THIS STILL L.A. OR IS IT ACTUALLY RIVERSIDE BY NOW?

SOMEONE SHOULD DO SOMETHING ABOUT ALL THIS (BILL COSBY)?

Joan shushes the group.

She stands on a lunch table, trembling under the fluorescents. And she says:

"I grew up in Ohio . . ."

A hush falls over the group.

"I grew up in Ohio," Joan repeats. "The public schools I went to had green grass, brownie-baking PTA's, and families who looked like Ozzie and Harriet . . ."

There are vague murmurs of assent.

"But we don't live in Ohio forty years ago. We live in Los Angeles today. Not only is it a desert, making even the growing of grass ecologically questionable, white children are now a minority in L.A. County—just one in five. So English speakers have a choice. We can turn and flee into our little Johannesburg-like enclaves, the supposed 'good schools' . . . But the fact is, there simply aren't enough of them."

Her arms fly up, like Evita, and she exhorts us:

"How long will we flee our neighborhood schools? How long before we learn to work all together! How long before we stop living in fear!"

The room falls dead silent.

Look at her! I think.

She is so strong! So certain! The fluorescents reflect off her chestnut pageboy! Her fingers point, touch, make circles! And through the sheer dint of her trembling passion, her body almost takes flight.

It is a rousing, epic *Lord of the Rings*–type moment.

What Joan is basically saying is, "Oh ye Gentle Hobbits of Kinderwood! Arise! Stand yer ground! In numbers ye are mighty! Take your kindergartens back!"

Now that I see her at work, I see that Joan Archer is a galvanizer! An Alpha Mom, or simply an Alpha . . .

For instance, in our family, it is Kaitlin, the oldest daughter, who is the Alpha. So when our quavering eighty-six-year-old elderly dad has a mysterious fall, is rushed to emergency, then is mysteriously discharged . . . and the two streams of conflicting information start coming in, our dad insisting irritably: "I'm fine! I'm fine! I just fell! Oops, dropped my pills. Let me count them. One, two, five, three, TWELVE, THIRTY-SEVEN—" And on the other line you have: "Paging you? Dr. Sanders. The cardiologist. It's urgent. Dr. Sanders." And you call back Dr. Sanders and . . . he's gone for the weekend?

I've found, even though it is I who live in town, since our family is lucky enough to have a family Alpha, all I have to do is to vaguely SUGGEST medical confusion, give a sigh, admit I'm at a loss, and within twenty-four hours, Alpha Sister has packed her bags, flown down (via her free airline miles—she knows all the codes, they're all at her fingertips), and set up camp in our father's living room. She is practically conducting medical tests herself, with her own equipment. All I have to do is murmur, "Wow—you're amazing," and respond to the continuing medical e-mail updates by occasionally typing things like: "Oh—so it's the bladder, then?" And the problem is handled.

As for my family, I have a Kaitlin now: For public school I have a Joan.

"When I and a group of just two other regular working mothers founded this *very* preschool we're standing in, Valley Co-Op . . ." Joan continues passionately.

Oh my gosh, that's right. Hazy memory now recalls that Joan actually founded this place. Which I'd gotten used to thinking of as a piece of random luck we just fell into, an unexpected lifeboat in Los Angeles, unbelievably cheap, convenient, and flexible, you can leave your kid in aftercare for like two dollars an hour—

"So, as parents today, in a large urban school district, unless we choose to move OUT of the city, we have to have a proactive attitude. As many times as you ask, 'What can this elementary do for me?' you have to ask, 'What can I do to help IT?' 'Where is a good public school?'" Joan pounds her fist to her chest. "'A good school is where

I am. A good school starts with me.' The number one factor determining your child's academic success is not the particular school she goes to but her parents. Or his! That's you! You, the parents, are POWERFUL!"

It's all so clear! I turn excitedly to the crowd, and realize . . .

No . . . Oh no . . . No . . .

Joan Archer is like one of the shiny elfin people, and we are like the raggedy hobbits. God, look at us: We are an unattractively lit roomful of wild-eyed, sweaty people. Bouncing babies. Faces hysterical. We can't do this. We can't. We are tired. We are panicked. We are already at our wit's end.

The reject parents—the clubfooted little hobbits—we are indeed in flight!

I glance down at the map of L.A. again. Look at this. No. It's too daunting.

This great, dark, overwhelming dragon threatening to crush us, this faceless thing called L.A. Unified, is a thing so much more vast and powerful than we are. It's a *Brazil*-like bureaucracy whose grim tentacles reach everywhere, poisoning the very kindergartens our children would attend.

I look back at Joan and now . . .

I watch in slow motion as she makes a fatal mistake.

Which is to say, after she stuns us with this rather shocking notion of "standing our ground," she fatally . . . turns. She turns away from a teeming mass of seventy-five people to fumble for a chart she has drawn up. The chart is in a scroll, she has to roll it out, but it keeps rolling itself back up—

"Oh my goodness," she says. "This thing keeps—"

Joan was clearly all prepped in the nursery, but now, since at the last minute we had to hastily move to the lunchroom, she doesn't have any of her traditional organizational weaponry around her.

Her Sharpies are rolling, her Tupperware containers are toppling.

"Walt?" she asks. "I think the humidity—it keeps curling—I just can't get this list of LAUSD schools to stick on this wall!"

"Let me get it," her husband says.

"It just—it's my list," Joan says helplessly. Her phrasing becomes broken, abrupt, tragic, William Shatner–ish ("Bones . . . The serum . . . My arm . . . Fading . . . I can't . . ."). "The chart is my list. It's my . . . 'Into Kindergarten' list—"

She turns back, but the mob is restive. This is not closure. They are being offered more questions than they started with, and it doesn't feel good. A baby in a stroller begins wailing. The mother doesn't shush her. She stands frozen in space, too anxious even to move.

"The thing is," Joan presses on, "our public schools—your public schools—can be improved. There are grants you can write! For beautification! Teaching gardens! New libraries! You can form booster clubs using a 501c3—"

A 501c3—what is she TALKING about? Our children are being abandoned like kittens in baskets and Joan is jabbering on and on about a 501c3.

"Take the handouts!" Joan cries. "Where are my handouts? It shows very simply how if you want to start a booster club or educational foundation using a 501c3—"

Or maybe it could make sense, but utterly depleted by the Vortex of the Snorl, I just can't follow it.

"Jonathan Kozol!" Walt cries out. "It's all about racial integration!" He holds up books showing a sad, dour, sheepdog-faced man. The books have TERRIFYING NAMES IN GIANT LETTERS! SAVAGE INEQUALITY! SHAME OF THE NATION!

It's all just too much.

"It's for your children!" Joan adds. "Don't be scared! Your children will thrive!"

Walt tries to get another banner to stick against the wall. It's supposed to read:

Parents for Public Schools

But the middle keeps collapsing, so it looks like it reads:

Parents f

ools

Or:

Parents fools!

Joan and Walt resemble elves encircled on all sides, waving their flimsy weapons, declaring an impossible plan. This year, what, armed with just a telephone tree, they are going to take on the entire city, and the Republicans, and Schwarzennegger?

I don't think so!

I think of what the sweaty dwarf perkily says in *The Lord of the Rings.* "Certainty of death. Small chance of success. What are we waiting for?"

3
Happy Lutherans: Island of the "B" Students

"I've made a new friend," I announce to Mike. "A mom from Valley Co-Op preschool. We have a lunch date!"

"Congratulations, honey," he says. "I knew you could do it. Which mom is it?"

"Brenda Runyon," I answer. "Mother of Cal. From the playdate."

"Wow!" he says.

And indeed, for our family, it is a whirlwind.

To begin with, Hannah has never before had a playdate. Until now, Hannah and her other classmates at Valley Co-Op—all the Colbys, Coleys, Codys, Colins, Coles—have roundly ignored one another (the polite term being "parallel play"). But all at once Hannah and Cal are BEST FRIENDS. Cal has been pestering and pestering his mother to invite Hannah for a playdate, which in my world means: "So you want to take my daughter for three hours for free? Gee—what's the downside?" (The downside is we'll have to then invite Cal over. Still.)

Part Two of the whirlwind is, as stated, my actually fraternizing with another mom from the preschool . . .

But Part Three may well be the most exciting . . . that I've decided in the fall, Hannah will be attending Lutheran School. And not just any. No less than the Valley's best-kept secret, the most up-and-coming Lutheran school around . . . Luther Hall!

That part Mike doesn't know about yet. That I've jumped our family onto the back of a new Alpha Mom. That I've changed pushy-mother-with-all-the-answers horses. Hitched my wagon to a totally new star.

It is true Brenda Runyon is a bit of a cipher for me. Brenda, with her shock of brown curls and faded AYSO SOCCER bumper sticker on her giant black Chevy Tahoe. While pleasant, Brenda has always seemed one of the more remote moms at Valley Co-Op. It is true my impression of Brenda's remoteness may relate to the fact that Brenda is most typically seen at a distance, halfway down the block, as if through a telescopic lens. And if you look closely, as I finally do, you'll see Brenda . . . stamping out what appears to be a cigarette—aha! That explains the remoteness! She's a smoker! Brenda doesn't smell like smoke, more like a breezy combo of peppermint gum, lemon, and Tic Tacs . . . But if she is a smoker in Motherland, that means she necessarily leads a secret life.

When I dropped Hannah off at her playdate with Cal, I noticed Brenda's home was immaculate (white couches, refreshing scent of cloves . . .). It was probably less smoky than my own house, given that we live under the Burbank Airport flight path.

And in that moment it struck me that Brenda was one of the few Co-Op moms I did NOT see at "Into Kindergarten" . . . which led me to believe she has a kindergarten "ace" up her sleeve . . .

So I jumped in, exclaiming, "Are you as confused as we are about this whole school thing? It's so crazy!" Then I casually asked for a stick of gum—which I consider mother-to-mother code, kind of a sly salute, a sort of polite tipping of the hat to say, "I know you're a smoker, baby, and Mama's okay with that." And it is, indeed, open sesame. Not only did Brenda give me several sticks of Juicy Fruit— one for now, two for the road—she has since opened the door to her secret Brenda Runyon world.

And at the center of that world is Luther Hall. As opposed to Joan Archer, with the futile, untenable, all-too-giant sweep of her Great Society vision, as regards kindergarten . . . Brenda has a laser-like focus.

In Hannah's cubby the next day, as though part of a covert spy operation, I find a crisp, white, unmarked $8\frac{1}{2}$-by-11 envelope, smelling lightly of mint. Inside, Brenda has not just printed out a MapQuest for Luther Hall, she has *clearly outlined my drive from Van Nuys to North Hollywood in yellow highlighter.* At first glance, the yellow route does not appear to be the straightest shot, but an accompanying note explains that since our ideal ETA for the Luther Hall parent tour is 8:45 A.M., we need to factor in TRAF-FIC CONTINGENCIES.

Given how sparingly Brenda uses actual dialogue, it's a revelation to glimpse inside her brain, to see the complex workings of her inner wheels and dials. She writes:

> There tends to be construction on the right side of Vanowen just before Colfax at that time in the morning, so while I know it seems counterintuitive, you'll actually want to take not Oxnard Boulevard over or even Magnolia or Victory but BURBANK.

I am a person who believes that in Los Angeles, people's innermost personalities, their philosophies even, are revealed in the driving routes they choose, the trails of bread crumbs they make as they weave their way through the city. And Burbank is such a bold, muscular choice! It is true I myself am more of a "resign myself to Victory" or even "consign myself to the ill winds of Victory" sort of driver. Yes, Victory Boulevard is butt-ugly and usually clogged, but so are the other east/west boulevards of The Nuys, in mysterious traffic patterns I'm not clever enough to divine, so I always simply commit to Victory and consider watching my life slowly seep away under the Jack in a Box signs part of my daily Zen practice.

But in Mike I see a bit of Brenda. He also believes in the bold, muscular choice of shooting all the way down to Burbank. Mike believes in Burbank so much he would take it straight to the sea if he could.

And thank God I have Brenda, because without her epistle on traffic, I may well have never been able to find the school. She continues:

> Luther Hall is a school you've probably driven by a lot but have never noticed before. Heading toward North Hollywood, it's up Laurel Canyon below Victory on the same side as the 170 Freeway and Coldwater.
>
> But here's the trick. When you make that left-hand turn, the first landmark you'll see to your right is El Pollo Loco (just beyond the Jiffy Lube, Target is beyond that) and you'll feel like you want to turn there
>
> BUT DON'T!
>
> If you don't quite complete that turn but continue on straight, into what first looks like an alley, it will zig left zig right . . .
>
> Then catty-corner from the chapel you'll see a low brick wall covered in ivy. Drive toward the guardhouse with the little coat of arms (sword and flame, indicates the eternal search for truth) and park. Gate arm should be open. I like parking way off to the right in slots numbered 110 and up because the shade is best between nine and eleven in the morning, which is during the time of our tour.

In addition to a School Fairy, it is clear that Brenda is also a Directions Fairy! With Kaitlin as my Medical Fairy, all I need is a Travel

Fairy. Which I bet Brenda could be as well ("Instead of using Hotels .com, cut and paste into your browser: 12312312$@@!$travelseats.org. You'll want to click on 'Menu A' BUT DON'T—!")

The directions totally play out, of course. As Brenda indicated, I COMPLETELY felt the urge—almost an overwhelming urge, like a bowel movement—to turn at the El Pollo Loco, but I stick with her zigzagging alley, and there it appears, almost as if in a dream . . . the guardhouse with the little coat of arms. I like this place, Luther Hall—I like its modesty, its caution, its tidiness, its quasi-hiddenness, and yet its ready accessibility (there's no guard in the guardhouse, the gate arm is indeed wide open). Its daffodil-yellow buildings are plain but clean, with many cheerful windows festooned with children's artwork. I pull toward the far, far right of the parking lot, where, indeed, are clearly marked numbers 110 and up . . .

Into one of the most leafy, cool, delightful parking slots I've ever enjoyed! It is a hot pocket, a saucy little oasis of excellent parking, tucked away, *counterintuitive.*

Brenda is waiting for me in front of her Chevy Tahoe, in slot number 111. She greets me with a large fresh Starbucks, which she lifts neatly up for me out of a tray. She has sagely pre-milked the coffee and arranged, in the center of the tray, a tidy fan of straight sugar, raw sugar, brown sugar, Equal, and Splenda. And . . .

"I like THIS," she murmurs, removing from her purse and splitting open a little Ziploc bag, which actually has, if you can believe it, a mini-shaker . . . of hazelnut powder.

I don't typically seek out hazelnut powder, but Brenda makes it all seem so easy, like falling into a bed that has already been turned down for you, and I'm still high from the excellent directions. (There was an interesting southward jog Brenda made me do on Fulton.)

So I say "Okay."

"All righty, then."

Brenda gives me a shake, a stir, I sip and I find . . .

I like it!

"Hazelnut powder!" I gurgle. "Who knew?"

"Hm!" she says, then all business: "Let's go."

The front offices of Luther Hall are laid out in a pleasant U. There are flowers, there are trophies, there are framed photos of neat lines of children in sports uniforms, there is typing.

Overall, a first impression is: gold, and navy blue.

"This is Doris Anderson, head of admissions—she's with our church," Brenda says.

A plump, white-haired woman with gold button earrings and an argyle cardigan behind the front desk waves (in my mind, she is "Mrs. Claus").

"Here's Hannah's application packet," Brenda says. "Just fill out the top section, leave the rest." I gratefully receive it. "Where it says 'Early Admit,' check yes." I do. "Here is a Luther Hall tote bag you can put it all into." It's navy blue, gold straps, canvas. "Oh, and here, as a souvenir bookmark . . . a Blue Ribbon—"

"The Blue Ribbon," Doris Anderson says. "Yes. You've heard about our Blue Ribbon. Everyone's talking about our Blue Ribbon."

"But for September, there are openings still?" asks a sloe-eyed brunette to my left. She is very thin, intense, long brown hair, in pale green Gunne Sax–style shift. Her accent is . . . ? French, it must be French.

"At this moment there are still plenty of spots open for Kinder— K—and Developmental Kinder—DK," says Doris. "However, we JUST heard the exciting news that Luther Hall has been designated, by California, as a California Blue Ribbon school—"

There is a portentous pause. We all murmur our approbation.

"And when that status is announced officially next week?" Doris continues. "All bets will be off. Already I'm getting calls. But we can't open any more spots in kindergarten. We are maxed out. Just this morning I started a waiting list—"

Gunne Sax is vibrating: "But we were told—!"

"Yes." Doris brings two hands forward, palms in, as though framing a small perfect gate. "All you families today who leave a check and an application will be guaranteed a kindergarten spot for September. No question. This is our last guaranteed-admission tour. You're lucky. You made it in right under the wire."

There are palpable exclamations of relief among the dozen or so parents gathered . . . And then a new surge of companionable relaxation, of sideways charming looks, of shy dimpling smiles. We made it! We've gotten in on a hot stock right before it doubled. We've landed the sensible brunette just before her makeover as a platinum blonde.

It is the complete opposite scenario of last week, of Valley Co-Op's sweaty, frantic, *Dr. Zhivago*–like panic. No, we are the lucky new family of Luther Hall parents. Instead of a frenzied Siberian train, we are pushing off together, festively, on a kind of laconically wending, Mosel River . . . party boat.

"Is your accent . . . French?" I ask Gunne Sax. "If you don't mind me asking. I hope it doesn't seem too rude."

She looks at me for a moment in surprise, then says, "Yes, we just moved here six months ago from Paris!"

"Well, welcome to Los Angeles!" I say. "This is my friend Brenda." Brenda gives a terse wave, her gaze already going reflective, and distant—thinking about a cigarette, I presume. "Her son is Cal, my daughter is Hannah . . ."

"Hannah?" asks a sandy-haired blonde in pince-nez glasses, standing next to Gunne Sax. Also with an accent.

"Actually, it's short for Hannelore. Although you can't tell by looking at me, my mother was German. From Danzig! My dad is Chinese, from Shanghai."

"Ah!" Both women blossom. Pince-Nez puts out her hand and says, "My name is Ilga. I am Swiss!"

"This is a lovely school, isn't it?" I exclaim as Doris leads us down the hall, toward the playground.

"Of the schools we've toured so far, we like it very much," says Gunne Sax. "Very cheerful. Very bright. It looks very safe."

"Not too stuffy," says Pince-Nez.

"How many schools have you toured?" I ask.

"Eleven," says Gunne Sax, with precision.

"Wow!" I exclaim. "What part of town do you live in?"

"Studio City," they reply at the same time, dolorous.

"Studio City!" I erupt. "Those schools down near the boulevard are supposed to be great!"

"Public school—no," Gunne Sax says firmly, a bit sadly. And thinking of the wild confusion, and the magnets, and the gerrymandering, (and then what about middle school? Ike Turner!), I can relate.

"I guess things are much simpler in Europe," I say.

"NO!" they exclaim in unison.

"It is the same situation as here," admits Pince-Nez. "You cannot send your children to public school in Europe anymore, either. My sister just moved out of Berlin. She had to move out of the city, actually."

"Berlin!" Gunne Sax shakes her head.

"Berlin?" I ask.

She murmurs something.

"What?" I say.

She repeats it.

It sounds like "Terken." Terken?

"The playground!" Doris exclaims, before a sweep of running, shouting children, verdant lawn, and a covered play area, with blue and yellow structures built in the form of child-sized rowboats and sailboats. "We just replaced all our concrete with this new rubberized surface, which, as you can see, the children just love—"

And now a bell rings. Teachers call out to their squads, begin herding, arranging. Children shuffle by in formations pleasing as flocks of birds in their white shirts and blue pants. "Luther Hall has a dress code, as you can see," Doris points out, "but it's fairly relaxed." And I like that, structure without rigor, like a guardhouse without a guard.

We follow one flock of children into their daffodil-yellow kindergarten classroom. Without much prompting, the kindergarteners wiggle down into their desks, pull out individual boxes, and seem to know to immediately busy themselves with cutting out little teddy bears, and pasting them onto different numbers.

"As you can see," Doris notes, "our kindergarten curriculum utilizes a full range of small motor skills."

"How many hours is kindergarten?" asks Gunne Sax.

"Six," Dories replies, with a kind of light regret that is then again NOT regret. "From nine to three."

"Whoof!" the parents exclaim, at once horrified and then . . . delighted.

"Kindergarten at Luther Hall IS a long day," Doris notes. "And it IS quite academic. That's one of the reasons we got the Blue Ribbon."

I must say, I love the academic, I love the Blue Ribbon, I love the fresh rubberized playground I feel I myself could do jumping jacks off of. I like the constant bustle, the clicking of typewriters, the cutting-up of bears. In the far corner, I see a heavy bespectacled woman Windexing a globe.

Lutherans . . . takin' care of business!

Windexing the globe!

"Is Wednesday chapel REQUIRED?" a white-lion-hair-maned dad asks.

"It is NOT required," Doris answers. "Although the children do enjoy it . . ."

"I will SO send Hannah to chapel," I whisper to Brenda. "She LOVES Bible stories."

"Hrmph?" Brenda replies. She is gazing longingly out the window, at trees, I think, at a small remote copse of trees. Smoking trees.

Happy Lutherans: Island of the "B" Students

"We used to send Hannah to Lutheran Sunday school up north, where my brother lives." (As with the Cal playdate, my attitude about Lutheran Sunday school was: "So you want to take my daughter for three hours for free? Gee—what's the downside?") "Man! There were songs, coloring books, finger puppets, cut-up bologna sandwiches, carrots, punch . . . The Lutherans ROCK at Sunday school!" I make a tight fist at the word *ROCK*.

"Yes, they do," Brenda manages, continuing to stare at the trees, in a glaze. But I sense she must, in some way, be enjoying my little ode to Lutherans. I press on:

"One time Hannah got invited to a picnic of UNITARIANS and . . . I don't know. There was too much drumming, they were disorganized, the field was cold and, let's face it, the children were hungry!"

Crossing back into the hallway, I see, on the wall, a poster for an impending biopic, *Luther,* starring . . . Joseph Fiennes! A Fiennes brother, no less! Up and coming, are these Lutherans!

So up and coming that, back in the front office, when I write out our application check, I notice the annual tuition for kindergarten has gone up. The original $4,500 has been crossed out. Next to it, in black pen, neat teacherly handwriting now indicates a fee of $5,200—

But the second child gets 10 percent off. And Lutherans, too, have got to eat! And someone has to pay for that pleasing sea of rubber.

I do the math in my head, and I figure it's still manageable for our family. In one stroke, two kids, Blue Ribbon school, K through 12, I already have the route highlighted, in yellow . . . AND the excellent parking spot . . .

We are done!

We go out to lunch at a restaurant that is as enigmatic as Brenda.

It is called RANDI'S!!!! It's on Moorpark. It's not quite American, not quite Mexican (although it does have a "Mexican omelet").

While it's not really a bar, little placards on the tables welcome you—hey, no judgments!—to have a glass of Chablis or rosé, or even a carafe, with lunch.

It is no genre at all. It is theme-free. It is RANDI'S!!!!

We sit in white, ornate, quasi–New Orleans–style steel chairs on the patio.

"Welcome, ladies! What can I do you for?" says our waitress jauntily. She is also chewing gum, as Brenda and I now busily chew gum.

And looking up into the weirdly tanned *Wizard of Oz* apple-tree face of our friendly waitress— Suddenly it occurs to me, maybe it's a smoker's restaurant! Maybe that's the genre—smokers! Biggest smoker of them all—RANDI!!!!

"Get the tuna melt," commands Brenda. "Small tomato salad, blue cheese, dressing on the side."

Not on my wildest day would I think of ordering a tuna melt, but after the hazelnut incident, I do it. I obey.

"I'll be back," Brenda announces, abruptly rising.

My phone chirps. It's Mike.

"How's your lunch date going?" he asks. "Having some laughs? Womanly laughs?"

"Sure," I say, uncertainly. "It's fun." I am burning to tell him that I've gone ahead and enrolled Hannah in a fantastic kindergarten—that in one blow I've solved our L.A. school problem (complete with secret knowledge of how to park)—but ... In marriages ... When the mother is manually overriding the father ... All information has a season.

"Hope you're letting your hair down," he says. "Enjoy yourself."

All right! He's right. When I hang up, I decide I should treat myself to something special and at least personally celebrate, so when Friendly Apple Tree returns with two ice waters, I ... well, I order a glass of Chablis! When it comes, I take a sip and instantly realize this is a mistake. As the Chablis enters my system, I almost cave over with the rank, even dank (can a white wine actually be "dank"?) Boone's Farm sweetness of it.

Brenda returns, sees me recoiling from my white wine.

"Oh!" she says. "Well."

"It's a bit sweet," I say.

"Yah!" she replies, like it's obvious. "THAT I would not order here."

And I realize that while I am IN Brenda's world, I can't stray even a foot off her yellow-highlit path.

"We put my older son, Daniel, into Luther Hall two years ago and he just loves it," Brenda says, newly invigorated by her short but clearly refreshing break from humanity. "And earlier this year, I got involved in the booster club. We threw a carnival last year and it was SO much fun. Through a special deal with my husband's company, we got one of those really giant Knott's Moonbounces—you know them? Those really big Moonbounces?"

"You mean the really—?"

I don't actually know what a Moonbounce is. Is it the same as a bounce house? To make things simple, I simply borrow Aimee's "hopelessly big as L.A. Unified" gesture again.

"THOSE Moonbounces?" I say, arms wide apart.

"Yes!" Brenda exclaims, making a pointing "You got it!" gesture at me, although her point is not a one-fingered one but a telltale two-fingered one.

"Hopefully, this year we can drum up more publicity. What with the Blue Ribbon Award, this is really going to be a big year! I'm on the PR committee—"

"PR," I proffer. "Well! Maybe I can help with that!"

"Yeah?" Brenda's voice sails up, interested.

"I don't know if you know, but I work at a radio station. I do weekly commentaries. Literary, sort of slice-of-life commentaries."

Brenda is enthused. "A radio station? Really? Which one?"

"KCRW," I answer, trying to sound casual, like it's nothing. For many in Los Angeles, KCRW is only the hippest radio station on the entire planet.

Still smiling, Brenda says, "I'm afraid I . . . don't know it. Oh, wait a minute—is it like a rock-and-roll station? Classic oldies? 93.1! I love KCRU!"

"No, it's . . . public radio. You know, NPR. Public radio."

Brenda shakes her head.

"Doesn't ring a bell."

I can't help feeling a tad . . . deflated.

Not knowing further what to say, I take a bite into my tuna melt . . . and . . .

Oh my God! It is so warm and toasty and good, I literally want to drop to the floor, rend my clothes, and scream. It is an amazingly good tuna melt.

Driving home up Burbank, then borrowing Brenda's tip and doing her weird little Fulton thing, which IS much nicer than my usual route, what with all its lovely picket-fenced farmhouse-like homes, why have I never noticed this—?

Well! I think. It's all right.

It's another of the curses of my forty-second year. A Law of the Universe. Kids and mothers never match. If your child and another child adore each other, you and the mother will have little in common. But when you and the mother are instant best friends, when you fall into each other's arms like long-lost sisters, as though she's the best friend you lost . . .

Perfect example: Leah at Gymboree. When I first saw Leah in the hallway, a too-bright jumble of parachutes and onesies and stuffed-animal toys, Leah was laughing. She had a chime in her laugh like one of my girlfriends of yore.

This was a stunning contrast to the continual gray drizzle of

Mothers of Small Children—their furrowed-brow looks, biting their lips as they strained to duck under strollers to pull out wipes, blankets, diapers, hats . . . No. Light on her heels, Leah was wearing a batik skirt, she had long brown hair, hoop earrings, and she was laughing.

Leah was a painter who was instantly wry and funny about our eerily corporate, relentlessly commercial Gymboree surroundings.

"Look at this!" she confided as we stood yet again at the flapping Sisyphean tent that was the parachute. "I could sew something better from scarves out of my own drawer!"

Later on we stood together in the parking lot . . . When I think back, I realize this is where some of my best conversations with mothers have occurred. It is the sheer transitoriness of the parking lot, the traffic blatting by, the fact that either mom may be spirited off in a second, via a gust of wind, the shriek of a child, the scree of a cell phone, or a sudden move across the country, a decision made in thirty seconds— It makes you want to open your heart immediately . . . because you may never see each other again. Leah confesses she just comes to Gymboree to get out of the house since, living up in Topanga, she has no mother network. She is surprised to find herself with two children so relatively late in life, everything has seemed so unplanned. She invites me for dinner in Topanga. Mike is so delighted at the prospect of my making a new "friend," he hugs the girls and waves me off.

I find myself driving up to Leah's home in Topanga with that breathless first-date anticipation—that shy junior-high gawkiness . . . Will this mom be my new friend?

I just love Leah's house! It's humble but charming, with skylights, winding decks, and Tibetan prayer flags. Leah's rustic bungalow is small, just three rooms really, but wonderfully livable, what with the ingenious system of loft beds and cozily built-in window seats custom-built by her husband, Finn, a sculptor/carpenter. Leah's is a perfect dollhouse, a cheery boat abob in life's ocean. There's a red velvet love seat and Leah's paintings hung everywhere, a torrent of horses, nudes, dragonflies, giant sunflowers, wild, arcing splashes of color.

"Welcome!" Leah exclaims, handing me a glass of (not dank but refreshing) Chardonnay, and leaning down, she puts on a record— "Yes, a record," she cries out, "we still have these!"—of, yes . . .

Joni Mitchell's *Blue*.

When I hear the familiar, gentle, slapping dulcimer opening, and then I hear Ms. Joni herself half laughing, half crying the long-forgotten words: "I am on a lonely road and I am traveling, traveling, traveling . . ." I am once again on that lonely road . . . that lonely road which, at twenty-four, I used to walk on, in my mind, so many times. But it was never a lonely road, it was a happy one. *Blue* was the road of my youth—above, the sky was a celestial blue bowl of endless potential. This was a time when I thought making Art would be life's greatest gift, my cosmic solution, as opposed to the Thing, in my thirties, it became.

In the gathering aromatic Topanga night, Leah shows me her marvelous forest world—her painting studio, her sketching deck, her Mother Garden.

"For when I need a break from the children. Here . . ." She bends down, pulls off a strip of plant, gives it to me.

"That's my crazy lavender. I call it that. Crazy lavender! I break it into my bath!"

"It smells incredible!"

"To Mothers Without Borders," Leah declares as we clink our wineglasses.

As she sets colorful hand-painted dinner plates out on the table (an antique chest) on the deck, Leah reveals that she, of course, loves KCRW, she seems to remember half my commentaries, half my whole life, she has read two books of mine, she even saw an old solo show I did—

"But then what happened to you?" she says. "After that you seemed to drop off the map!"

"Well, in a nutshell, I guess you could say I started my career planning to be the next Amy Tan . . . unaware that decades later there would still *be* an Amy Tan," is what I lamely say. Which is part of the truth.

Leah grasps my wrist, urgent.

"NEVER stop creating. Never stop writing. No . . . matter . . . what. We women artists are fierce, fierce, and we have to be fierce! And you know who are fuckers? Men! The men are fuckers! Men!"

Although I am not ready to leave the small, safe hammock of public radio obscurity I've carved out in the middle of my life, hiding out in the leafy enclosed hamlet of Motherland, it does my heart good to hear her voice her "Rock on!" support.

In short, Leah and myself . . . We are a match made in heaven!

At which point I feel an odd sort of . . . stinging sensation in my right ankle. And I look down in the gathering aromatic darkness to see . . . Well, it appears to be Leah's six-year-old son, Coltrane, curled around my leg. He is—FUCK! Biting my ankle! He is literally BITING MY ANKLE!

"Shi—!" I squat down to extract him. "Jesu—"

I hold the wriggling boy at bay, jaws first, like a rattler. "It's nothing," I find myself babbling, "I'm sure Cole didn't mean to . . ."

And to my greater surprise . . . Leah doesn't leap up in alarm! She just gently coos, holding out her arms: "Come on, baby. Mama doesn't want you to do that."

Cole utters a strange gibbering howl and flies to Leah, who sinks down in a rocking chair, and cradles him, dreamy-voiced.

"Boys—in particular indigo children, like Cole is? They have such a hard path in this world. Such a hard path. This teacher Cole had, at his other school? She would just snap at him, snap!" Leah makes a little snapping gesture with her forefinger and thumb. "Snap! That teacher! Mrs. Arnold." Her voice slides into high-pitched mocking. "She was all 'Sit in your chair, Cole! Sit in your chair.' Or 'It's a pencil, Cole. It's called a pencil.' Or 'Now it's lunchtime. Now we eat lunch.' Fuck it!" she exclaims angrily, now veering into a more widely free-ranging monologue about how society willfully oppresses boys and will stop at nothing to punish and put down their questing human spirits. I've never seen anyone become so viciously *rageful* on white wine. It is truly an eye-opener.

On cue, Leah's two-year-old, Nita, begins shrieking, shrieking, shrieking, like a coyote in the glen . . .

And now, materializing behind me in the dark, is Leah's husband, Finn. He was clearly once a ruggedly handsome man but now is somewhat grizzled, and has an unsettling thousand-yard Vietnam stare. Finn stands so close behind me, light and cat-like, I can feel his breath on my neck. And hey—I know I'm one to talk with my kale farts, but I must say that Finn is exuding this kind of weird Moroccan rotting tobacco/henna/bargain-persimmon smell. What can I say? Parents—we just smell worse than other people.

Without asking, Finn starts giving me what I can only describe as an inappropriately slow shoulder rub.

"I lo-o-ove the music on KCRW," he breathes. *"Nocturna* is my favorite show. You wanna smoke something?"

I have to fight the urge to turn to them all and say, "Oh, I know who YOU are. You're the Crazy Family! It's not just your lavender that's crazy . . ."

And now, as though sent straight from central casting, drifting down the stone stairs, comes the fat sixty-something seminude Topanga neighbor, crooning Van Morrison, flip-flops slapping. He is wearing only a falling-open Japanese gee. No! What will I be asked to do next? Oil his belly? *Is* it a marvelous night for a moon dance? I think not!

Compare to little Cal, star of the first playdate I have ever thrown.

I can see why Hannah is in love with him.

Cal is the dream four-year-old. He's like a little Sun. Blond, blue-eyed, a perfectly formed little human. Like Hannah, when he sees me, he bolts to me, his arms fling around me. Why? I guess simply . . . because I'm related to Hannah.

Cal thinks our small, incredibly messy house is a wonderland. All Mike's guitars everywhere! And my cluttered back office, and computer!

"What is it all FOR?" Cal wonders.

"Well!" Mike says. "I play music."

"And I teach," I say. "And write!"

Cal's eyes open in amazement. "That's why Hannah is so smart! When we play Candyland and checkers, she always wins. Don't you, Hannah?" He turns to her, batting big blue eyes.

"Eh . . ." she says, though you can tell she is deeply pleased.

"Hannah is just so smart! Her big brain works so fast! It's like . . ." Here Cal does a little tap dance of surprise and delight. "Wow!"

I put out twin plates of all I actually have in my pantry . . . toast with peanut butter and honey.

Cal leans cautiously forward, takes a tentative bite. Oh!

"This is so . . . good!" he enthuses, as though I, too, were some sort of genius.

"Would you like another?" I ask. This is amazing. Many kids at the preschool respond to even a plain bowl of noodles with a piercing scream: "Euwwww!!!!!! I'm going to BARF!!!!!!!!!!!!!!" And then suddenly Hannah, too, is barfing.

But this guy, no, Cal's mind is open. Indeed, I think I can expand his world even further. My voice drops a half-octave: "Cal honey, would you like to try, on the peanut-butter-and-honey toast . . . raisins?"

When he takes a bite, his small body slumps backward with exhaustion and even a kind of gusty relief, it is so good. "Wow!" he says.

I'm literally out of kid food, so unused am I to actually line-producing a playdate. Rummaging through the fridge, I locate an expired strawberry Danimal—at least two months past its expiration date. I toss it to Cal. He inhales it as though it were truffles. "So good!" He hasn't changed color. Seems none the worse for the wear. What the heck. I toss him the remaining expired Danimal. This is fantastic—Cal is actually helping me empty out the fridge!

Strengthened and invigorated by his expired, processed, artificially colored food, Cal now suggests to Hannah how fun it would be if they . . . make all the beds in the house! Now he suggests a game of putting all the toys away! Next I hear the whine of the DustBuster. Cal is DustBusting . . . !

It occurs to me that Cal may in fact be a small gay child . . . which may be why he and Hannah are so in love. Their palace all neatened up and ready to receive them, now Cal and Hannah step into matching tutus, carefully slip each other's feet into high-heeled princess slippers, lifting and draping each other with boas.

Well! It's the NEW Luther Hall! Their lapis lazuli Cinderella outfits will coordinate just fetchingly with the Blue Ribbons.

Speaking of which . . .

"Lemonade?" I say, offering my husband an icy glass. He is in the backyard assembling his brand-new fish smoker (which he probably read about in *Popular Mechanics*). I follow his gaze to the children. I have cannily set up, also in the backyard, twin water tables where the children now bathe a frothing snarl of My Little Ponies. In matching red aprons, Cal, Hannah, and now The Squid look adorable together.

"They are having fun, aren't they?" I say.

"It's nice that age to have a friend," he replies.

Mike still maintains ties with many of his childhood friends from South Dakota. He used to walk home from kindergarten with Vicki, wife of his best friend, Dave. They've all known one another more than forty years and, unbelievably, still like one another. In Sioux Falls, apparently people remain friends for life. What's the secret? Perhaps unlike in Los Angeles, one's old friends don't seize one's wrist across the table and ask you what school district you're in, gibber on about a wild string of charter schools, and then suddenly reveal that their children have Asperger's.

As far as I know, South Dakotan children do not have Asperger's.

Mike says, "I almost REMEMBER being four . . ."

"They ARE enjoying it!" I enthuse.

"I remember being that little. How uncomplicated everything was . . ."

"Hannah and Cal?" I shake my head with telling sadness. "Well . . . They have to get their time in now . . ."

And I let it portentously hang.

Mike frowns as he lines up two trays in the fish smoker . . .

"Where is Cal going to kindergarten? Do they know yet?"

I do not tell him about the Blue Ribbon, the tote bag, the yellow-highlit MapQuest. And the fact that I have already put in the application, and paid the two-hundred-dollar fee . . .

Because that might seem not "delegatory" and not "trusting" . . .

I say vaguely, "Oh, I think . . . you know, I think . . . Oh wait, it's coming to me! But don't mock," I warn, stern. I fold my arms across my chest. I put two smoker's fingers up. "Because it's a decision they're really happy about."

"I won't mock!"

"It's just that Brenda's older kid goes there, and they just love it."

"Okay . . ."

"And it's not expensive, and of course for their family, saving money is—"

"What's the school?" Mike asks, a little hysterical.

"Hannah—no!" I suddenly yell.

She has dropped trou and is . . . peeing! A great stream. While standing up!

"Hannah, no! Wait!" Cal picks up a beach towel and runs over to shield her with it. The picture of a gallant young cavalier, he holds the towel up like a wall, discreetly averting his eyes. (The young Joseph Fiennes, in . . . *Luther*!)

Crisis handled, I turn back to my husband. "I know how against organized religion you are, so don't mock. It's actually . . . a Lutheran school. Luther Hall. Cal's family is Lutheran."

"I think that's great!" Mike says in surprise, and in interest . . . And just as I knew he would, Mike falls in love with the idea of Luther Hall.

Because here's the thing. Although we grew up in different parts of the country, by coincidence, because of his Midwestern background and my German mother, both Mike and I were actually raised Lutheran. And though our church membership has long lapsed, in the crazy patchwork that is Los Angeles, what with all the Lindsay Lohans falling out of limos without underpants, it's nice to be able to scratch out . . . a little familiar solid ground. To go home again. To get a little LUTHER back into our lives.

Squinting ahead, envisioning the future of his little girl—a girl who at four is already a bit too brassy in the nudity department—Mike soon realizes he loves the idea of semi-uniforms, a little bit of structure, and a whole lot of chapel. To L.A. adolescence and beyond, it is, if you will, the Lutheran Solution.

"But if it's a private school . . . I don't know," he worries. "Do you think we'd have to kiss ass to get in?"

"Are you kidding?" I reply. "They don't know from ass . . . They're Lutheran!

He calls Brenda, who, with a nudge and a wink to me, manages everything. Paperwork is in process, space is no problem, acceptance letters will be mailed after fifteen-minute meetings with the children, which are just a formality . . .

It will be Mike, the dad, who takes Hannah to the meeting, because as he tells me:

"You need to take that vacation. Go."

4
Auberge du Fenouil

The thing is, I would still have my best girlfriend today—she whose name cannot be uttered—if it weren't for the Ocean of Money. The Ocean of Money separating us. Or at least that has been my theory.

I am talking, of course, about my ex–best friend of fifteen years. Celeste.

Celeste and I were best friends in grad school, we were housemates, we were aspiring sister writers, we were fellow Joni Mitchell travelers . . .

And then we became separated by the O. of M.

Which is to say I went into prose and theater. Celeste went into television, and it consumed her whole. Oh, her career began, in her twenties, like mine. She was writing things, submitting things, getting close calls, nothing big, then rounding thirty, she sells a pilot! I whoop for her! At first I get daily updates . . . ! Then things enter this second phase where there's no regular phone contact, only the occasional e-mail full of up-and-down emotions: "It's horrible. They're changing everything. But did I tell you? James L. Brooks, who as you know has been my hero all my life? Well, he said . . ."

Then things went dark. I left a few messages . . . Then I finally got a return call one Thursday night, after eleven.

Celeste's voice had changed. It was a breathy croak. It was as though her blood had all been sucked out by a—a Nosferatu.

"I don't think I can go on," she whispered. "I think I'm going insane. I've been there seventy-four straight hours. I really feel I might . . . hurt myself."

In panic, I called our mutual friend and Celeste's neighbor Kim, sent her over to to knock on the door. But unbelievably, like the hypnotized virgin of Klaus Kinski, Celeste had already actually driven BACK to the studio, to the heinous beast masters she so loathed, who she said were killing her, killing her, killing her!

The next week, cue the enormous gift basket—like something sent from a tropical jungle—from Celeste, with a polite two-line thank-you note saying that things were much better.

A gift basket? I have to admit, the cheeses were fabulous, things I'd never tasted, but . . . a gift basket?

It was the very opposite of intimacy.

Who were we?

The answer would come six years later in the form of a wedding announcement.

I am used to having friends in Los Angeles who make more money than I do. I'm used to visiting the homes of those who live just one class bumped up from us. I remember a barbecue at my writer friend Tom's where I was surprised to find not just one Hispanic lady busily washing wineglasses but an actual crew. My feeling is, if you have enough Hispanic women in your kitchen that they could play pinochle together, you are Rich. Ish.

But then you open an invite—like Celeste's, one saying she had eloped, and now to share their joy, she, her new husband, Bran, and his five-year-old daughter, Skyler, were inviting us all to a house-warming party ("No gifts. We mean it. No gifts")—

And here comes the classic L.A. moment where out of the invite falls a map. A very complicated map.

It's not just that they have moved from the corner of Higgledy Avenue and Yucca (or as my friend Roger used to say, "from the corner of Crack and Liquor") to some place like Canyonview Terrace, Bluebird Circle, or Ravenna Lane (as in the Palisades, where winding avenues sound suddenly Tuscan and Lake Como–like).

It's that this folded-up map is no simple MapQuest. MapQuest won't help you here. Nor anything tawdry and common and yahoo.

The map . . . Well, it's a bunch of wildly squiggling lines in remote canyons labeled with references to things you wouldn't even expect to find in Los Angeles. "Go 8.3 miles into canyon," then make left at "old railroad car," "miner's cabin," "flamingo preserve," "Trappist monastery" . . .

That's when you know you're really into Money. When the only signposts indicating the whereabouts of your friends' vast, rolling, private acreage are fire roads, water tanks, or perhaps a capsized model of the original *Hindenburg*.

(You live WHERE, Mr. Darcy? Pemberloo. Pemberleaugh. Pember-what?)

The only thing I can tell you about the location of Celeste and Bran's house was it was somewhere near Santa Barbara. Montecito looks to me like just a tiny town, and yet within Montecito they had a property the size of San Pedro. Is that even possible? Or maybe it was ABOVE Montecito.

All I can say is after you drive 8.3 miles up a canyon, everything totally unmarked, at the eleventh hairpin turn, out leaps a small army of red-vested Hispanic valet parkers, like a paramilitary junta. Not only could this number of valet parkers play pinochle together,

I imagine they could get together a rousing game of cricket, perhaps even form a modest national league.

After shrugging off your car, you follow a winding set of stone stairs down, down, down . . . You're vaguely aware of natural moss, on all sides, enclosing . . .

Then all at once it opens before you.

Bright sunshine.

Oh my God!

It is as if you are flying over the giant, scooped-out blue bowl of the Pacific Ocean. Below you, holding you almost aloft, is what looks like a crashed starship, a massive rock pile of slate-colored wings, shearing geometrically away from one another. When you look closer you realize the wings are, unbelievably, roofs of many buildings, each roof individually nubbled with discretely and artfully broken stone. Each sheared roof nestles amid floating islands of frosted glass.

I look down and realize . . .

This is no housewarming party, where Celeste and I are going to reunite. It is a houseCOLDING party . . . The frosted glass and slate THING—the crashed starship? It is the ice sculpture centerpiece of a bon voyage party to our friendship, a memorial, if you will, a wake. It is the glacier Celeste will be sailing irrevocably off on. I should smack a champagne bottle against its prow.

Mike pushes our two kids off in the double-stroller while I wander alone through the compound, and . . . No wonder there were no gifts. I can't imagine an object a civilian could bring to this house. There is not a single conventional or even conventionally sized item on display. The vases are, I want to say, fifth-century Egyptian granite, the toilet paper rolls hammered steel, the art is . . . important. And . . . archaeological. Turning along charcoal-colored slate, I pass a Balinese gargoyle . . . A Thai snarling goddess waving two fistfuls of twisting snakes . . . A giant bowl that is . . . Etruscan? A pop-eyed head, with an ear missing, that is . . . Mayan?

And there, at the end of a berber-carpeted hall . . . Celeste's office. It has to be. There's a silver iMac, piles of scripts, and just beyond, on a long wooden table huddles a menagerie of photos. Large ones, small ones, in frames of gold, brass, silver, probably Tiffany, and then, at the very end . . . Could it be?

I gasp.

"Aw," I breathe out, caught unexpectedly by emotion.

It is a small, circular blue-and-yellow daisy frame, reminiscent of the late eighties. It cradles a faded Polaroid showing a tiny Celeste and myself crashed together on a sleeping bag, hysterically laughing. Celeste and myself, ages twenty-seven, forever caught in time. But it is so small, so half-hidden, clinging to the edge, as though Celeste is embarrassed about this tchotchke, artifact, relic from that ancient, faraway time when Celeste was poor.

Feeling like a rather elderly, distressed, and weathered artifact myself now, I locate the child area, easily visible via its large pink Princess bouncy house. Perhaps half a dozen children, presumably including Celeste's new stepdaughter, Skyler, are jumping, in safety, cordoned off from cliffs and ravines that plunge dramatically away.

I grab myself a glass of wine and make myself a plate from the buffet—the good thing with Celeste being that she has always believed in feeding people. I must say, I've often been startled by the experience of going to rich people's houses and there is either Domino's pizza or a Costco vegetable tray or some really bland pasta ordered in from the local strange canyon trattoria. There really shouldn't BE trattorias in canyons. One mega-wealthy screenwriter friend of mine is, if you can believe this, a vegan. We drove forty minutes up a canyon past haunted goldfields to his house only to discover this. Honestly, to have to listen to his pompous movie monologues and not see a tray of sushi or paper-thin prosciutto for our pains—it was really NOT WORTH IT. Because Greg will never throw any work anyone's way—he's really consistent about that.

So I approach the bouncy house with my globe of wine and my plate of food, my plan being to perch on the nearby low wall and enjoy my feast while keeping an eye on my girls, when out of the Princess bouncy castle, a snub-nosed girl with blond ringlets pokes her freckled nose.

She says to me, flatly: "You can go away."

"Well, maybe I don't WANT to go away!" I respond, pertly.

The girl waves a small hand. *"No comida."*

"Wha—?" I say.

To clarify, the girl says three amazing words, which I have never forgotten:

"Skyler isn't hungry."

Of Chinese-German extraction, I could be said to look Hispanic. And with my two blond daughters . . . ? We're the polar opposite of the white forty-something mothers you see in parks, pushing, in strollers, their adorable Chinese girl babies. From a racial point of view, it looks like either I'm their Third World nanny or I stole my white babies.

At the same time, I suddenly realize that even with my LIGHT mocha-colored skin, I am by far the brownest person at the party! Which is to say, the brownest person not washing glasses, hefting trays, or parking cars. And looking around, it dawns on me that Celeste and Bran's guests, here in Santa Barbara . . . The tall blond women and their short, bald, homunculus husbands? They aren't just white, they are iridescent! They have that kind of bluish look you get from spending every day in dark screening rooms or in end-less film-scoring sessions.

And in the meantime, stop the presses:

Skyler isn't hungry!

After that, it is true that I don't try hard.

I eat my food. I take seconds. I drain a second glass of exquisite wine. I slip off my sandals. I enjoy my view of the Pacific.

Then I round the family up, locate Celeste in her half-mile-long kitchen, and lob back, like a sock of poo, my own version of the coldly luxurious tropical gift basket:

"Congratulations, sweetie, the house is so fantastic happy marriage Bran seems wonderful oh my God the view this is amazing! WE ARE LEAVING."

"Oh no!" Celeste exclaims in alarm, clinging to me. "You just got here! I wanted to show you what we've done in the study, where I have a whole shelf of your—"

"Long drive back," I say, "lo-o-o-ng. But congratulations. Really. Wonderful!"

When, the next day, Celeste sends me an e-mail, this time it is I who doesn't respond. Really? What can one say? No gifts. Really. We mean it. No gifts. (No! We REALLY mean it! Our architect will KILL us!)

But now, two years later, Celeste has written me a letter.

A long letter.

S—

I've started writing this letter so many times so many different ways and then I thought, fuck it, I'll just rip the bandaid off.

You know and I know that these past few years we have not been close.

In many ways I know I have disappeared, into my career, into the WB, into that hell train called Everlywood, *which destroyed the lives of just about everyone—*

What on earth was *Everlywood?* It was a mark of how MUCH Celeste had disappeared that even the major signposts of her life made absolutely no sense to me. ("Go 8.3 miles and make right at Balinese mongoose farm.")

Anyway:

Taking stock upon turning 40, surveying the major ups and downs of my thirties, a clear mistake I made was placing too much faith in that feckless weasel Bran, his not-so-covert affair with my 22 year old assistant

Kayla being just the tip of an iceberg so big it should be its own Arctic sub-continent penguins included.

In that run-on sentence, particularly when I hit the penguins, I actually felt I could hear the faintest lilt, the faintest familiar melody of the old Celeste I knew so long, long ago.

Then last January, my mother died.

Oh no! LOVED her mother!

Emotionally burnt in every way, I went down alone to our beach house in Isla V. and took stock.

I am now emotionally invested in this letter, but once again, "Isla V."? A blank.

S—I don't know if we can ever be the friends we were. I don't know if we can even be the people we were. But I honestly love you, and have missed you, and wonder if perhaps there is some new version of our friendship we can try in our forties . . .

"Auberge de Feneuil?" Kaitlin exclaims on the phone. "For three days? That's like the most expensive spa in Napa!"

"Apparently she got this huge divorce settlement! And I think . . . I honestly think . . . divorce has brought her down a peg."

"Down a peg?"

"Well, there was something in the tone of the letter where I saw a flash of the old Celeste, when she'd let you see right down into the core. As opposed to how she became after she entered TV land. Where she always seemed oddly stressed, jangly, harsh . . . impatient with anyone not successful in TV. One time I was complaining about one thing or another and she said, 'Liquidate some stock!'

Just like that. She actually snapped her fingers. 'Liquidate some stock!' "

"Maybe she's just the same . . . but it's you who've changed." There is a crunching sound. Kaitlin seems to be at her computer, eating. "Celeste was always a bit fabulous. Even when she wasn't rich she was fabulous. You always liked that. You couldn't wait to rush to her house and eat all those gourmet cheeses."

I hadn't remembered that . . . But it was true!

Kaitlin continues: "You guys were always strong on the wine and cheese. And you're going to Napa, all expenses paid. Wine and cheese. Just stick with that—focus on that."

"I always think you're not really listening to me, that you're always doing something else on the phone, distracted, but in fact, that advice is very wise!"

"It's amazing how wise I am: Conversation number 922."

A buzzer goes off.

"What was that?"

"I've just been defragging my hard drive. But no worries. I was really listening!"

I stand on the curb at the Oakland airport. Southwest. The sky is a gray haze. Traffic brays by. My flight was early.

I stand waiting, all I can do. I'm actually not quite sure what I'm looking for. Celeste said, "I'll pick you up," but does that mean town car, limo, Hummer?

I look up one way—Asian family of five, a slim blond college student bent over a tennis racket. I look the other way—a gaggle of mop-haired trustafarians, all typing things into laptops—

I hear a familiar voice from behind me.

"You."

I whirl. There Celeste is, in T-shirt and khakis, with that big, toothy smile of yore . . .

"'lest!'"

She tackles me into an embrace. She holds me. Hard. Her body is shaking, she is wordlessly crying, now I am, too . . .

And all at once, the years roll off. The decades melt away. The cage of my heart opens. We are those girls again. We are those girls laughing on the sleeping bag.

We hug. We squeeze. We laugh. We weep.

Now there is more laughing . . . at the weeping, weeping after laughing . . .

We stroke each other's hair, murmuring our apologies. So many years have I been wearing this body armor. To be putting it down at long last. To once again find the place—the comfortable bathrobe—where I fit.

"Okay," she says, wiping her nose. "This is very *Beaches*. It's just a bit too *Beaches*."

"Yes, it's very much like how movies jump-cut from twenty-six, and then suddenly the women are standing in an airport weeping at forty-two."

"And then you're sixty doing a solo cabaret act for the armed forces—"

"And you're walking through a snowstorm with James Brolin—"

"Let's not do that," she says. "Let's just get this messy reunion done. We're now forty-two, I am divorced, you are still married to—" She gives me a gentle punch in the ribs. "Good old Mike, salt of the earth. The years have spooled by, what in the world happened, we have become like strangers—We don't know who we are—Regrets, we've had a few—Women in transition, blah blah blah—Cue Carly Simon—"

She opens the car doors of a slate-blue convertible Saab thing, its innards a welcoming living room, a step-down Jacuzzi, of cream-colored leather.

"And it's now the weekend!" She raises her fist in exultation. "We are going to ENJOY our vacation. 'Women Getting On to the Next Page!' "

Celeste and I are now winging our way, fast, through Napa.

We have been laughing since Oakland.

I have come on this weekend determined to suspend my judgment about all her money . . . And I must say, I have found it ridiculously easy.

It's hard to feel sour in this glorious countryside, vineyards falling open all around us, under the most golden, perfect, late-afternoon Northern California sky.

It's hard to feel sour while cupped in soft leather that, thanks to the seat warmers, is artificially warm beneath my ass. While surrounded by a magical constellation of invisible German microspeakers.

Celeste has programmed into her iPod an eclectic-mix of all the old music we used to listen to—Joni Mitchell, Prince, Aretha, James Taylor, Sly and the Family Stone . . .

"Sly and the Family Stone!" I scream.

Our conversation is seamless. We are yelling insights at each other. We are vomiting out all the thoughts that have been collecting in our innards, over ten years.

I have talked, she has talked, I have talked, and now she is talking again.

"Here is the problem with women's friendships, in the forties. No one has the time. All I find myself doing is 'bookmarking' women. I run across an interesting woman at work or somewhere and I 'bookmark' her—I say, 'I like you. I'm bookmarking you. I'm mentally making a note that I'd like to know you better.' So last year I 'bookmark' my music supervisor, we go out for lunch and suddenly we decide to order a glass of wine with lunch, which no one ever does anymore, and then we have more wine, and now all at once we've been sitting there three hours and this door to a whole new universe has opened and she is telling me about who she was in her twenties, going to school at Columbia and studying composition, she thought she was going to be a female John Cage, or Yoko Ono—

"And I look at this woman I've been working side by side with for five years and I realize . . . I have no idea who she is! All this stuff she is telling me about herself is fascinating! And we realize we have become just these working automatons, pushing all this work THROUGH, on a constant SCHEDULE, and that in fact we know at least twenty women just like us! Not only should we all go out to lunch together, with mandatory wine, we should throw a midsummer's night bash for all the other stressed forty-something women we know who never make time for a mental-health day!"

"A mental-health day! I love the idea!" I cry out.

"This would be a fabulous evening where everyone would wear—"

"Sarongs!"

"Exactly!" Celeste lifts a hand from the wheel to snap her fingers. "Just like in *28 Beads*—"

"Although that Paolo, I must admit he seems—"

"Gay!" Celeste snaps her fingers again. "I believe those are toreador pants he's wearing on the cover."

I feel like saying, "Conversation #207: Paolo is gay," but for once it's fun to actually HAVE the conversation.

"So," Celeste continues, "at the dinner, our idea is all the women would wear sarongs and no one would talk about their jobs or their children or their allergies or any other enervating topics! We would call it 'Women Getting On to the Next Page.'"

"I love it," I say, taking another swig of . . . the flask. That's right. Celeste has handed me a flask of chilled Stoli and tonic, from our youth, our signature beverage.

"Unfortunately," Celeste continues, "when the week in question rolls around, neither Lynn nor I can stand anyone we are currently working with, let alone each other. There are scheduling issues, there are cat issues, our executive producer has that thing—" Celeste makes a vague gesture down her back.

"Chronic fatigue syndrome?"

"Close."

"Epstein-Barr?"

"Closer."

"Fibermyalgia?"

"Fibermylagia, YES!" Celeste snaps her fingers. "So I tell her just take a Vicodin and a bath, and she says, weepily, 'Then I have to wash my tub. And baths—they're so complicated these days. I don't even know what to put INTO the bath anymore.' WOMEN! I want to say." Celeste pounds the steering wheel. "WE'RE TRYING TO GET ON TO THE NEXT PAGE!"

"Then again," I say, "bath crap is complicated."

"TELL me about it!" Celeste erupts. "Just last month I was going through the things in the house—"

"The one in Santa Barbara?"

"Yes—the nightmare house."

"I thought it was fabulous," I said, putting in a college try of loyalty.

"You liked it? That stone-and-glass monstrosity? I hated it. It was Bran's project. And all the people who live in Santa Barbara? I thought I would go insane."

"I've missed you," I say.

She puts her hand on my arm, squeezes it, continues.

"So I'm going through the things in the house, and just the tonnage of bath products . . . ! Lavender bath bombs, driftwood-shaped loofah sponges, eucalyptus-scented candles, clay jars of Dead Sea mud, aloe vera lotions, masks, exfoliants, a complete unto-itself oatmeal scrub unit, one crusty bat of—I think—New Mexican sage, a small glycerin nest of seashell-shaped soaplets . . ."

"Yes!" I say. "I have that kind of stuff, too, under my bathroom sink. I don't even know where it came from. I think it's the accumulation of years of bath gifts—graduation, marriage, baby showers, birthdays—it seems there's no rite of female passage that can't be marked, in some vague way, by a little hay-strewn basket of bath items. As if to say 'Happy Graduation! Have a bath.' 'So you're thirty-seven! Have a bath.'"

"Yes!" Celeste lifts a hand off the steering wheel again, to gesture. "I even got a DIVORCE bath basket! It's like 'Wishing you a fabulous divorce, and menopause! Rock on, sister, and what, I guess? Try a bath.' And I look at this giant pile of unopened bath crap, and I mean to re-sort it, or re-gift it. But the sheer hugeness of the task daunts me—the sheer amount of relaxation woman-hours it represents. A hundred females soaking in a hundred tubs for a hundred days could not soak up these oils."

"Maybe we've reached a point where we simply have more aromatherapy than the nation can use . . ."

"And you know what's funny? We do a lot of cross-advertising through New York, and you know who the most stressed magazine editors in the world are? The ones who work at *Real Simple.* Apparently it's a real sweat factory. A eucalyptus-scented sweat factory."

"How much more blood can you get from a loofah sponge? Oh! And then the herbal teas!" I exclaim.

"The herbal teas!" she shrieks. "How many types of noncaffeinated green tea can you *have?*"

"And the gourmet hot sauces. Which I think our nation also has enough of. Particularly those with cartoon labels featuring devils or gleefully self-designated insane guys named Dave! The demand peaked about 1994, to judge by the untouched bottles in our pantry, slumped together like once-irrepressible frat boys now permanently hung over."

"YES!" Celeste says. "Dave! Who WAS Dave?"

"I, too, have given up on women friends," I declare. "Since entering my forties, I've sort of gone into hiding. I feel like maybe my twenties and thirties were my social time, but now I've retreated into my shell." I don't know why I've suddenly plunged into such candid territory, but the vodka has enlivened me, the sun is shining, and Celeste is playing me, drawing me out like a brilliant conductor, a Toscanini.

"I know what you mean!" she says. "The shell. In a way, it's just easier."

"I guess I feel like I'm at the point of my life where I've met most of the people I'm going to meet, and there are no more new people or ideas under the sun." I think of people like Joan, and her sweaty, fluorescent-lit *Lord of the Rings* flailings, and I amend it to say, "Well, I mean no ideas that are really workable. Like saving the whales? I'm not going to save the whales. I know my limits."

Celeste leans in: "Can I admit something?"

"Please."

"I have not seen *An Inconvenient Truth.* I mean to, and I'm for it, but admit to anyone you just haven't gotten around to it and it's like you're burning coal."

"Exactly. I'm in sensory overload. Too much information!"

"Exactly! That's the problem now! There's too much information! Did you know that an average weekday edition of the *New York Times* contains more information than a typical seventeenth-century villager would come across in his or her entire life!"

"Where did you hear that?"

"On NPR!

"Forget the bath. My own favorite evening—my own favorite form of 'me' time—is sitting glamorously alone at the computer and playing Solitaire. My laptop nub is worn from all the satisfying squeezing and snapping of cards. It's my version of worry beads. I've always got a secret game going—while on hold with Blue Cross, in between reading irritating e-mails that flock to my in-box like crows, for that last delicious two minutes in the day before returning to husband and children. Those last two minutes of the day being penultimate time when my otherwise ever-cheerful sixties mom used to retire to the back porch, alone, Greta Garbo–like, for her one grim cigarette."

"Supposedly, Hillary Clinton's preferred mode of 'relaxation' is playing Tetris on a Game Boy.

"You know HILLARY has a pile of unused bath products!"

"You don't still stay up all night in a ratty leotard anymore, eating popcorn, playing games on the computer, do you?"

"Noooo," I say, alarmed that she remembers that about me. "Of course not!"

Auberge du Fenouil—which, loosely translated, means "hotel of the fennel"—is so exquisite, you can't see it. Which is to say, the buildings are actually built into the hillside, and covered with wildflowers, sage, moss. The only sound is the occasional distant squawk of a jay, and the discreet whine of a golf cart.

We pad our way across what appears to be ancient rock and salvaged farmhouse wood into less a lobby than a gently glowing orange orb.

From within her cartouche of maple, a young supermodel tilts her chin up to us. One glimpse of us and, I kid you not, her face has lit up. The plucked eyebrows have spontaneously risen. In honeyed tones of perfect German-accented English, she says, "Welcome!

That is, she would be a supermodel—glowing skin, cheekbones slanting outward under clear blue eyes, white-blond chignon—except for the fact that she is totally devoid of hauteur. Brita—that is her name—appears to have been placed on the planet for the sole purpose of serving us.

"I parked in the—?" Celeste waves an arm.

"Of course," Brita says. She rings a bell.

"Ms. Walden," she says automatically, placing a cream-colored

envelope on the counter. Clearly no formal introductions are needed—
there's no nasty-ass check-in. At Auberge, apparently guests are
tracked in by GPS. She slides a second cream-colored envelope
forward. "Your key, your map, your schedule, spa pass...? Ms.
Tsing Loh."

"Ooh!" I say.

A brunette appears at Brita's side. She is just as long and lovely,
also with a chignon, but...brunette. Indeed, it's hard to know...
who is lovelier! They look like impossibly leggy Euro air hostesses
from some zeppelin in a James Bond movie.

The brunette's name is Gisele and she is also "aus Dusseldorf."
Brita and Gisele met in "international hotelier school," whatever the
hell that is.

"Mein mutter war Deutsche!" I say ham-handedly, with my extremely bad German.

Brita and Gisele cry out in delight, fluttering around me like birds.
I feel like some kind of linguistic genius. They love me! In this room,
I am actually killing.

"I just want to make a note of where we are on the Auberge
map..." I say.

"Natürlich—" says Brita, who is tearing something off a printer.

Celeste leans into me and whispers, "Brita and Gisele remind me
of the prettiest girl in high school who you desperately want to like
you and then you finally meet her and, unbelievably enough, she
actually IS...*really, really nice."*

"Because secretly she's Christian," I whisper.

"I have placed the cheeses in your suite," Gisele murmurs. She
leans her chignon into the radio, nods, informs us, tersely: "Warm
fresh bread is on its way."

I don't know that I've ever been happier than in the perfectly
warmed infinity pool at Auberge du Fenouil.

We have been discreetly attended to by chiseled young men in white—not in white suits, you know, or in white gloves, or in outfits so stuffy and formal you feel bad for them . . . No, these young men, with brown eyes you could melt in and clearly the souls of poets? While they have apparently also been placed on this whirling blue marble to serve us, they're clad in the relaxed natural fibers they themselves might choose to wear, while relaxing at the Auberge. Fueled less by duty than by breathless inspiration, they keep bringing us little tiny plates of things—a kiwi tart, a raspberry sorbet, adorable chilled glasslets of things . . .

And I realize I may have to handcuff myself to the Auberge's infinity pool, in case the authorities ever try to make me leave Napa.

Celeste and I are joined by her friend Lynn, same age as us, but with wild dark curly hair, big hoop earrings, a sparkly Stockard Channing, very attractive.

"Are you also from the Women's Divorce group?" Lynn asks as she doffs her terry-cloth robe.

"Oh no!" Celeste cries out. "Sandra is married! Been living with her husband for eighteen years! Great guy! Mike, salt of the earth."

"No!" Lynn says in amazement, settling herself into the pool. "Oh my GOD, this feels good." She raises a glass to clink with mine. "Eighteen years! How do you do it?"

My marriage feels so remote right now. I almost forgot I had a husband, and children. I'm not so sure I'm eager to fly back to them, to, in particular, my daughters' many tiny socks. All those tiny, tiny little socks.

I look down over the gentle rolling hills of Napa Valley. Slowly, a hot-air balloon wafts by. Down the hill before us, two bicycles zing. An extremely lean man, and an extremely lean woman. In matching green jerseys, and helmets.

"You know couples like that who do everything together?" I say. "Bike together, hike together, kayak together? You know? They literally KAYAK together in matching visors, their paddles dipping neatly up and down like synchronized swimmers . . ."

"Yes?" Celeste and Lynn say.

"Mike and I," I say. "We do NOTHING together. We can't even bear to GROCERY SHOP together! That's the secret to our longevity. I have this writer friend Joe. He WAS dating Liz, the most fabulous woman in the world . . . with the exception of this thing she calls the 'stay 'n' dart.' Shopping together, at Costco—"

"Which could be the problem right there," Lynn points out.

"Well, Liz will ask Joe to STAY with the cart in one aisle while she DARTS one, two, maybe even three aisles over to fetch a forgotten item—that's what she calls it, as though that term solves the whole thing, the 'stay 'n' dart'—and they broke up over it!"

"No kidding!" Celeste and Lynn exclaim.

"More advice," I say. "Beyond the Sisyphean futility of trying to load the dishwasher together, in light of the perennial gender-incompatible question of knives up or knives down—"

"What?" says Lynn.

"I'm guessing . . . Women do knives down for safety, men do knives up for cleanliness?" Celeste wonders.

"Yes!" I say. "But more importantly than that, do not pack together. Men and women: packing, total incompatibility. My husband, Mike, packs a car by placing each bag in the car as he packs it. I pack a car by packing and then methodically lining each bag up ALONG THE WALL next to the front door in sort of a necklace-like STRING OF BAGS so I can VISUALLY SEE WHAT I HAVE ALL AT ONCE. When the line of bags is totally complete, then the bags go into the car. So you can see how if Person A imposes his car-packing method on Person B . . . If while she is carefully COMPILING her string of bags—her own alphabet of bags—he starts removing the bags and putting them into the car willy-nilly, à la an *I Love Lucy* episode, slowly driving Person B mad, in a *Gaslight*-type manner—

"I sound insane," I cut myself off, suddenly.

"Not at all!" Celeste says stoutly. "Bran and I divorced over a house. A really UGLY house."

"Well, and a few affairs," Lynn adds.

"Lying about the vasectomy," Celeste observes, "that was another one."

Lynn exclaims, "Ah! And the hidden four million!"

Celeste throws up her hands. "Scientology!"

My cell cheeps. It startles me.

"I'm sorry," I say. "It's . . . kindergarten. We're trying to get my daughter into—"

"Absolutely!" the women cry, raising their hands. I flap open my cell and wade into a far alcove—that's how big this infinity pool/ Jacuzzi/spa thingy is: There are alcoves.

It's Mike on the phone. He is bubbling with excitement. They just got back from the Luther Hall "Meet and Greet" . . .

"Did Hannah have fun?" I ask.

"Sure!" he says. "It was actually sort of a . . . test."

"A test?" I feel a slight dimming of my perfect world. A distant . . . crow.

"No, no, no," he assures me. "She did great. They just asked her some simple questions . . . 'What's your favorite ice cream?' 'Mango.' 'What was your favorite present you got at your birthday?' 'Uni the Unicorn.' They gave her some drawings to copy, even this kind of crazy British flag thing, which she did. They asked her to write her name—"

"What?" I put my hand over my heart.

"She did great!" he says. "Wrote her first AND last name . . . perfectly!"

"I've never even seen her do that at home!" I laugh, feeling my cheeks flush with warmth and relief.

"They asked her to name some animals. She said, 'Lion, tiger, hip-popotamus . . .' "

"Hippopotamus!" I exclaim.

"Four years old, this kid is!" Mike exults. "We're going to Siz-zler!"

"What? What?" Celeste and Lynn exclaim when I snap shut the cell and slosh back, beaming.

I give them news of my daughter's genius ("Lion, tiger, hippopota-mus," "Said her favorite ice cream was *mango*—bet they never heard that one!") and they raise their glasses.

"Cheers!"

"That's my marital secret," I announce. "Delegation. He does his thing, I do mine."

"Hear! Hear!" they say.

"Of course," I laugh, "I make sure I do the IMPORTANT PART. I filled out the forms already, put down the deposit, secured the deal. He just does the follow-up. In that way I give him the . . . illusion of control."

"It's what I do at work all the time," Celeste laughs. "Give people what I call 'a comfortable Siberia.' With photos of palm trees taped over, masking the ice of their igloo walls."

"What school?" Lynn asks.

"Luther Hall," I say.

Lynn and Celeste raise their glasses automatically.

"Bravo!"

"Good for you!" Lynn says. "My ex's assistant's son goes there."

"Schools in L.A. are impossible," Celeste complains.

"And so expensive!" Lynn agrees. "So overpriced. At least you won't be paying an arm and a leg at Luther Hall. If I could do it over!" She turns to me. "Three children. Campbell Hall. Never again."

"Well, there won't BE an ever again," Celeste says.

"Hear! Hear!" Lynn says stoutly, clinking her glass.

"What was the . . . um . . . problem, at Campbell Hall?" I venture. In Los Angeles, it has come to feel weirdly personal to ask about specific *schools*. As if to say, where is the hidden stop to YOUR underground railroad? Can I and my party of fifty crowd into it? Into your secret bomb shelter? Got room?

"Campbell Hall has JUST become so SNOTTY!" Lynn cries out. "That guy Ray Romano—*Everybody Loves Raymond*! He dropped ten thousand dollars at the auction to win this prime parking place on campus—not that he EVER drops his own kids off. I tried to park there last year for just a minute, I was running late, and they SNAPPED at me! Just SNAPPED! Three kids I've put through that school, full tuition, no breaks, and no, suddenly it's Everyone Loves Raymond. It has become such conspicuous consumption I hate it. And the kids, I'm sorry—I just don't think they're that smart. It's all jocks. They've got this equestrian program now, it's an Episcopalian school, meanwhile everyone's Jewish—"

"You're Jewish," Celeste says.

"I know, but in a way, not so much. Stephen Wise Temple—feh."

"I like Campbell Hall," Celeste says. "Lovely campus. Very pretty."

"Right—said by a parent of Wonder Canyon."

"Wonder Canyon!" I erupt. "Where have I heard that name?"

Celeste puts her hand up, waggles it. "It's not really MY daughter. She's Bran's. Poor Skyler." She sighs. "It's really been tough for her."

"Wonder Canyon—it's the super-gifted school up on Mulholland," Lynn explains. "You have to be some kind of genius."

"Or have a father who gave the school two-point-seven million," Celeste mutters, shaking her head. "You have to use whatever currency is in your pocketbook. Even though, sad thing is, I think Skyler herself would be happier out there on the flatlands, riding ponies."

And as the women chatter on, I realize, okay . . .

If *Pride and Prejudice* were my life—and took place in L.A.—and schools were suitors—

Wonder Canyon, clearly the stratospheric ideal, would be like Mr. Darcy.

Campbell Hall would be like Mr. Bingley.

And Luther Hall is clearly like (blat of flügelhorn) Mr. Collins. People are so staunchly "Way to go!" for me, "Your cancer's in remission!" before turning back to their much more interesting Campbell Hall/Wonder Canyon business.

The fact is, Luther Hall is a third-tier school.

And yet, sipping wine in Napa on this exquisite day, sun on my shoulders, I'm not at all bothered to be bound to Mr. Collins . . .

Who, after all, dwells on the estate of Lady Catherine de Bourgh. Who while dull—and aren't most people?—took pretty good care of him and, as I recall, was NOT a vegetarian!

Like Elizabeth Bennet's friend Charlotte Lucas, I'm happy to be anywhere at all! And hell, at least it's not like I've run off with . . .

Wickham!

I mean, look at that creature in front of us. Off the grid entirely. Twenty-two, vulpine, eucalyptus-rubbed, in a fluffy white spa robe . . . the new mink.

She is telling the young man squatting next to her, who is offering a Napa peach tartlet: "Hm-hm. We just arrived Sunday, we'll be here for a week."

At which point a door opens and in a waft of steam he emerges, her date, who is about fifty years older and two feet shorter. He moves so slowly, painfully, practically wincing with every step . . . My goodness, this goes beyond what we expect from May-December relationships. Forget the sex, she must actually be deeding him body parts . . . perhaps a kidney!

Whereas here I am with my gal pal Celeste, who shoots me a look and mouths, "Are you okay?" Then she tilts her head toward Lynn and gives a wry flap of her fingers, so much talking. She mouths another word: "Sor-ry!"

I laugh, and shake my head: It's okay.

She squeezes my arm again, mouths: "Thanks."

We are now at dinner.

"The tasting menu!" Celeste declares, waving away all menus. "It's fabulous! Trust me!"

I giggle, very happy to be her ho'. All I have to do is chat, listen, veg.

By contrast, I feel sad for the vixen in the spa robe. The next table over, there she is, seated woodenly, with her horrible homunculus. And then after dinner she'll have to first put out, then donate the kidney. It's so much better in this postfeminist age, where WOMEN have money.

It turns out, unlike Celeste, Lynn has, overall, had a FABULOUS divorce.

"The first years were hard," Lynn reveals. "Before I got a whole synergy working with the nanny, the au pairs, AND the grandmother. But eventually, Charlie and I realized it was easiest to just stay best friends. We actually have therapy together twice a week now, and yoga."

"No!" Celeste and I laugh. But then Celeste becomes thoughtful.

"You know," she says. "The other day . . . I actually had a nice conversation with Bran. I don't hate him. I just hated being married to him, which makes me wonder . . ."

She leans forward. "Do we even need husbands, every day, in our lives? Maybe they're no longer necessary. I mean, the sex is . . ."

Lynn's face goes sly.

"Oh! With anyone NOT your husband, the sex is better . . ."

"Morgan!" Celeste screams.

Lynn throws back her curly head and chuckles throatily.

"Who is Morgan?" I ask.

Celeste explains: "Oh, Morgan is just a thirty-one-year-old British bad boy who flies into town now and then, and then . . . flies away. On days when Charlie has the kids, Morgan comes over and he and Lynn have wild sex. And then the housekeeper changes all the sheets."

"All the frenetic sheet-changing!" I exclaim. "I simply don't have the staff to do it!"

We are now all laughing and yelling: "I'm drunk! I'm drunk!"

The hot young maître d' with his ponytail is eyeing us, smiling at us, enjoying us . . . Bowing slightly, he says, "I will bring a dessert menu. Just to—"

"Look at you!" Lynn exclaims bawdily, practically taking—I kid you not—two fistfuls of maître d' bun and squeezing! And he . . .

Only laughs, raises a teasing finger. "Oh now. I could get fired." Either he is honestly charmed by us or is just getting paid a lot—

That's the beautiful thing about good service—you can't tell the difference!

"And, oh my God, Morgan," Lynn says huskily, leaning into the candlelight.

"Thirty-one," Celeste repeats.

"Oh my God!" we scream.

"Even at forty-nine he makes me feel like a peach . . . a delicious, juicy peach."

"*28 Beads!*" Celeste and I scream, at the same time.

"Paolo the Swordfisherman!" I say.

"But not *gay* at all," says Celeste.

"Oh no," says Lynn. "He's quite the swordsMAN."

We scream again, but—

"Is there dryness?" Celeste asks.

"No!" Lynn says, swatting her. "For that there are vitamin E creams and aloe vera unguents—NEVER MIND. The point is, Morgan says he PREFERS older women. He thinks our confidence is refreshing, our laughing sensuality, our lack of inhibition. Two words . . ."

"What?" we say.

"Nude Pilates. Nude nude Pilates."

"Oh my God," we scream.

I say, "I sometimes wonder if my own husband, after eighteen years of cohabitation, has grown, well, too lazy to have an affair. Like me, my soul mate has developed a certain endearing reluctance to change out of his sweatpants and leave the house after five P.M., and all those kittenish young *Sex and the City* gals seem demanding, they require meals eaten sitting up in restaurants, chilled crantinis, vigorous discoing . . . If my beloved husband were to embark on an affair with a twenty-six-year-old, I would be hurt, of course, but also impressed . . . All that showering, the micro-trimming, the grooming, the continual anointing, of all the body parts . . . !"

Lynn leans in.

"Are you kidding? I find as I get older, the sex only gets more interesting. My fantasies only get more exciting. Whatever is politically correct, I imagine its diametric, polar opposite . . . and that is what is hot. It's not Jodie Foster getting the Oscar for her brilliant acting—no, it's all the victim movie roles she plays to get the Oscar, the waitress raped on a pool table by a bunch of rednecks—'Yeah!'"

"Euw!" Celeste and I cry out.

"Or here's another," Lynn says. "THEY are a passel of fifty-something Kuwaiti businessmen—oil?—at some hideous downtown hotel with glass elevators. I am a nineteen-year-old blonde, slightly chunky, and bored telecommunications heiress with a taste for Amaretto sours. The oil men offer money for a private party. Thirty dollars? No. Five hundred dollars? Better. Two thousand seems a tad high. Five thousand is too much—for some odd reason (because the high price seems too call-girl professional, proper licensing in the state of Nevada and vaginal health exams now becoming involved), at five thousand dollars the fantasy loses traction."

"I'm still a sucker for Richard Gere," Celeste admits, moonily.

"Are you kidding?" Lynn retorts. "With our movie stars today . . . All that political idealism, earnestness, and altruism has become a real problem. I've never ONCE had a fantasy involving Richard Gere and Tibet. Brad Pitt these days seems completely desexed, what with the close-cropped hair, the relentless pussy-whipping by Anjelina Jolie. He is always trooping somewhere, saving Africa or something, hamstrung every which way by multiple BabyBjorns."

"Ralph Fiennes," Celeste sighs.

I turn to her. "Did you know Joseph Fiennes is now playing Martin Luther?"

"Mmm!"

"Ralph Fiennes," Lynn declares. "I feel nothing for Ralph Fiennes now, or even back in *The English Patient*. Oh no . . . Only in his debut in *Schindler's List*—forty pounds heavier, the chunky Nazi captain tying up young Jewish women in his basement . . . hot!"

"People do change," Celeste agrees. "I used to be so in love with the YOUNG Mel Gibson, before—"

"Forget the YOUNG Mel," Lynn barrels on. "I'm actually turned on by OLD Mel, the sheer BADNESS of him, anti-Semitically ranting by the side of the freeway, mad-dog drunk on tequila, his career in ruins . . . I could easily construct this fantasy where I am Cop Lady and Gibson is taking me right there in the squad car, oddly gleeful, pretending to flay me as in *The Passion of the Christ*. 'D-girl! Go! Fetch my coffee!' Hot hot hot!"

Celeste and I look askance.

"Too far!"

Lynn raises an arm. "What-ever!"

For dessert there are cheeses.

"Oh my God!" Celeste exclaims. "That's the problem with Napa. Never do they just give you a cheese. They're always compelled to drape it with a fig, a lingonberry, or an herb."

"And then the whole mess is drizzled over a chop of venison, and julienned . . . !" adds Lynn.

"And this whole place!" Celeste moans. "Auberge du Fenouil? Hotel of Fennel? I hate fennel!"

"I just want chocolate smeared ON my cheese, with a bowl of Cabernet!" I say.

And we fall over our cheeses, laughing.

The next morning it is time for our treatments.

Celeste has booked us not two-handed but four-handed massages.

"A four-handed massage?" I ask.

"Yes," she says.

"What," I say, "a kind of Leon Fleisher . . . four-handed massage?"

"I think Leon Fleisher played piano with just the ONE hand," Celeste says. "I think you mean a LABÈQUE sisters massage, Katia and Marielle."

"Or maybe it's four people but they just put in the one hand!" I muse.

Celeste and I don spa robes and meet in the meditation room, which features a tinkling Zen fountain, crystal bowls of fruit, and of course the customary townhouse units of exquisitely appointed herbal teas.

The names are all Mystic Meditation, Chamomile Rivulets, Orange Kaboom . . .

"How come Orange is always kind of a Kaboom?"

"I don't even read these anymore," says Celeste.

"Au contraire," I say. "I feel like I can't actually HAVE the tea unless I read it. Like it may go down the wrong chakra or something. Or like I might choose the wrong mood alterer. Look at these. It's all ORANGE KABOOM. MINT MIST CLEARER. SHOUT OF CHAMOMILE. OUCH: IT'S LEMON."

"GREEN TEA WITH MANY OTHER NON-GREEN-TEA THINGS

ATTACHED TO MITIGATE ITS ESSENTIAL UNFORTUNATE GREEN TEANESS," Celeste adds.

"CALM INFUSION," I say. "WHERE YOU ACTUALLY TAKE A TEN-CC. SYRINGE OF CALM AND INJECT IT DIRECTLY INTO YOUR STOMACH FAT."

"Perhaps Mel Gibson could come out with his own line of herbal teas," Celeste suggests. "Hallucinogenic teas."

"MEL GIBSON MADMAN TEA," I say. "Or OOPS, I SAID IT AGAIN: CHAMOMILE!"

"CRRRAZY MAN LEMON," she says.

"Or HONKING BAZOOMS OF CHAMOMILE."

In thé candle-lit hallway that leads into our massage rooms, we pass a bamboo plant upon whose thin green stalks hang small tiles with words on them, which you're supposed to hurl into a glass urn of bubbling water. In this way, you're able to mentally rid yourself of things like "GUILT," "SADNESS," "WORRY" . . .

All my crows, I hurl into the fountain. Tile, tile, tile. Down they drop.

And as I watch the white tiles lazily spiral downward, I feel my cares lift off my shoulders. I close my eyes, and for once, I can picture it . . . The unbroken white cliffs, on that perfect cloudless day. From beyond wafts the scent of pine, on a fresh breeze bringing with it a cool, calm . . . serenity.

For so long has my life seemed this frenetic wild-goose chase of female searching, a psychic wind tunnel of worry, anxiety, and obsession. It feels as if I never know where I stand. I've never known what role I'm supposed to be playing, from age fifteen to age nineteen to age twenty-four to age thirty-one to . . . ? Hello? What's my job this year? Good daughter, promising ingenue, loyal best friend, foxy girlfriend, brilliant artist, understanding wife . . . I never know how moist my skin is supposed to be, how high my boobs, how much a liberated independent woman should be making, or how organic should be the snacks in my kids' lunch boxes, the snacks they won't eat. My whole life I've felt like a square peg in a round hole. Whoever I am, I should be someone else. Whereas secretly the real me is an ungainly blob, a blight on the face of the earth, pimply, in wrinkled sweatpants.

But standing here now in my fluffy white spa robe, no makeup on, my skin aglow, tossing my worries away—clearly worries everyone else secretly has!—amid other women in their fluffy white spa robes . . . Finally we are all as one. There is no longer any competition. It is enough. I am enough. I have found my rung on the ladder, my coordinates on the grid, my nesting place in the honeycomb. Massage Room C.

In my airy, skylit, vanilla-hued massage room, my reverent male and female massagepersons meet me, clad in matching crisp white polo shirts and shorts, like Wimbledon ball people.

I lie on the table, and with the four-handed massage, I must tell you . . .

It is beyond exquisite, unspeakably so, to have one's shoulder blades butterflied by two therapists at once. At first the hardest thing is to keep from laughing—but then I come to feel as though I'm being held by the giant palm of God, cradled, in radiant light—

And then, eyes closed, in such a state of ecstasy, I see it . . .

I see the Bodhisattva. Looking exactly like he does in all those quaint-colored Eastern hangings. Lotus position, forehead dot, the big hanging earlobes. And emanating from his chest, I see what my perennially hectoring therapist, Ruth, with her waving turquoise-beringed hands, is always trying to get me to visualize before bed.

The orb! Red, gold, yellow, red, gold, yellow . . .

And in waves, I can feel it all rolling off of me.

Worry.

Stress.

Guilt.

I think of Hannah saying *mango, lion, hippopotamus,* and a warm ring of contentment encloses me. Lutheran school.

And I realize this, finally, is a story, a movie, I can be the hero of. Because what I am this year, above all, is a loving mother who is taking good care of her family. To be a mother who fights for her children, who finds safe nestling spots in the vast, perplexing honeycomb grid for *them,* that alone is a hard job, I am doing it well, and for all other perceived failings . . . I forgive myself. I accept myself. Without irony, I give myself a giant, universal hug.

Afterward, we women lie on the sleeping porch in our fluffy spa robes, creamed, pummeled, lotioned, with cucumber slices over our eyes . . .

A mandala of sleeping beauties.

Ringed protectively by mystic circles of *Spa* and *Real Simple* magazines . . .

Like creamed sleeping beauties . . .

Under the blue sky of Napa, perfectly clear with, only occasionally, a passing hot-air balloon.

Not a crow in the cloudless sky.

Oh no. That would be waiting for me upon my return home.

When word comes that, upon interviewing her, Luther Hall has concluded that my daughter is not developmentally ready for kindergarten. The protective amulet I have fashioned for my daughter has revealed a crack. According to Hannah's test, the school has decided she will have to be held back a year.

5
Fear in the Milk

This is the 2001: A Space Odyssey moment where lights and colors around you smear into tunnels. My gut turned to ice, I vault into the minivan, bouncing crazily down the rainy boulevards to Luther Hall—

Brenda's MapQuest has disappeared into the passenger-seat pile— I try to reconstruct the route in my head, but even reliable Burbank . . . It's totally backed up! Squeal of tires, I reverse, turn across a double yellow line, blare of horns. There is construction everywhere—red flashing lights, white-and-orange sawhorses. I'm driving like a maniac, like a wild-eyed Mother Tiger, stoplights flaring orange, knuckles turned to white.

I'm panting, I'm panting . . . Left at El Pollo Loco, zig left, zig right, there is the guard gate, which is . . . closed! Even worse . . . There is a guard in the guardhouse!

In just three weeks, so much has changed at Luther Hall. Ahead, above the administration building, stretches a large, ominous new blue-and-white banner . . .

BLUE RIBBON SCHOOL.

I force myself to breathe slower as the guard picks up the telephone, as the white arm of the gate reluctantly creaks open, as I hurry across the parking lot from my formerly perfect spot . . . SPLAT! goes the puddle I step into. Good Lord—I don't remember all this construction. Everywhere around me lawns are dug up, rectangular ditches yawn, yellow tape is strung every which way—what are they building?

"There has been a mix-up," I tell Doris Anderson, smiling through my teeth.

"Well I sure hope not!" Mrs. Claus says pleasantly. Today she is wearing a snowman cardigan with gold buttons that match the gold chain on her glasses.

"My daughter is Hannah? She came in for her—her 'meeting' the other week with my husband, Mike!"

"Yes!" Doris says, brightly. She picks up a thick pink pile of what appear to be . . . tests, and begins paging through them. "Let's see now . . . Here we are!" she says brightly. "Hannah! Yes, she has been assigned to . . . DK."

"DK," I repeat.

"Developmental kindergarten," Doris says, smiling up at me, and her smile is so cheerful, for a moment I almost imagine that this is good news.

"Well, what about kindergarten, REGULAR kindergarten?"

"THAT Hannah will start the year after," Doris Anderson says smartly, not changing her body language. It occurs to me that the counter in front of her is like . . . its own kind of guardhouse. Which I notice also bears the little coat of arms.

"So what—when she comes to Luther Hall in September, you're going to stick her into an extra year of preschool?"

"Not preschool. Kindergarten. DEVELOPMENTAL kinder-garten. It's a WONDERFUL program."

"You mean you're . . . holding her back a year?"

"We are not holding her BACK. In fact . . ." Here Doris leans forward, takes her glasses off, kind. "You might ask yourself, why are you pushing her FORWARD?"

The problem is that I have no Brenda. I am devoid of Brenda. Brenda is in Tennessee for two weeks. Without Brenda I'm lost. I have no idea how to negotiate.

I do a quick panicked scan of what cards I might be holding.

Celeste's voice comes back to me: "You have to use whatever currency is in your pocketbook."

My voice comes out very rushed and wobbly:

"It's just that as a media person? Who has authored books and written for the *Los Angeles Times* and does regular commentaries on KCRW? And teaches at Marymount? We think we can be a useful addition to the—the Luther Hall FAMILY—?"

"I'm sure you can be," Doris replies, unflapped.

There is a beat.

There is no Open Sesame.

"I guess—I guess we didn't know you were TESTING them!" I finally wail.

"The Gesell isn't a TEST, it's an assessment," Doris says.

Ah, so the horrible thing has a name. Doris holds Hannah's packet up. I can now read the front of it: "Gesell Kindergarten Readiness Assessment."

Doris continues: "Apparently, Mrs. Crandall—and our evaluators are very good; they all have extensive training in the Gesell . . ." Doris opens the test, puts her glasses back on, pleasant, anticipatory. "Well! Let's see what she wrote here."

I gaze down.

At the top of the first pink page is Hannah's name and age—4.4.

And below . . . ? Below is not a description of a child I recognize. It's a sea of scarifying ADD-like phrases like "intermittent eye contact," "not focused," "attention seemed to wander."

"Hm," says Doris, turning the page. "So she's a little wiggly—they can be."

"Wiggly?" Was that bad?

"Here we go," says Doris, sweeping her hand down the new page.

The main categories listed on the page are Conversation, Blocks, and Pencilwork, which are accompanied with many small technical diagrams. I feel a pang in my heart when I see Hannah's brave pencil work, her careful scratching. I can imagine the frizzy yellow head of my love bent dutifully over this paper.

And to the right of her drawings, well, look! There's an age-appropriate score spray of 4.0s and 4.5s!

"That's good, isn't it?" I erupt, in relief. So it IS all a mistake! "Hannah is 4.4 years old and, hey, check it out, she's doing some 4.5s, 4.6s!"

"Yes, but by January," Doris says in that way she has that is both regretful and not regretful, "for Luther Hall students? Because our kindergarten curriculum fully utilizes both large and small motor skills, even at this point in the game we want to see more 4.5s moving into 5.0s."

"Well, look at this British flag thing!" I half scream. Oh my God! Hannah replicated an entire British flag! I will tear this Mrs. Claus's cardigan to bits if I need to to get my point across. I tap the British flag, hard.

"The British flag! Look at the score Mrs.—Mrs. Crandall put! 6.0! Six-point-oh years old, I believe that is!"

Doris leans over the British flag, moves down her pen to keep reading. I have to admit that I'm grateful, at the very least, that she is giving such careful attention to Hannah's test, studying it as though it were a fascinating unfolding mystery.

"But look what the evaluator wrote," Doris replies. "Because after drawing the flag, Hannah did not want THEN to try the much simpler diamond . . . That drops her score down to 4.0. In some interpretations, that would even scored be 3.5."

My voice is shaking.

"You get nothing for doing something brilliant and then get docked for not trying something simple? What kind of—of . . . test is this?"

"Kindergarten is a long day, nine to three," Doris says. "We don't want Hannah to be frustrated. We want her to thrive. Kindergarten at Luther Hall is academically demanding."

Academically demanding? They were cutting up teddy bears!

"She said 'hippopotamus'!" I shrill. "I know for a fact she said 'hippopotamus'!"

There is a moment of silence while Doris turns to the next page.

"Yes, animal naming, here it is—lion, tiger, hippopotamus. But you see—" Now she tilts her head back and fixes her eyes on a faraway, dreamy point.

And in this moment I hate her for not even acknowledging the word *hippopotamus*. She just said "hippopotamus" and went on, refusing to even say, "Hippopotamus—very nice." To give said sparkling vocabulary word just the polite tip of a hat. No, Mrs. Claus said "hippopotamus" and went straight to the "But—" Argh! Suddenly I understand a drunken Leah railing away at AUTHORITY on her Topanga deck. I, too, could locate boiling dark rage, in a light and whimsical Chardonnay.

"But you see," Doris continues, in that same dreamy way, "this is interesting about the Gesell, that's why it's such an interesting ASSESSMENT. The animal naming is timed."

"Timed?"

"With a stopwatch."

A stopwatch?

Why did my husband not tell me this?

All that marital hooey about Delegation . . . and fuckin' . . . Trust.

In the madness of my past few years of sleep deprivation, I seem to have conveniently forgotten that my husband is *the world's worst messenger of vital information*. Any information! One time he came back from lunch with an old friend of ours whose wife of twenty years had just moved out. I met Mike at the front door, beseechingly: "How is Alan?" "Alan? He's fine," Mike said. "But what about Caroline!" I ejaculated. "Her moving out, hitting Alan with the divorce papers, the affair?" And my South Dakotan husband actually said, "Oh! We didn't talk about that." *And this is the man to whom I've entrusted my daughter's education . . . !*

Mrs. Claus is still talking.

"What the Gesell evaluator is looking for is not WHAT animals the child names, but how LONG the child keeps going. Hannah stopped naming animals at, what? It says nine seconds. More developmentally mature children will continue trying to name animals for fifteen, even twenty—"

"You mean you could say 'Dog, dog, dog' over again for twenty seconds and that would get you a higher score than 'hippopotamus'?"

Doris brightens. "That's what makes the Gesell so interesting!"

And suddenly, horribly, I can picture Hannah during the test. I can picture what happened.

She became . . . me. At four.

Because if I were four and said 'hippopotamus'? This is a very big word for a very small person! I, too, would have paused. I, too, would have to have been prompted, as the evaluator noted, for the far more tedious "farm animals" . . . Farm animals! Yawn!

In life I, too, tend to make a big splash . . . and then wait for applause . . . before gathering strength to go further. In our family? Well, I guess we're show people! In our house, an unexamined life is simply not worth living.

Maybe we don't flower so much during a test so boring you can hear the *tick tick tick* of the wall clock. Maybe we need a teacher with maybe a LITTLE BIT of a lively face to get us interested, to get us going— Who WAS this Mrs. Crandall?

My voice drops down.

"Look, maybe Hannah had a bad day. We didn't prepare."

"We don't want you to prepare. Preparing doesn't help."

"It's inhuman, the testing of children!" I plead. "They're four! You should see Hannah and her little friend Cal play together!"

Cal! I suddenly think. Poor Cal! If Hannah with her big brain couldn't swing this test, poor Cal, what did he get, 2s? 1s?

"Cal?" Doris asks.

"Cal Runyon!" I exclaim. "Poor Cal took the test, too!"

Doris looks back down under the counter, brightens.

She places another pink packet on the counter.

"Actually, Cal Runyon got one of the top scores on the Gesell assessment. He has been placed into kindergarten."

My stomach drops through the floor.

"Cal has been placed a year AHEAD of Hannah? You mean they won't even be in the same CLASS? You mean I have to tell Hannah that Cal . . . ?"

Doris reads aloud to herself: " 'Excellent focus. Pleasure to be with. Follows instructions.' "

That *kiss-ass*! I think.

In the dream version of what happens now, I leap over the counter and take Doris by her floppy wool cardigan lapels.

And this is what I say . . . my voice as low as Clint Eastwood's in *Dirty Harry*:

"Let me tell you something, Mrs. Claus. We didn't even want to GO to this third-place school! We were doing you a FAVOR! Do you know why Hannah stopped naming animals, and why she didn't try the diamond? Because she was bored. She was bored with you all. Look at you, Luther Hall, this sad little campus behind, let's face it, a Target and an El Pollo Loco. Your wall of ivy? Just a bit tattered. Your coat of arms? Doesn't stand for ANYTHING. I believe you people made that little coat of arms up!

"A Catholic nun with mustache and a ruler? That would have gotten my daughter's attention, but no . . . Look at you. Look in the mirror. You are LUTHERANS. The most BORING of all Christian religions.

"Maybe you Lutherans are suddenly on your high horse, what with your pompous Blue Ribbon, because you've got an entire city of desperate Los Angeles parents—and even a couple of Europeans—washing up at your door. But try as you might, friends—you may close that white gate down, you may put a guard in that guardhouse, but you will never be Baptists with their lovable kitschy color! Or Catholics, with their mesmerizing drama-queen flair! Or our Evangelicals, who actually run the country . . . badly, but then again, I ask you . . .

"What do YOU do . . . Lutherans? What do YOU have to say for yourselves? I once saw on the coffee table of my South Dakotan mother-in-law a book called *Reclaiming the "L" Word*—" Here my voice would go high and pretend-weepy. "Oh! It's like a twelve-step program to help Lutherans feel PROUD again about being Lutherans—

"Oh, poor Lutherans— You feel like the dark horses in the Christian world, infamous, ignored, overlooked— You inspire nobody's passion—

"Well, boo-hoo!" Here I get up on the counter, Norma Rae–like. "From this day on, as God is my witness, it's going to stay that way! More PR for your Blue Ribbon? I know Appalachian SNAKE handlers who are going to get more ink than you! Grim lockstep followers of Martin Luther, with your seven-and-a-half-hour kindergarten, here's MY Augsburg Confession, and that confession is that I curse you!"

My accusing finger stabs the air:

"YOU WILL NOT . . . REVIEW . . . MY CHILD . . . BADLY."

And then I would turn back for one more zinger:

"So you got Joseph Fiennes to play Martin Luther? Not exactly Ralph, is he?"

Then I toss a match into gasoline and Luther Hall erupts into flames.

In reality, so shocked am I over the news that Cal is a genius while my own four-and-a-half-year-old has all sorts of cognitive and emotional problems, that I awkwardly thank Doris for her time, go into the parking lot, get into my minivan, fold my arms across the steering wheel, and cry.

I do this for a while, eventually desisting, and blowing my nose on all I can find on the passenger's seat—what's this? Another old to-do list:

Frsdrggb???

⬩♌⬈⬩ℳ⬤◻&ᐟᥱᖇ⬩ℳ◻⬩⬈⬩♌&ᐟᥴ❺ᥱᖇ⬩♌⬈⬩ᥢ⌒ᥢ⌒ᥢ⌒

CUPCAKES

Bouncing home in the construction, in the rain, wandering, lost, taking every wrong turn, I pass by the hunched, brown, chain-link-fenced LAUSD elementary that I realize is . . .

Guavatorina.

The sign in front—it is in Spanish.

I can't even make out the sign.

It says something about "Matriculación!" Something about "12 Janero!"

And then at the bottom:

"Feliz Navidad!"

What haunts me in the following days is that the items Hannah missed on the Gesell could have been coached. Easily.

But I see the blowing of the test was due to a fatal combination of two blondes . . .

Mike and Hannah. The happy-go-lucky's. Father and daughter.

I watch Mike and Hannah like a spy in my own house.

I watch them play Strawberry Shortcake gin rummy with jelly-smeared cards. Thirty-seven and a half of them. The rules are arbitrary, Strawberry Shortcake–ish. They do this while sitting on the deck, on Homer Simpson towels, in dripping-wet swimsuits.

I notice both Hannah and The Squid in the backyard, dropping trou and peeing on the bushes. STANDING UP. PROJECTILE PEEING. It's their favorite thing to do. And I ask you, from whom did they learn this charming habit?

I notice that there is quite a bit of pointless dancing around in underwear in this house, to wild keenings of jazz. There is much fussy making of messy blanket nests in discarded cardboard boxes. There is much random shampooing of bears.

Breakfast may involve chocolate chips and peppermint-flavored spray-on whipped cream. Chants Mike: "Fluffy are my pancakes!"

And did I mention that Mike, being from the Midwest, is not comfortable unless at least four televisions are on at once?

I awake from a troubled nap to find something pulling, pulling at my head like bats. It's Hannah and The Squid. They are brushing, brushing, brushing my hair with tiny doll hairbrushes as though I myself were a stuffed unicorn.

"STOP IT!" I yell.

I now see, tragically, that Jonathan and Aimee were right, with their Mozart in the womb, and their baby mobiles, and all that kinder-jazzerbastics (which I suddenly recall had a lot of blockwork, and chanting, and letters, and was there even . . . a British flag?). How I used to mock them what with all the natural birthing, the Baby

Einstein, the getting on to two-year waiting lists for super preschools, for starting piano lessons at two . . .

I see now, in retrospect, that Jonathan and Aimee weren't crazy, no, they were . . . sensible, prudent, sagacious. I had no idea then how easily children get tracked into the "slow" group, even at the third-tier schools! Any ONE of kinderjazzerbastics class would certainly have gotten us over the hump of 4.3s at 4.4 to probably more like 4.7s, 4.8s, maybe even a couple of 5.2s.

If her mother had been paying *any* attention, I think, my daughter would not be sitting alone, come September, with no kindergarten to go to, One Child Left Behind.

I suppose we could send Hannah to DK, but . . . $5,500 (the annual tuition has ticked up one last time) for DK? It's preschool! We pay half that at Valley Co-Op.

And bottom line, the whole Luther Hall PROMISE . . . The promise was that Lutheran school would be sort of like the Payless SHOES of schools . . . free of hassle!

And Hannah is so set on going to KINDERGARTEN. She loves carefully laying out all of her crayons, at her little play desk, and writing festive if meaningless symbols on her little chalkboard. Going off to school!

And frankly, I don't understand that damned TEST!

Oh, am I reaping the rewards of my forty-something idiocy.

I have been asleep at the wheel. I have been living in a fog. What delusional trance was I in—trying not to "angst"?

I should have remembered my own good advice. It was during our breast-feeding fiasco during that first Year of Hell, when baby Hannah was hungry and crying but wouldn't feed because I was engorged. (Meaning the breasticle is stretched so tight with milk, it's like an overinflated basketball, and the hungry baby can't latch on—in case you ever need to know this!)

Mike's mom, Bernice, thought the baby was choosing not to feed because, she said, with her implacable farm wisdom, babies can sense "fear in the milk." Fear in the milk! Oh, so it's MY fault! Thanks a lot, Mom-in-Law!

"In short, what she is saying is the number one thing you should do is NOT PANIC!" Mike screamed.

And I screamed back: "Panic is efficient. Panic is effective. Panic is . . . the way I get things done! Panic attacks are my booster rockets!"

It's called ADRENALINE! The adrenaline fires, sweat pours, I make lists, I harangue people, like a rat pressing a lever to get a pellet, and I get a result!

When I don't PANIC, I stop being vigilant and I become an idiot!

My first 911 cry goes out to Kaitlin, but . . . childless in the north, she knows less than I about the Byzantine world of L.A. schools.

The second 911 is to Brenda, who—small comfort at least—is horrified. "DK? What? That's not fair! I'm going to try to talk to someone."

But I wait, and wait, and wait . . . for a phone call back.

Brenda finally does call back, very apologetic, her older son has had some kind of diarrhea flu thing, she promises she'll try back again at Luther Hall on Monday. But in the meantime, at least to be safe, I should reserve the DK spot with a subsequent deposit, apparently a waiting list is already forming . . .

I think for a second of calling Celeste, but . . . this—Hannah's flunking her kindergarten test at Mr. Collins U—I'm not ready to try Celeste on this. I'm just not.

Aimee?

I have never in fifteen years placed a call to Aimee. The woman is always traveling, always away, always on her BlackBerry . . .

I punt. I creep out in front of the house, shove myself into the backseat of my white Toyota mini-barge of failure. Hidden from the gaze of my family, the Clampetts, I covertly dial an old number I have for Aimee's office at Glaxa.

"And what may I say this is about?" her bland male assistant asks. I make him write down every word.

"School. Luther Hall. Gesell Kindergarten Readiness Assessment. SOS."

Even though there is no way the ever-busy, ever-BlackBerrying Aimee is going to call me back, I feel powerless to get up off the backseat. I'm sort of half curled up, in the fetal position. This is what it's come to.

My cell phone jumps to life.

"Tell me exactly what happened," Aimee says, flat, like a paramedic.

"Aimee!"

Tears spring to my eyes. I cannot conceive of this kindness. I actually start crying again, sobbing.

Aimee registers no surprise. She says, flatly again, "Deep breaths."

"I called you on a whim— I wasn't even sure you were in town—"

"I'm not. I'm in Dallas."

"In Dallas?" Now I'm even more touched to have penetrated the inside of Aimee's world. Somewhere in Dallas, a group of people are looking at Aimee, who, earpiece in her ear, is slightly turned away from them in private conversation, private conversation . . . with ME!!!!!!!!

I tell her the whole baleful story, punctuated with 4.4s and 6.0s and 3.5s and British flags and wailing. Aimee listens without judgment, then speaks.

"The Gesell is a standard test—the block formations, the pencil figures to replicate, the animals, very typical. If you want, schedule a reevaluation for two months from now. I'll have my office FedEx you a copy of Connell's."

"What's Connell's?"

"Everyone knows Connell's. It's the private school testing cheat book."

"But the admissions director said the test can't be coached."

Aimee emits a flat, dry, papery sound that is almost like a laugh.

"That's ridiculous. ALL the placement tests can be coached. That's why we've had the boys tutored since two. All this testing is a bad system ESPECIALLY for gifted children—gifted children who are enviro-sensitive. That British flag thing? If Hannah replicated that, she may well be EXTREMELY gifted. Which may actually show up as what we used to call retarded!"

All the times I mocked Aimee for her obsession with IQ testing and early education and child psychology . . . Suddenly I understand.

Feeling as though I can breathe again, I hang up, wipe my face off, re-enter the house.

"When can I have another playdate with Cal?" Hannah wonders, with the cry of the lovelorn.

"Cal you can see at preschool," I reply evenly, even cheerfully. Yes, I think, you can see Cal at Valley Co-Op, that empty shell, to where I make Mike drive now, because I don't want to see any of those mothers anymore, not any of them.

And after school, instead of bathing her stuffed animals, and Uni the Unicorn, Hannah sits with me now, in my office. We practice flashcards I have copied out of the Connell's guide, which arrived the very next day from Aimee. Fast. It flopped on my doormat before ten A.M. The woman is good. I see why she gets paid the big bucks.

I read Hannah the questions, in a relaxing, upbeat voice:

What is ice when it melts?
What is a key for?
Where does meat come from?
If today is Monday, what day will tomorrow be?
Mother is a woman; father is a _____?
An airplane goes fast; a turtle goes _____?
Repeat: 3725 _____ 4531 _____ 8694 _____

. . .

Mike watches me as I slice tomatoes for a healthy snack, full of vitamin C and riboflavin, as well as carrots, for good concentration.

"Are you okay?" he asks.

"I'm great!" I say lightly.

"I know the whole Luther Hall thing was . . . squirrely, but no worries. Kindergarten is nine months away! We've got irons in the fire. It's going to work out."

I'm married to an idiot.

With the same light voice, I say, "I'm just concerned that the magnet thing may not work out right away, as I know the odds are kind of tough. And that if we don't GET that magic letter—IN MAY—in September, Hannah will be attending kindergarten—ha-ha—in Mexico."

"What do you mean?"

"Guavatorina? I don't know if you've driven by recently, but the signs are all in Spanish."

Mike is unperturbed. "I'd love Hannah to be bilingual."

My voice remains light, even slightly whimsical: "Maybe two languages is not a good idea for someone whose favorite ice cream is . . . MANGO."

Watching Mike smoke fish in the backyard, with his beloved new *Popular Mechanics* smoker . . .

I realize now that I am the idiot. Because I married an idiot. And had children with him. Yeah, as a foolish twenty-six-year-old, I made the mistake of falling in love—like I did—with an affable, funny, creative fellow with a bread-making machine—!

The marrying was understandable, when you are young and foolish.

But clearly the problem is, I forgot to divorce him. Was too lazy.

Never got around to it. Couldn't find a pen to sign the papers, in this wreck of a house!

I could have married Jonathan, or someone like him . . . I could have married, instead of a warm, funny musician, a conveniently traveling, absent, distant periodontal surgeon—perhaps one having an affair, a string of affairs . . . My wealthy, cheating husband could be traveling and sending home fabulous guilt-induced tropical gift baskets while I could be rattling around alone in a spacious mansion in La Cañada Flintridge, getting massages, drinking Napa Viognier, eating cheese!

And look at this house we bought. What were we thinking? It seemed so charming, this thirteen-hundred-square-foot 1926 Spanish-style bungalow. We were the sort of wide-eyed, barefoot, idealistic, Joni Mitchell–style bohemians who were so amazed we could buy a structure that we bought it without FIRST VETTING THE NEIGHBORHOOD. Our method of buying a house? Look at that sunshine! Look at that cactus! So pretty! Pretty cactus! Pretty, pretty cactus! Idiots! (Where would Joni Mitchell have sent her daughter to school? I mean the one she gave away? Well, even if Joni Mitchell had *kept* that daughter, she would clearly never have such pathetic kindergarten problems. Joni Mitchell's daughter would immediately be wafted into a magical elementary charter progressive Waldorf kingdom!)

No, us, we failed to vet our neighborhood. We paid little attention as to whether we were doing the smart thing—moving to a good school district, next to lawyers or bankers or periodontal surgeons. Idiots, we would have insisted on NOT living next to such bourgeois sellouts! Oh, how we laughed and partied on this sagging deck, with its Chinese paper lanterns and Miles Davis records and Two Buck Chuck from Trader Joe's.

We were completely unaware that we were living in a public-school MINEFIELD, our Van Nuys neighborhood a mishmash of apartment-dwelling immigrants and a few unemployed actors who, as soon as they have babies, are now, I am suddenly noticing . . .

Moving to Dallas. Moving to North Carolina. Moving to . . .

Portland.

All around us, Los Angeles bohemian families are suddenly moving to Portland. I get the notices daily. They are throwing kid car seats into their aging Volvo station wagons with the peeling Kerry/Edwards stickers and heading north.

I get a note from Leah . . . Portland! Topanga had become too "heavy" for them.

I get a note from Kim, Celeste's old neighbor, in Echo Park. Now that she has a three-year-old . . . Portland? Why? The air! The culture! The much more liberal politics! And—what else—juicy blueberries!

I imagine, in Portland, if you threw down $700,000 you could get a house in a decent neighborhood, as opposed to ours, which I'd thought was gentrifying . . .

But it's starting to dawn on me. I can't deny it anymore. Our Van Nuys block has really NOT gentrified. I'd thought we were middle class but our middle-class house seems, increasingly, to be no longer in the middle of—how shall I put this?—a middle-class neighborhood. Rather, ours seemed to have become the sort of block nice middle-class people . . . Oh, what's the word? Flee. Now look, I have nothing against six-foot-tall neon Virgins of Guadalupe, or old couches with the stuffing coming out being used as furniture on that plein air front parlor known as the lawn. After all, it gets hot here in The Nuys, and not all of us have central air, window units, electric fans, or even (to judge from the astonishingly leathery Third World denizens I find rooting around in my recycling), quite frankly, teeth.

Who are our neighbors of The Nuys?

I get an e-mail from Aimee . . .

SENT BY MY BLACKBERRY WIRELESS.

It contains a link to the indispensable school search Web site, www.greatschools.net.

Two clicks of the mouse and there you are, at our LAUSD elementary, Guavatorina.

Greatschools.net rates schools from 1 (lowest) to 10 (highest). The ratings are based on API (Academic Performance Index) scores. In California, API's range from 0 to 1000, 800+ being the ideal.

Guavatorina's greatschools.net rating is a 3 out of 10.

Its API is 682.

It is 96 percent Hispanic; 93 percent poor (aka free and reduced lunch—I take it that means food stamps); 89 percent English learners.

That's like weight = 191 and *Consumer Reports'* rating is a D.

How can these families even AFFORD Los Angeles? is my question.

It's 2:07 A.M. My eyes pop open.

I don't even pretend to sleep anymore. What is the point?

Everything I assumed about running my life is wrong.

I pad over to Mike's computer pile—the one I swore I would never disturb. Without emotion, I locate the folder marked "SCHOOL," open it . . .

It is a snarl, a jumble, a chaos! Look at this. It looks like ants! A sweater!

The actual LAUSD magnet application looks like a thirty-two-page booklet from the DMV, in Tom Ridge panic alert colors of red and yellow.

I study the magnet booklet. The school we are apparently trying for, we are HOPING for, our supposed savior, is Valley Alternative Magnet. Valley Alternative Magnet—which I recall parents at the "Into Kindergarten" meeting dubbing sad and "grubby." One dad I talked to, an actor, Dennis, was so horrified, they are now moving to West Virginia. Why? "It's so green!"

Valley Alternative Magnet. It says last year there were 2,400 applications for 100 spots. What are those odds, 1 in 24,000? 10 in 240? 100 in 24? 1000 in 240,000? I suddenly can't do the math! I can't do the

QUESTIONS TO PARENTS THERE,
"WHAT'S IMPORTANT TO YOU?"
"WHY DO YOU LIKE?"
" " " " " THE TEACHER?"

<u>Kindergarten and Beyond</u>

GREATSCHOOLS.NET API/AYI
TEST SCORES !
LOOK AT SCHOOLS.
STANDARD BASE TEST

1. Home School "BAD NEIGHBORHOOD"
WEBSITE, REALTOR, — GO TO SCHOOL, GET I COPY
ACCOUNTABILITY (SAR) # IN CLASSROOM, INFO ON
REPORT TEACHERS, POPULAR ALL

2. School Accountability Report   www.lausd.k12.ca.edu TEST SCORES
MID-70S DESEGREGATION. TAKE STUDENT INTERESTS
60% MINORITY 40% CAUCASIAN, OR 70/30 "RACE" MARKS
ARE CONSISTENT FOR 13 YEARS. BETTER CHANCE IF YOU ARE

3. Magnet Schools A MINORITY, BUT CAN BE CONTESTED.
2 LISTS: %. ELEMENTARY ONLY A COUPLE OF TYPES
60%   40 Types of magnets 1. GIFTED
)   2. MATH/SCIENCE 3. THERE'S ONE KESTER!
5 1ST GRADE CLASSES 1. GIFTED
HIGH ABILITY

Advantages and Disadvantages

4. QUALIFICATIONS TO GIFTED/HIGH ABILITY (GHA) ALL 1-5
1. VOCABULARY
2. FORMULATES ALTERNATIVE WAYS TO SOLVE
3. USES ALTERNATIVE WAYS TO SOLVE   3 PTS   DESIGNATED BY
4. CREATIVE 3. SCHOOL IS   "Points"   5 WAYS 1. SIBLING 2. HOME SCHOOL
KINDERGARTEN   IS OVERCROWDED
TEACHER MUST SAY   "PHBAO"   4 PTS. 5.
THIS BY FEB.   PREDOMINANTLY   4. WAIT LIST
GHA TEACHERS   HISPANIC   Other qualifications IF APPLY TO MAGNET   MATRICULA-
REALLY WANT   BLACK OR   AND REJECTED, 4 PTS,   TION (GRAD-
TO BE THERE   ASIAN OR OTHER   UATION)-
EMULATES   UP TO 12, MAGNET 12 PTS
GHA CURRICULUM   Choices Brochure   KINDERG. KINDERGARTEN   MATH/
70S INTEGRATION   APPLY FOR KINDERGARTEN   SCIENCE
B 1/21!! BALBOA, VAN OWEN
4. S.A.S. Programs   VALLEY ALTERNATIVE SCHOOL   VINTAGE
"LANAI" SCHOOL DEADLINE 12/1 — IF CHILD IS   MAGNET
"RIVERSIDE" 5 ON SHE CAN BEGIN K   1-5 BALBOA
GIFTED
5. Permits: child care, <u>instructional</u>, open enrollment   ORANGE FOLDER
LOTTERY ANY SCHOOL W/ OPENINGS   (HANDY IN
IF YOU CAN STAY IN, DITTO SIBLINGS   JUNIOR HIGH)
CALL IN FOR # OF OPEN ENROLLMENTS
6. Charter Schools   COMMUNITY CHARTER   2 YRS IN
NO OPEN COURT PRIVATE SCHOOL, YOU DO NOT   A ROW
BUT API SCORES LOSE POINTS MAIL RETURN   CAT 6
MUST STAY HIGH   KEEP YOUR RECEIPT!   TEST
7. Private schools
LOSE CHARTER   TEACHER MUST SIGN OFF ON GIFTED TESTING

math! Throat closing! Crows descending! Panic attack coming! Panic attack coming!

And the other musicians assured Mike it would work out fine. Right! Just like those clams in Ensenada! Eat them off a streetcart! No refrigeration! *What can go wrong?*

School will be no problem? A tale told by an idiot!

Clearly, we're never going to get into that magnet school. Not unless I personally start literally KILLING OFF school-aged LAUSD children.

Rummaging around in the pantry at 2:30 A.M., I find my own late-night friends.

Rum. Diet Coke. Microwave popcorn. To which I add—here they are—Parmesan cheese and cayenne. It's my traditional late-night recipe. The cayenne lends a pleasing burning sensation, which the rum and Coke cuts through.

I pad to my office and do what my therapist, Ruth, has expressly forbidden: I turn on the computer. Her actual quote: "Sandra: Trolling on the computer late at night is the absolutely worst possible thing you can do."

Tough luck. Get to know me.

And if I stay up past four? Past the Hour of the Wolf? FUCK IT.

In my late twenties I had the habit of staying up by myself past midnight in a ratty old leotard, ingesting rum and Diet Cokes and popcorn, and obsessively playing Solitaire. ("It could be worse!" I'd protest to Mike. "What with my half-Asian background, at least I'm not in some casino out somewhere in San Dimas . . . gambling!")

In my thirties, I would stay up late and obsessively Google myself. I would throw my back out with the self-harming self-Google.

But now . . .

I pull all the shades in my office. I lock the door against any intruders or, more likely, against my family, possible nocturnally wandering children, a judgmentally tapping-on-glass husband. I flick my fingers reflexively, sit at the controls.

It feels inevitable, that I have finally arrived back here, in my Panic Room. Which, in a way, I knew I would all along. Frankly, it feels good to be BACK IN THE DRIVER'S SEAT, WHERE I BELONG, EXPERTLY TWIDDLING WITH THE KNOBS.

I delve into the information Snorl I have been avoiding.

It is true that public school is attractive from the point of view that it is free, and there is no testing for kindergarten. Perhaps we should just move to . . . Well, not La Cañada, as those are million-dollar homes, or at least $950,000 (with their 950 API scores). How about Sherman Oaks, right next door to us, whose elementary school API score is a still-sumptuous 850—but damn, look at typical Sherman Oaks houses, those are $850,000! I jaggedly jot the numbers down on the back of an envelope, and oh my God, combine rum and Diet Coke and popcorn and I become some kind of mathematical genius! Cross-referencing API scores with home prices, look at this formula!

1 API point = $1,000 worth of real estate.

Clearly, you have to pay all this money for good public schools because you want to keep clear of the poor! They tend to drag school API scores down. Typical greatschools.net bar graph:

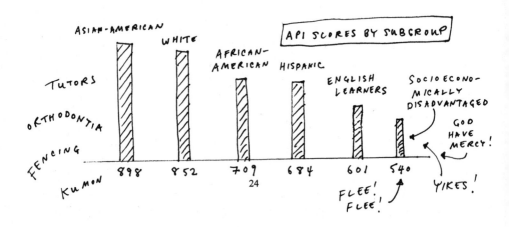

Just *look* at the poor! With their tiny, little bar, their short, wan tenement of stank API!

In my prior life as a liberal, politically progressive person, I might feel horrible about even casting my eyes on such a hideous bar graph, demeaning as it is to African-Americans and Hispanics, but our family crisis—this personal 911—has given me, blessedly, finally, a laser-like focus. In a way, it's a relief not to have to worry about any of those vague, gauzy, distant, important-sounding NPR things any-more—Chechnya, Botswana, global warming, pediatric tooth decay, the eternal flounderings of our oppressed minorities. Finally, I have a short, manageable agenda I can actually act upon—MY FAMILY. HANNAH. ME.

But in Los Angeles, exciting news: I appear to have found a loop-hole! I think you can actually get a house in the $700,000s in Thousand Oaks, whose school's API is in the 800s, even 900s! I guesstimate you can buy the same house you'd get in South Pasadena for $40,000 less in Thousand Oaks. But you'll also add *forty* minutes to your drive, which, okay— For every *ten* minutes of white-knuckled free-way driving (even on that far-flung 118 everyone swears by) (five minutes on the 118 equaling *fifteen* on the 405), you'll bag 10 API points—one API point per minute. But that's with no traffic. One big rig turns over and there you sit, hyperventilating, heart pound-ing . . . LITERALLY HEMORRHAGING API!

And then there's PROPERTY TAX!

Shit—! Fuck—!

I forgot property tax!

It's a good rhythm I now settle into, good. I rise every night at mid-night, down a Tylenol PM and get myself a rum and Coke and the popcorn, put in two or three good hours of school computer trolling, and am back in bed by three, up at eight . . . I've had five straight hours of sleep, which is plenty—! I'm very calm now that I under-stand the numbers, very calm.

Knowing I'm gaining control allows me to be incredibly even and cheerful with my family. And Aimee continues to help me, the wind beneath my wings. For instance, she has subscribed me to a Web site that gives news flashes for all the educational things kids can do around Los Angeles. Instead of all of us lounging around in the yard in our underpants, napping, I am able to plan all sorts of delightful educational activities for the children.

I pitch things to Mike in a voice that has a happy upswing.

"Let's take the kids to see this fun concert on Saturday called . . . KidMozart!"

Or: "I thought Hannah would love taking this class . . . Kindertanz! Which has a neat, fun unit in . . . counting! You love counting, don't you, honey? Girls ROCK at counting!"

I use the word *rock* a lot, make a cheerful, educational—but fun—fist.

I buy us a membership for a new place in Pasadena, the KidSmart Museum.

"Where you'll learn about SCIENCE!" Uh-oh. My voice has gone too shrill.

My snub-nosed mostly Midwestern family looks at me, suspicious. They freeze in the driveway. I make a comedic dismissive motion.

"Oh, you know what I mean! Less science than bugs . . . and mud! Messy things!"

"Let's play a driving game!" I sing out to the kids as we fly along the 101. I chant out the playful questions, making a game of it:

"Why does ice melt?"

"What is a key for?"

"Open door," says The Squid.

I whirl in surprise. Just two years old . . . but clearly has promise. Perhaps we started too late with Hannah, but if we do what Jonathan and Aimee did . . . start drilling now . . .

Cannily I have MapQuested the KidSmart museum and, à la Brenda, have marked our route in yellow highlighter . . . It is an admittedly circuitous route that takes us home from Pasadena to Van Nuys through . . . La Cañada.

"What do you know?" I erupt in exaggerated surprise, twisting in my seat. "Look at all these open houses!"

I know one thing my husband cannot resist is an open house. Conversation #703.

From my late nights on the computer, I have learned that the shining Twin Towers of L.A. public education are La Cañada and Calabasas, lovely bedroom neighborhoods where single-family homes run from $850,000 to $1.5 million (giving rise to my new favorite real-estate phrase: "$1.1 million and it's on septic!").

However, Aimee has just sent me a La Cañada listing that has NOT YET GONE ON THE MARKET.

It is a La Cañada house in a cul-de-sac listed at the IKEA-like Impossibly Low Price! of $830,000. It is a small house but—if you check the stats on the Internet—on a surprisingly big lot. I figure if we sell our house, put 10 percent down, get an adjustable loan and I get another regular, lucrative teaching job, parlay my Marymount currency—

I say lightly to Mike, "You know, memory recalls . . . I think that crazy Aimee said . . . Maybe there's a house somewhere around here . . . ? Not yet on the market . . . ? Hence no one will know about it . . . ?"

But no.

Pulling up in our pockmarked 1998 Toyota, I feel my hopes crumble upon seeing a mob of sleek-sunglassed parents, all business, plus their children, piling like vermin out of their gleaming black Mercedes and Lexus SUV Horror-Mobiles, tossing ever-escalating sealed bids like jaunty paper airplanes through the squat house's peeling, ranch-style windows.

"If it weren't for all these *Asians*!" I hiss under my breath, crumpling Aimee's e-mail in my fist. "Asians—they over-fetishize education, drive up the real-estate market, and P.S. I hate their tile!"

"What did you say?" Mike says.

"Asian food!" I reply, smiling widely. "Haven't had it in a WHILE!"

I'm always punching up API's on the Internet like a rat seeking pellets. When a Berkeley friend calls to complain about her daughter's third-grade teacher, I log on to greatschools.net, check her school's API score, and call back angrily to exclaim: "Count your blessings, baby! I wouldn't complain if I were you! Your school's API score is 824!"

I have a new message from Aimee:

SENT BY MY BLACKBERRY WIRELESS.

Kentwood Elementary. API = 907. There may be one or two open spots, due to its remote location high up on a hill, and the fact that no new families with children are moving up there. A colleague of mine at Glaxa East (our NY affil.) is the husband of the assistant principal Franny who is a HUGE FAN OF YOUR WORK ON KCRW.

Awesome news: They would LOVE YOU TO HOST THEIR SPRING AUCTION!

Call me ASAP!

I do, catching her in New York, where Glaxa is holding a sales conference for a new woman-targeted relaxation pharmaceutical called Quellna. "I just had lunch with some editors from *Real Simple*," Aimee says. "These women are nightmares! So high strung! So competitive!"

"They've got a LOT of relaxation to push," I say. "They have to move A LOT of loofah sponges."

"Kentwood," Aimee says. "This spring auction thing is a big breakthrough. It's a fantastic invite. Kentwood hasn't done open enrollment in years."

"So if I host the spring auction . . . that means Hannah's IN, right?"

"Yes. Probably. Ninety-five percent sure. Okay. The thing is, while FRANNY is a huge fan, she's just the assistant principal. It's the actual PRINCIPAL who pulls the trigger . . ."

"Is she LUTHERAN?" I ask, suddenly gloomy, feeling the sourness of futility come over me.

"I think Belgian. Her name is Mrs. Carla Feninger. Problem is, while she is not exactly a NON-fan, she's never heard of you."

"Great."

"However, the good news is Mrs. Carla Feninger has just recently developed a mania for fund-raising because of the new computer center. In a meeting this morning, Franny convinced Mrs. Carla Feninger that a public radio celeb—albeit one she has never heard of—will be a crack fund-raiser. As soon as we hang up, put together a gift basket of signed books and letter, introducing yourself and Mike and describing your own MANIA FOR FUND-RAISING . . . for Kentwood . . ."

"Argh," I groan. The whole wobbly enterprise is making me feel a little like Sean Young in a Catwoman suit, rattling the gates of Paramount.

"I know it's horrible," says Aimee. "But API equals 907! There's nothing you shouldn't stoop to for your children. And Mrs. Carla Feninger is a big fan of KCRW! She LOVES KCRW! She's a huge admirer of your station manager, Ruth Seymour."

"Maybe KCRW can be some kind of a media sponsor," I suddenly realize.

The various seemingly unrelated strands of my life! They're coming together! Perhaps there actually *is* a larger, divine plan at work!

"Absolutely," Aimee agrees. "KCRW a sponsor, you have Kentwood in the bag."

6
F&*(&*(!!!!

It is at this highly unfortunate moment that I am scheduled to give the annual "Women on Fire" talk at Marymount College, as I am the "Woman on Fire" writer in residence.

In my contract, the "Women on Fire" program is described as an opportunity for the older generation to inspire the newer generation of female writers to Be Fierce! Speak Out! And, of course . . . Get Creative!

My talk is to take place on campus at the Kahlo Café . . . which brews its own blend of Kahlo Koffee. I don't know if Frida Kahlo actually drank coffee. I always imagine the woman more on the exotic painkillers I hope her Mexican doctors were able to prescribe for her. I imagine coffee would make Ms. Kahlo rather more jittery.

Coffee-averse or no, Frida Kahlo's accusing visage gazes down from every wall. Frida Kahlo with braids on head, Frida Kahlo with nails in neck, Frida Kahlo in her Spanish headdress thingy, looking all the world as though she is MOCKING the headdress, as if to say, "I HATE this thing Mexican men make me wear!"

Or maybe Frida's just too . . . warm. I don't know if it's because I'm a Woman on Fire, but to me this coffeehouse feels uncomfortably . . . MUGGY.

I need to pull myself together. Maybe with something iced.

The Kahlo Café counter is a tattered collage of hand-lettered signs delineating a complex web of relationships between global sustainable farming practices, the oppressions of minimum wage for the counter employees, Marymount student food allergies, and the politics of fat-free cinnamon buns. 100,000 TREES CUT DOWN EVERY DAY — RECYCLE YOUR CUPS. CHANGE FOR DARFUR. SOY HAZELNUT LATTES ARE MADE EXCLUSIVELY FROM LOCAL, ORGANIC, SHADE GROWN FARMS. PLEASE KEEP USED DAIRY ITEMS SEPARATE FROM VEGAN COUNTER — PLEASE!!! YES BROWNIE NUT CINNAMON SWIRL CUPCAKES DO UTILIZE EGG WHITES BUT ARE 100% CRUELTY FREE.

A safe choice, surely, is herbal tea. But at the Kahlo Café, not even tea is simple. Improving on the original concept, the Kahlo Café offers neither teabags nor teapots nor tea balls but an invention all its own, the tea sock. Which appears to be made of hemp. It's the four-dollar hemp tea sock.

The two dozen or so female students gathered around the Kahlo Café stage area are a colorful melange of dreadlocks, tattoos, and even braids on top of heads, in the manner of Frida. Too, there are some beautiful straight preppies. A tall thin girl with a short red mop top has toted in her lacrosse stick. Her girlfriend wears a T-shirt: TRANSGENDERED HUMAN RIGHTS DAY. At which point it occurs to me that Ms. Lacrosse might actually be a man. I don't know! Brownie nut cinnamon swirl! Egg whites only! Cruelty free!

I do a short reading about my Chinese father, from my long-ago next-Amy-Tan glory days. How I miss them. And now the floor is open for questions, from young Marymount College students, about writing. Women's writing. About women's careers in writing. It's women on women on writing.

In my compromised state, I find the questions bewildering.

"In my experimental-fiction writing class, we've been discussing the fact that MALE critics always read WOMEN writers biographically. Why do they insist on categorizing us, on limiting us . . ."

I had lost her back at "experimental fiction." Why was this still being taught? So few people can write an intelligible story to begin with. Now we are actually TEACHING our young women to confuse?

Another hand. Big square glasses, breathy Ani DiFranco voice.

"After graduation, do you think I should go right into the MFA? I've already completed three chapbooks of poetry. But last week at a conference an editor from Viking said it's wiser to take a year off to get a book started and THEN apply for the MFA, when you have one hundred pages of a novel to show?"

Aren't my students already IN an MFA? I'm confused about all these degrees. Degrees and chapbooks. GOD, it's stuffy in here. Could someone open a window?

Another hand. It's my rebel student, Ms. Frida Kahlo shirt. I notice she actually seems to be growing a bit of a mustache, possibly in homage.

"I've heard some publishers LIKE you to have a journalism background, but some DON'T. But I'm interested in studying journalism. Should I study some journalism or do you think it will blow my chances with a publisher who wants something more pure?"

Tuition at Marymount, I've been told, is $48,000 a year. If someone was footing the bill, I for one would stay in school. That's the ticket. I would stay in school forever if I could.

Another hand. A Sinead O'Connor type with peach fuzz, cheek tattoo, and black turtleneck.

"I know this may seem off topic, but I want to ask some personal advice. My boyfriend is five years older than me, and although he's a painter, he really wants children. Because I want to give everything to my artistic career, I feel I definitely DO NOT WANT to have children. That is what my mother did, she had children, put everything into her family, and she says she has really regretted it. She is the one who pushed me to study poetry at Marymount. 'Find your dreams,' she said. 'Pursue your art.' "

Just beyond, a fifty-something woman with braids across her head, in a white shawl, romanced with lavender "key of life" appliqués, cheerfully waves. The girl turns in acknowledgment, mouths, "Hi, Mom!"

"Does your mother go here?" I ask in surprise.

"No. She . . . audits."

"How old are you?"

"Twenty-two."

"Name?"

"Chelsea."

I feel sweat beads burst out on my upper lip and suddenly I lose it.

"I understand," I say. "Your plan is to have a glamorous career. At twenty-two you cannot envision any other track. But Chelsea, I PROMISE that after the small craft of you shoots past the age of thirty, and then rounds the bobbing breakwater buoy of forty, you, too, will obtain a baby."

Chelsea exclaims, "I don't THINK so!"

I lift my hand up.

"Will it be a human baby? Perhaps not. Oh no. It could well be: A collection of Beanie Babies. A pair of pug babies. Or perhaps an adult baby in the form of a lactose-intolerant bachelor you found on match.com named Grigr. This is what happens, Chelsea. Who knows what form this all-consuming baby into which you pour all your emotions will come—a small sailboat named *Liz*, scrapbooking, a nonprofit corporation, a writing class of eight neurotic adults you teach in a caftan and turban from your own home!

"It is all inevitable, this being thrown off track of your artistic career . . . But you will take my advice, none of it, because you are young!"

The room is riveted—possibly they, too, have experienced one of those teachers in a caftan and turban . . .

"Youth," I wend on, "I remember youth. In my youth I was a person who plotted out my future very carefully. At twenty-two—your age, Chelsea—teetering on a sticky red bar stool, pretending to pump my moussed, grape-Kool-Aid-smelling hair in time to horrible pop music—mine was the regrettable era of the Pet Shop Boys and Flock of Seagulls—on various beer-soaked cocktail napkins I was secretly diagramming out, planning my escape from the ghastly, fetid, fashion-impaired obscurity that was my youth."

I go to the whiteboard and start drawing.

"My goal was to achieve early success as a writer, preferably by the age of twenty-five. This was how it was done in the mid-eighties. Everywhere you looked, young writers were publishing searing short stories in hot literary quarterlies, then smash cut!"—at this, I actually leap down off the stage—"electrifying both coasts with debut short-story collections that were but a hundred pages long. Then would come the six-figure advance for a novel. Then would come . . . what? I guess more novels. Yes, if following that professional path, that's what my continual, churning output would now lithely braid itself into: novel novel novel . . . novel novel novel . . . novel novel novel—

"Maintaining that continous background chant—'novel novel novel . . . novel novel novel'—let us now step back from The Work, grab a bottle of water, and move down into the main auditorium." I wave my arms to indicate an imaginary screen before us. "The over-heads dim and there they are! All the decades of my life—past, present, and future—laid out on the big screen. And when we consider the chapters, the movements, of my career, we see a grander pattern emerging, in discrete 'themes,' along the lines of:

20s.	Ascension!
30s.	Arrival!
40s.	Mastery!

"Looking ahead, I saw that my forties promised to be less a maturing than a kind of extraordinary goldening. I envisioned these as my Yo Yo Ma/Amy Tan years. This would be a seasoned, a leavened time of life when the artist travels around the country accepting lifetime awards and honorary medals from the President, the Queen, Bill Moyers. These would be the PBS years, the Lincoln Center years—'Live from Wolf Trap,' perhaps, would be a special Christmas/Hanukkah/Kwanzaa concert featuring readings from my early work before a chorus of one thousand white-haired tuxe-doed singers. One would be inducted into the Smithsonian as a National Treasure, and it was now that one would be issued one's own stamp, if not actually one's own U.S. currency. Maya Angelou is an incandescent spirit, yes, irreplaceable, but at some point She will choose to gear down and younger female spokesauthors of color will be solemnly called into the wake of Her distinguished service.

"But what really happened?" I exhort them. "What really hap-pened . . . to me?"

No one moves. Frankly, they have no clue. As is the case with most visiting professors, my bio is fuzzy to them.

"When I was twenty-two, I thought to be an Artist was to be like a Silver Arrow shot across a Magical Sky. If you could only express your true Self, your true Soul in the moment of flight, you would be

bestowed the magical Amulet of—as regarded a book—actual pub-
lication or—as regarded any of the one-woman shows I was always
working on—an actual booking. And this AMULET of external
Validation would be as your magical cape, shield, eternal protection.

"And lo and behold, I actually had this miraculous experience.
After ten years of, like any good Girl Scout, twisting and twisting my
metaphorical pencil into a rock, trying to make a curl of smoke . . .
at thirty-four it happened. My first solo show in New York, off-
Broadway! Eight shows a week for five weeks!"

"Ah," the room sighs, as together we inhale—we snort a line of—
the dream.

I lower my voice, bend forward, striking the hammy pose of a poi-
soned William Shatner.

"But *The New York Times* review . . . It all hinges on *The New York
Times* review . . . And my excitable director calls me at midnight
from a newsstand, with three words: 'Ben! Brantley! GOOD!"

Another crowd exhalation: "Ah!"

"And with that the Art Gates swing open! First thing the next
morning, I spring down four flights from my tiny sublet-from-a-
seventy-something-Dutch-opera-queen-with-a-Danny-Kaye-fixation
apartment at Seventy-sixth and Columbus . . .

"I am Gene Kelly in *An American in Paris,* in white pants and
striped tee, jeté-ing down the boulevards. All around me, New York
City bobs up like a sparkling lake, like a luminous dream. Literally
everything I see around me reflects the wonder, the goldenness, the
rightness of my good reviews. On the newspaper kiosk, lines of festive *New York* magazines—I still remember the cover—white, with
gold writing—gaily flap like pennants. Below, from the ground,
rises a congratulatory stack of *Variety.* And there to the left, at the
Tully's Coffee window, sits the dark-suited and bespectacled forty-
something Manhattan stockbroker, reading his *New York Times.* On
the very next page, he will see my review! My review! Crossing the
street, I step on something mushy. I look down. A *New Yorker.* Did

it have—? Could it be—? Yes, I kid you not, unbelievably, even *The New Yorker* has a flattering little blurb about me, me, me!

"I am literally WEARING THE AMULET! And the magic cape! I am invincible!

"Of course, that was my FIRST show. *Aliens in America.*

"Two years later I return with my SECOND show, *Bad Sex with Bud Kemp.*

"Note to self: In future, do not place word *bad* in title.

"Which is to say I am now in my Second Act and this time, Review Morning . . . Well, instead of Paris in the spring, it is West Gaza in . . . well, presumably at any time of the year . . . I would check with the NPR people—they know when times are PARTICU-LARLY BAD in West Gaza. It was like a horror movie, starring Gene Kelly. All the bad reviews are like nail-bombs going off all around me, a hailstorm of shit.

"Ahead of me now bobs the newspaper kiosk, with one hundred derisively waving copies of *Time Out New York,* containing my small but EXTREMELY HATEFUL REVIEW. There to my left sits the stockbroker reading *The New York Times,* containing—desultory backhanded slap—NO REVIEW. I step down into mushy *New Yorker* . . . This week *The New Yorker* is kvelling about a new photo exhibit at the Natural History Museum, Yo Yo Ma going Appalachian at Lincoln Center, and—what's this? A hilarious new one-woman show . . . ! Starring the toast of the town . . . ! A transgendered African-American rap poet who goes by just one name. Amid the standing-room-only opening-night audience at P.S. 122, Meryl Streep has been seen front-row center, doubled over in hysterics—that's how funny and surprisingly poignant that other new solo show NOT MINE was.

"Please picture now, instead of the Gene Kelly sun of two years ago, a gray sky, and a lowering oily rain. I duck into a Broadway deli and, by hurrying midtown workers, am literally pushed into a waist-high stack of slightly damp New York *Posts*. My body is splayed—I think of the spread-armed stance of the helpless man in the Goya execution painting—across a low wall of damp New York *Post*s.

"My throat tightens as in warning.

"But I can't help myself. As though hypnotized, I reach a hand down. Knowing this is a door I probably shouldn't open—it hums and buzzes, foreboding—I nonetheless flap open . . . the New York *Post*. Flip through its damp pages and articles, featuring . . .

" 'TWO-HEADED BABY!'

" 'ELEVEN-CAR CRASH ON THE NEW JERSEY TURN-PIKE!'

" 'DOUGHBOY SWIMMING POOL BURSTS INTO FLAMES!'

"And my review. Certainly, any artist who has worked professionally for any length of time will have some bad reviews. But there are some that particularly haunt, and claw. This one was by Clive Barnes."

Dramatic, I reach into my fanny packet, remove it, and unfold it . . . my Clive Barnes review from 1998 that I always carry with me . . . like a grounding talisman.

"For those who can't see all the way up here," I murmur, like a dark sorcerer, "the headline reads 'Bad Sex . . . with Loh.' Below is a small awful photo of me, mid-expression, as though I am chewing a bit of gristle, looking, frankly, a bit crazy. And then underneath THAT photo is a blunt Gaza Strip caption, as though titling the scene of an accident, or a maiming. 'Tsing Loh . . . Manic.'

"What Mr. Barnes very much wants the ninety-six million or so readers of the New York *Post* to know is that, for him, watching me perform onstage was an experience literally as painful as dental surgery. That's the exact phrase he uses. 'Dental surgery.'

"I am, clearly, one of the most annoying women he has ever witnessed trot across the boards, fatally unaware that no one could possibly care about my tedious life. Mr. Barnes describes me eagerly blabbering on and on, unstoppable, zooming manically about the stage 'cute as a button.' " I take a beat. " 'A desperate button.' "

I raise my arm in the air, proffering the yellowed review like a trophy, or severed head—mine.

The girls huddle their dreadlocks in closer, cradling their hemp-tea socks and cruelty-free cinnamon buns, as though in protection.

"From a distance of six years now, I can almost laugh. 'Desperate Buttons!' It almost sounds like a back-stabbing *All About Eve*–like theatrical comedy about a glitteringly tattered cadre of aging forty-something Broadway actresses starring Kaye Ballard and Ruth Buzzi . . . 'Tomorrow at two and eight, half-price tix, laugh till you cry: *Desperate Buttons.'* And in fact I do manage a few brave chuckles as I raise my gin and tonic with an almost too eerily sympathetic stage manager later that night, after the show. Which had been performed to a suddenly half-empty theater. Why? Because it's . . . New York!

"But it is safe to say, my youthful confidence is . . . just a bit shattered. And in the years that follow that one magical Gene Kelly morning, I come to know my life in Art as not like a Magical Arrow shot just once, but a continuing journey fueled by two forces. Like the Good Fairies gathered around Baby Aurora in *Sleeping Beauty*, the good reviewers granted me a career. But the Bad Fairy—the late arrival—he haunts me now too.

"Because from this day on, it seems bad reviews follow me everywhere. I started to dread finding them slumped in the morning, like the body of Jimmy Hoffa, against my hotel room door. I started avoiding public transportation for fear the local alternative weekly would be lying open on a seat, to the theater section, and my bad review—which actually happened to me in Seattle! Everywhere I go he follows me—the spirit of Clive Barnes, the Bad Fairy! Even at home I'm not safe because hurled at our porch daily, like a missile, is the *L.A. Times*. Sometimes, via a PR person, you're warned ahead that your *Times* review is going to be a smeller . . . I would literally lie in bed dreading the dawn, when, like a foul-odored red tide, the *L.A. Times* would wash up on every driveway in Los Angeles with . . . MY BAD REVIEW.

"And further, I humbly submit, in the same way as there is no bad food worse than bad CHINESE food—even with bad Mexican food or bad Italian food, you can always find melted cheese—there is no prose more searing than when critics are given a forum to detail how much they hate . . . the one-woman show! Who doesn't hate a one-woman show? I hate the one-woman show just think-ing about it! So many opening lines of the reviews were like the pulling back of a feathered shaft on a bow, the twine singing with deliciously unreleased tension: 'Let me begin by admitting I am not a fan of the one-woman show. For me? Nails on a chalkboard is the one-woman show. Even TWO women is better than ONE woman . . . Even THREE women! Eleven women! And, as every-one knows, I am a man who HATES women! And yet, as fast as I run screaming from a room of eleven performing women with their nattering, shrill, cacophonic keening, even more unendurable to me is a SOLO WOMAN, as in ONE WOMAN, as in a ONE-WOMAN . . . SHOW.' "

"Why don't you stop READING the reviews?" Chelsea's braid-over-the-top-of-the-head mother asks. She stands now in her mysti-cal, white shawl, like Glinda of the Good, protector of young bohemian girls' dreams. She is like a soft-focus Glenn Close in *The Natural,* or like some kind of wizard-like Gandalf figure, lifting a scepter in an attempt to ward off the evil of my tale.

"I did!" I exclaim. "Soldiering on, I continue to perform in ever new cities at ever new repertory theaters, eight shows a week. And I'm gradually starting to realize that most of the people you'll find in theaters are eighty-plus-year-old Jewish subscribers—and God bless them!—who would prefer to be seeing *Tuesdays with Morrie* or even *A Midsummer Night's Dream* with a cast of forty harlequin, leotard-clad acrobats. But no, to their bewilderment, out you bounce onto the stage instead, a—Multicultural Female, that was the slot I was in—desperate button, blabbering . . .

"And there will always be this moment just a few minutes in, when you can see individual audience members start to realize that no refreshing second person will be soon joining you on the stage. No! You are it! And in slow-dawning horror—that's the thing, you can see them!—they look first beseechingly at one another, then, getting no answer, they seek solace in their programs. They pick them up, page worriedly through them, hunting down some kind of explanation as to why it is YOU up there on the stage . . .

"And so I write another solo show—post–September eleventh—about worry, called *I Worry*. My theory being that we worry when we cannot STAY IN THE MOMENT . . . and by reading one's program instead of watching the LIVE PERFORMANCE GOING ON IN FRONT OF YOU, well, that's a metaphor for not being in the moment—! So midway through the show, to make this profound spiritual point, I plan to break through the fourth wall, the houselights will come up, I will rush out into the audience, totally Dadaesque . . . and I will locate some stockbroker with his head down in his program—or perhaps holding it up in front of him, STILL READING IT, like a magic talisman to ward me off—and I will grab the program RIGHT OUT OF HIS HAND and sort of . . . hit him over the head with it!"

The Kahlo Café crowd laughs, in relief. Sinead O'Connor Head makes a fist: "Givin' to the stockbroker, yeah!"

I press on:

"So I'm premiering *I Worry* at the Kennedy Center, we're thirty-five minutes in, the houselights come up, I rush into the audience . . . and I realize, in slow motion, that the usual left center aisle I attack—the section that we lit in rehearsal—is full of men scribbling busily on pads . . .

"It's opening night and they are the critics! It is a fateful moment that hangs in time. And I think … Probably I should skip that row and go to the next, so the Washington, D.C., critics can keep making their important journalistic notes … But to change ANYTHING would destroy the intent, the mission, the MOMENT …

"So I attack! I RUSH the front guy, a bespectacled fiftyish man with his overcoat next to him on a chair, writing. I snatch his notebook out of his lap and heave it over the railing! I'm yelling at him: 'You need to stop writing, sir! You need to … be in the moment!' And the whole audience … erupts! It's a circus! The man smiles but, head still down, he simply whips out another notebook, keeps writing. But I am committed. I rip the SECOND notebook out of his hands, hurl THAT over the railing! The audience roars again!

"Now I grab his coat— He really does not want me to take his coat. We wrestle. Afterward, I learn that the man was the theater critic for *The Washington Post*."

"Oh!" the café crowd exclaims, charged up, kind of excited.

"And STILL I say fine! I don't READ reviews! As everyone involved with the production knows—the staff, crew, PR people— I keep telling them: 'I don't want to see any reviews. No reviews!' And in the meantime, another performance art–y innovation I've put in *I Worry* is to have the audience write down their worries as they come into the theater … about Iraq, which was just brewing, about illness in the family, personal finances, about where they parked the car, or even their worries about, if you will, the evening. A young intern plucks out—and places into a hat—what he thinks are the funniest worries, for me to read aloud during the show. And lo and behold, onstage, mid-performance, the first Worry I pull out of the hat: 'I worry that Sandra Tsing Loh's one-woman show tonight won't be funny because of what I read in yesterday's *Washington Post*—THE BAD REVIEW!' Argh!!!!!!!!!!!!!"

There is a gasp, followed by a wobbly silence. Chelsea looks stunned. Then whispers: "It just never occurred to me that … you could get a bad review."

① ORIGINAL PLAN FOR MY ADULT LIFE

MARTHA'S VINEYARD YEARS

(circa mid-1980s)

START GRAD SCHOOL → COMPLETE 8 SHORT STORIES* → $200,000 ADVANCE BOOK DEAL → NEW YORKER PUBLICATION → NEA BOOK AWARD (ESQUIRE COVER, ETC.)

AGES — 21 — 22 — 23 — 24 — 25 →

(* TWO SEMESTERS' WORTH, 4 PER CLASS)

② REVISED PLAN FOR MY ADULT LIFE

WHITE HOUSE HONORING

(circa mid-1990s)

(SOMEWHERE IN HERE) ARTISTIC CAREER EXPLODES!!!

PRODUCTIVE AND SURE GAINING OF MOMENTUM → $250,000 CHECK ARRIVES → THE GENIUS GRANT/PBS/SMITHSONIAN/AMY TAN/CHEESE YEARS

(EXPANDED)
AGES — "20's" — "30's" — "40's" →

③ CURRENT PLAN FOR MY ADULT LIFE

"SHOWS IN NY" ~ WHOA!

MIDLIST BOOK PUBLISHED (34)

(BARGAIN CHEESE)

(THE LICKING ONE'S WOUNDS IN $150 A WEEK PUBLIC RADIO GIG YEARS)

(REVISED)
AGES 30's — 40's — 50's →

WHOA!

WHOA!

... /// THE CLIVE BARNES HORROR STORY BAD REVIEW YEARS

(GREG LOUGANIS HITING HEAD ON DIVING BOARD AND RECOVERING TYPE MOVEMENT)

The crowd is dispirited. Too many turns in this story have gone badly. When they came to "Women on Fire," they didn't actually have a sweating forty-something midlist artist on a flaming pyre in mind. It was supposed to be more: "Let's get fired up! Let's get rowdy!" Not gloomy!

The first pair of girls stand, pointing at their watches, apologetic: "Seven o'clock: Gender Studies Seminar," one mouths.

But I must finish. My voice is a plea:

"And I realized, my youthful expectations had been so wrong. Fame is no magical amulet PROTECTING the Artist from harm. Indeed, if you actually get to Act Two, a modest measure of success may actually BEGIN to become a harm CATCHER.

"And that is why I quit theater. I guess at a certain point . . . it was wonderful to me to safely open the paper and know I would not see ANYTHING about myself. It was great to be invisible. To be free. I can't tell you how DELICIOUS it is not to be working." My voice gets shaky. "Motherhood has been such an unexpected GIFT. I love my two girls. They make me so happy. Many are the times I've said, midafternoon, 'Come on, kids, time for your NAP!' And two small, warm bundles will climb onto me, as I fluff pillows on the warm bed in the sunshine, and oh so sweetly . . . everyone will drift off. To the warm thump of the dryer, and the smell, thanks to my salt-of-the-earth husband, of baking bread.

"Chelsea's mother?" I say.

"Yes," she croaks.

"In raising Chelsea, you have already BEEN creative. EXTREM-ELY creative. Just those appliqués on your shawl—I can tell how much fun you had putting them on! I, too, have had SUCH creative fun mothering my kids. With children, like a temperamental New York director, you can make all the wild artistic decisions you want and never get a bad review. Pink shoes with yellow socks? Paper-cutout hand turkey with green polka-dot head? I tell my daughters stories that MAKE NO SENSE AT ALL . . . There is no coherent plot, the theme is whatever, the characters are repetitive—One story last week had ten Barney dinosaurs, their only distinguishing characteristic was color, and three of those were yellow . . . We've left entire sets of characters, mid–tea party, cups halfway up to their lips, marooned on imaginary jungle islands that we have simply forgotten about. My stories go on for days, some might say they GRIND on . . .

"And here's what . . . my daughters beg for more! Take THAT, Clive Barnes! Another favorite quote of my daughters'? 'Mama, we love your big, fat belly.' Good heavens—that unconditional love I yearned for? I found that in my children! I found that *as a mother.*"

More girls are leaving. I wave my arms.

"By contrast, when you're an Artist . . . you never really arrive!

"Here is my template for Carnegie Hall.

"One: Congratulations! You're playing at Carnegie Hall!

"Two: Exciting news—what a beautiful poster they've designed to put up all around New York, including the subways, and you know all the foot traffic THEY get, to promote your debut at Carnegie Hall!

"Three: This is Jennifer, publicist for Carnegie Hall. She is very excited about booking some local media coverage to drum up tickets sales for your upcoming date that is now fast approaching at Carnegie Hall.

"Four: The wrinkle is, no one as obscure as you has ever been booked into Carnegie Hall, and of course there is the depressed local economy to deal with. So that it doesn't look too empty, as seat-fillers, we are seeing about busing some senior groups from New Jersey over the bridge to Carnegie Hall.

"Five: News flash—CARNEGIE HALL HAS BURNED DOWN."

Now we're down to half a Kahlo Café. There is some avoidance of eye contact going on. But like a bus without brakes, hurtling down a hill out of control, I can't stop myself:

"Each of the books I've published were at some point deemed a failure by some twenty-two-year-old publicist in New York named Jennifer. They were all named Jennifer. All my Jennifers—they're a bit like my discarded wives. My Jennifers were all graduates of Brown, they deserved so much better than me as an author, they had such beautiful hair, beautiful educations . . . They'd been groomed to have much bigger successes. But I and my incorrigably midlist work destroyed them.

"Somewhere, in some hip bar in Manhattan, are my Jennifers, about thirty-three now, still cutting great figures in the dark, but with hard lines around their mouths. It is my career that put them there." I gesture wildly. "I mean, look at Frida Kahlo! Look at the walls of this café! She was one of the most famous women artists of her time, and in any ONE painting, I ask you . . . does Frida ever look happy? Nails in the neck—that's the life of the Artist! And poor Frida Kahlo, did she have her own Jennifer to disappoint? Her own Jennifer? Or maybe, in Mexico, a Yennifer? Or maybe an Xchtl, a disappointed Xchtl!"

As if to punctuate, there is a crash of glassware. A murmuring clot forms around a capsized barrista.

Certainly I have blown it—blown to smithereens my students' fondest hopes, the already flimsy veil of my classroom comportment and whatever I had left of my reputation for groovy, simpatico hipness on the Marymount campus. No matter: What my coffeehouse meltdown has shown me is that I am not a calm, sedate, resting-on-my-laurels teacher but a bold, vibrant, and still passionate writer with interesting things to say. In this year of fog, what I've forgotten is that the important thing is my work—my weekly witty, sharply literary musings about city life for KCRW. And KCRW is after all the key to Kentwood: All my Marymount embarrassment will soon fall away when Hannah's kindergarten acceptance is finally nailed. (And I'm still glowing from Kentwood's amazing API . . . 907!)

But here comes the next rude turn. I am just headed out the door to record for KCRW when the phone rings.

It is the KCRW station manager, whom we will call Ruth, as that is her name. By coincidence she has the same name as my therapist, Ruth, but the call is not therapeutic.

"SANDRA!" my station manager exclaims. "DO YOU KNOW WHAT YOU DID OVER THE WEEKEND? YOU SAID 'FUCK' ON THE RADIO! HOW COULD YOU SAY 'FUCK' ON THE RADIO? OF COURSE, I HAVE NO CHOICE BUT TO FIRE YOU IMMEDIATELY, AND PLEASE, SANDRA," she adds, "GET SOME HELP. GET . . . PROFESSIONAL . . . HELP. GOOD-BYE."

I fail to stammer out a request to see if KCRW could be a media sponsor for the Kentwood Elementary fund-raiser, so my daughter can go to kindergarten there.

But it's ever so much worse than that.

Clearly, a horrible error has occurred.

Over the years, my engineer and I have worked out a system, in our sleepy basement control room. If the text colloquially yearns for it, to highlight some personal frustration or other, I'll record an expletive . . . and mark it for him to bleep out later.

Like me, he has recently suffered some sleep deprivation. Like me, he has two small children.

He has clearly forgotten to bleep and now I've been fired, not just fired but . . .

"Fired for obscenity . . . on public radio," Kaitlin says in wonderment. "There is actually no conversational number for this."

I call Aimee, give her the bad news about KCRW, how I will not be able to "bring it" for the Kentwood Elementary fund-raiser . . . My ex-boss hates me, now Mrs. Carla Feninger will too . . .

"I'm so sorry," Aimee says tersely. "In a meeting. Gotta run."

And now I may even lose my Marymount College job. The dean is a devotee of public radio—that is how I got hired. That KCRW radio gig was the last shred of a professional, creative toehold I had in this world . . .

I am such a fuck-up. I'm utterly fucked. Fuck!

It's all too much for me.

I can't do any of it anymore.

I take to bed.

I give up.

I shred my KidSmart Museum card.

I holler, "Kids? It's watch-all-the-TV-you-want time! And look . . ." I open the cupboard, pour it out into a bucket. "Stale Halloween candy!"

There are cries of joy, cheering. It's Christmas!

My daughters dance around me, hugging me! Apparently I am the greatest mom who ever walked the planet!

Chewing furiously on their lollipops like Teamsters chewing cud, my girls get right down to business in the bathroom, bathing all of their stuffed animals. What with all the educational flashcards and rushing about to science museums, all their ponies, unicorns, Doodle Bears have gotten so dirty . . . They need shampooing, and rinsing, and much brushing, with tiny doll hairbrushes. Jonathan and Aimee's children are violining their way into Carnegie Hall by age nine, fencing their way to the Olympics, and completing all the leading-to-Harvard-early-admission math puzzles of the danger-ously highly gifted. By contrast, here in The Nuys, if we gauge our spawn's eventual careers by their current interests, it appears we have a small tribe of pint-sized future beauticians, or cosmetologists.

But then I get to thinking, gloomily, as I click on the television, maybe it's okay. Why does EVERY child have to be exceptional? Per-haps Bill and Melinda Gates could create a kind of wilderness sanc-tuary called "The Island of the C Students," a safe place for children to go who are not exceptional. When they turn twenty-one and are still flailing, not having graduated early from Princeton, they can move to our island to enjoy responsible and fulfilling citizenry. Our

F&*(&*(!!!!

C students can perform extremely useful tasks such as inputing checkbook data into Quicken, separating out everyone's recycling, and cutting up watermelon. (Recently I was at a brunch with a roomful of Ph.D.'s, Ivy Leaguers, and various other media professionals. Did ANYONE make the slightest move to cut up the watermelon! No-o-o-o-o!!!)

C students have many other attractive features. They don't destroy a Scrabble game like 1600 SAT's do, and are fun to play cards and watch television with. They also don't play the violin, practice the violin, or sit around boring people with long monologues about how they have fallen behind on their violin— How they just saw Nadia Sadja-Salerno or whatever her name is do some *Live at Wolf Trap* thing on PBS and fell into depression and went to therapy for four weeks over somehow not finding their true potential on the violin and being stifled by their dad.

(I remember when Jonathan and Aimee's son Ben first developed his extraordinary childhood gift for the violin. Jonathan was especially thrilled at how much Ben clearly loved playing, how passionate Ben was about music. "I never had that," Jonathan said, "that love of music. For me growing up, practicing was always a chore." "That's wonderful," I said. "Perhaps Ben can grow up to become a musician, a real working musician like Mike, and move out to where we live, in Van Nuys." Jonathan visibly started, checked himself. Then added: "Well, there are plenty of surgeons who enjoy playing the violin!")

Or massage! That's what our C students can do: massage. As I lay in bed and watch the Home Shopping Network—which is amazingly interesting—my girls sit on my back, roll over me, walk on me with their clammy, slightly sticky feet. It actually doesn't feel too bad. Instead of a four-hand massage as at the Auberge, it's a four-feet massage . . . At a price I can afford.

And perhaps my firing—it's all for the better. My slot was so obscure, no one even wrote me at the station anymore. And, in fact, when the expletive ran at 7:30 A.M., no one even called the station to report it, so it ran again at 9:30 A.M.! My KCRW pay was only $150 a week, anyway.

So no one knows about it. The humiliation is contained. I can probably keep my Marymount job at least. Things will be okay.

Mike comes by. Sits gently by the side of the bed.

"Honey?"

"Wha—?"

"The *L.A. Times* is preparing an item on your, well, your being fired for saying 'fuck' on the radio. Apparently your boss gave them some pretty choice quotes about you."

"That I'm an insane raving maniac who will never be hired again?"

"Something like that. Do you want to give them a quote?"

"No," I say.

I close my eyes.

In a way—the obliteration—it feels good. What a relief not to even pretend to write anymore. Anything. This'll give me time to take up some new hobbies. For instance . . .

Where's that knitting kit?

Here it is!

Turquoise wool! Fluffy! Nice!

Via much long-distance phone calling, Kaitlin and Mike busily arrange an emergency I-CHAT with my therapist, Ruth, who has been on leave in the San Juan Islands.

Mike props his Mac up on the bed, opens it, adjusts the tube-shaped camera eye.

There is static fritzing in, fritzing out . . . But suddenly an image pops up. I see Ruth, my Ruth—the nice one, not the mean one. Her cloud of dark gray-and-silver hair bobs gently in front of me. She is resplendent in an orange-and-gold caftan.

"Sandra dear heart!" she cries out waving her turquoise-beringed hands. Then she looks to the side. "I can't hear anything. Is she there?"

"Look right," an offscreen voice says.

"Oh, THERE you are!" she cries out. "Sandra dear heart! Trust me!" She hugs herself. "You will survive this! You will survive this! Another public radio station will snap you up right away! You're THAT good!"

I lean up on one elbow, the better to get at the jalapeño Kettle Chips my husband has been kind enough to procure for me, at my request.

"Let me tell you something, other Ruth."

"I am here," she says, moving her arms in an aura-like circle. "Boy, I wish I could hear better. But go on."

"Public radio commentators—those gentle, trusted souls, characters, and types who venture into your car or into your home five minutes before the hour? The bond they build, with their audience, is through their quirkiness. But it must be a gentle quirkiness, a charming quirkiness. No one will want you after that 'quirk' sheers off into something grotesque and pervy like, for instance, saying the word *fuck*!"

"Well, you didn't mean to," Ruth says. "It was a technical error. Surely when you get your story out—"

I pick out another chip, a great big fat one, curled over in grease.

"Oh no no no, my friend, I'm afraid the damage is done! It's the sort of gaffe that is irreparable. It's that Gary-Hart-on-the-yacht moment. Let me explain.

"NPR listeners do not want to see:

"Andrei Codrescu exposing himself in a Louisiana adult movie theater, à la Pee-wee Herman.

"Garrison Keillor caught red-eyed and wild-haired in a police mug shot, raving, drunken, bedraggled, Nick Nolte–esque.

"Five words no one wants to hear? 'Bailey White is in rehab.' "

The enormity of the injustice hits me.

"God! The forties . . . These were supposed to be my Maya Angelou years! My *Live at Wolf Trap* years! Amy Tan! When is she going to retire! I ... want ... her ... spot! But I guess my judgment is shitty. The older I get, the more I seem to be just ... LOSING it. My forties have been just some kind of debacle. Worse and worse. The last time scary radio Ruth called me, two years ago, was to inform me she was cutting my commentary that week as, in case I was unaware of it, public radio commentators cannot call Osama Bin Laden 'the Towelatollah.' Which, I admit, sounds bad—'Towelatollah'—but you have to understand this word came three-quarters of the way through a painstakingly framed essay about language, political correctness, and the complex vagaries of our post–September eleventh world. I mean, is it worse for ME to call the Taliban the 'Toweleban' than for them to herd women into the backs of pickup trucks and, before howling football stadiums, shoot them in the head?

"See—to me, 'Toweleban' seems like something brave to say, a searing linguistic/semitoic point of some kind, but to other people it's just ... stupid. I'm losing it! Thank God for that Marymount College job. I hope I don't lose that. All I want to do is keep my little teaching job." Now I'm babbling. "In a way, it's great to be finally totally out of the public eye, even if the last bit of that eye was at seven-thirty on a Sunday morning. The public eye was basically closed. Still, it's kind of a relief. After the Clive Barnes years, I'm just tired of being attacked and paraded."

"GET A HOLD OF YOURSELF!" Ruth suddenly screams. My Ruth. My therapist.

She has my attention.

Ruth raises one fist.

"You are in a cauldron now. You are in the pressure cooker. You are in the battle zone."

She raises the other fist.

"You are in the hot seat. You are in the cockpit. You are in the gladiator pen. You must ... strap on your armor!!!"

F&*(&*(!!!!

I have to admit, it is rather mesmerizing to see my tiny therapist floating on Mike's computer screen. She's like my own miniature little destroying Shiva goddess.

She shakes both fists, screams!

"The only way home is through Bagdad!"

"What are you talking about?" I say.

"Was it right for her to fire you? Did you mean to have that word spoken on the radio?"

"Well, no."

"It was wrong, and if you don't say it, you're a PUSSY! The buck stops with you! What are you going to do in life, just roll over and roll over and roll over? You keep giving others the power!"

"I'm just too tired to have . . . my own power," I admit. "It's like I had the power, didn't enjoy it. It gave me indigestion. I guess I really didn't want the power. Power is exhausting. I just wanted inner peace."

"You have NO CHOICE now! Destiny has thrust you into this position! The power wants you. The power CALLS to you."

Ruth raises her hand in a fist again, but which now has the thumb through it, in the Italian way.

"You must tap into your inner FUCK YOU!"

"I'm just so tired," I say.

"Apparently she also said that your work is trivial and that you're emotionally unstable, that you tried to harm the station, and that you should get therapy! And guess what—I AM YOUR THERAPIST. You need to fight back at that toxic being!"

I make a dismissive motion with my hand.

"That's just Ruth. You have to understand her. She always fires people like that. She's kind of, I don't know, a ferocious mother bear. She fires you, starts yelling, says YOU look depressed . . . you should get therapy. Although, as with Joe Frank, I hear she usually does it at Peet's Coffee in Santa Monica. The only thing I didn't get was the

157

Peet's coffee. But really, in the long run, you'd have to agree she has done more good at that station than harm—she's a talent picker—I owe my career to her!"

Ruth makes two fists, with two thumbs poking through them.

"You are calling the *L.A. Times*. You are giving them the quote that you are sad . . . AND ANGRY—"

"I guess I'm not really angry. I'm just humiliated and depressed."

"That's called anger!" she yells.

"Really?" I ask. "That's what anger feels like? It's just kind of a headache."

"You're ANGRY!"

So I upgrade my emotion to anger.

And as soon as I say I am angry, my dominant emotion morphs into fear, fear of repercussions . . .

But here instead is what happens.

Here is how my small tragedy of being fired from a $150-a-week job shears off into surrealism, like something out of Woody Allen's *Zelig*.

The complication is my firing occurs just weeks after Janet Jackson's Super Bowl breast baring, and it seems there's a new FCC filing every day.

Because of the FCC/Janet Jackson thing, any obscenity firing in any media outlet is major news, no matter how little known the person. And as most of the firings occurring are of morning shock jocks, how fresh and interesting is the firing of a forty-something minivan-driving mother? Who talks a lot about sorting her daughters' socks. Subsequent instant headlines read HOWARD STERN, BUBBA THE LOVE SPONGE, AND . . . SANDRA TSING LOH? WHO THE HELL IS SHE? Inquiring minds wanted to know.

And, like pings on a radar, all my friends and acquaintances—even very old acquaintances, people I haven't spoken to in years—

are calling me with excited media updates. All at once, my removal from a three-minute time slot so obscure the FCC actually slept through it (twice) is starting to make ink.

Jonathan calls: "Oh my God—look at this . . . you're on the *Drudge Report!*"

Rachel e-mails me from Europe: "You're on the BBC!"

Even Brenda phones in, slack-jawed in wonderment: "So I'm standing here in the elevator taking Cal to the dentist, and on the wall, they have one of those new red teletype things, and it says . . .

" 'RADIO COMMENTATOR SANDRA TSING LOH FIRED FOR OBSCENITY! RADIO COMMENTATOR SANDRA TSING LOH FIRED FOR OBSCENITY!' "

Which my dad now actually sees on the crawl under Larry King—"RADIO COMMENTATOR SANDRA TSING LOH FIRED FOR OBSCENITY! RADIO COMMENTATOR SANDRA TSING LOH FIRED FOR OBSCENITY!" Or sometimes it's just "SANDRA TSING LOH! FIRED! OBSCENE!"

And like a rolling stone gathering moss, lichen, and other peaty things, the meaning of my firing is now flipping. Like the little "fuck" that could, the shooting media star of my obscenity takes on a glamour—a cultural heat—my actual employment never has. And I mean NONE of my actual employment, twenty years' worth of books, theater shows, and numerous radio pieces. Of all the thousands of painstakingly labored-over literary words I have written by age forty-two, it is but four magic letters—F-U-C-K—that have vaulted me to the next level.

The congratulations are pouring in—"You're in *Rolling Stone!*" It's like winning an Oscar!

Even my agent calls . . . a man I practically forgot existed! NBC Casting called—they want me to come in IMMEDIATELY to read for the part of Jeff Goldblum's therapist in this new pilot!

That's the way Hollywood works—WHY I'm in the news doesn't matter. For them it's just "Asian person on radar: Call her in."

Even my gloomy ex-boyfriend Bruce interrupts his Dick-Cheney-is-behind-every-evil-Republican-conspiracy mass e-mails long enough to place a bitter personal call: "Man, I wish I could get fired. You're lucky, Sandra. I wish I could get a career break like that."

Instead of a forty-something loser, overnight I am transformed into a First Amendment heroine, free-speech pioneer, inheritor of the mantle of Lenny Bruce.

And my heroism . . . feeds on itself. The more my boss colorfully insists I am an emotionally unstable person who tried to destroy her station by pulling a Janet Jackson, the more reporters demand a response. I don't have to be witty. All I have to do is suggest the difficulty of—of smooshing—a pre-edited breast . . . into the radio? and I look like some kind of comic *genius*. And in the *L.A. Times,* every day it's "she says, I say, she says, I say"—this kind of wild, over-the-top "Mothra versus Godzilla" battle! Which people have never seen anything like in public radio! I mean, this is like *Jerry Springer,* but the NPR version, with two haggard women in flat-heeled shoes hitting each other over the head with like 100 percent recycled-material tote bags, coffee mugs, and special pledge-drive CDs. "And here—Yo Yo Ma! Bill Frisell! And what's this? The Kronos Quartet doing the songs of Elvis Costello—take that!"

The more we fight, the more media outlets love it! These are the best reviews of my career . . . !

Celeste calls me, voice purring.

"Did you see *The New York Times*? Unbelievable. Two words: Frank Rich."

FRANK . . . RICH???

Until now, my local public radio commentaries have never been heard east of Barstow. But now, within the bowels of Manhattan, Frank Rich has cited MY firing as an outrage. Even better, and this is like every fired misfit creative person's wet dream come true, he deems MY boss . . . like the Taliban!

F&*(&*(!!!!

Forget Clive Barnes and the *Post*. This is Frank Rich in the FUCKING *Times* of New York!

"Frank Rich," Celeste repeats. "The reason I'm calling is the ACLU wants you to be a V.I.P. guest at this huge 'Speak Truth to Power' event Friday in Hancock Park. It's the Clintons, Bill Gates . . . Al Pacino actually requested you. Personally. He was outraged after reading the Frank Rich column."

A town car is sent for me. Celeste rides along. When we arrive at the giant stone castle in Hancock Park, the street is already mobbed with town cars and limos. I know the guest list of performers includes Anjelica Huston, Kathy Bates, Carrie Fisher, Jeffrey Tambor, Eddie Izzard, Johnny Rotten, Eva Longoria . . . Which tends to only strike me with dread, because I know how low in the celeb pecking order I'm going to be.

But unbelievably, when Celeste says my name to the guard, the gates explode open and we are waved in toward rows of security guards, listening to earpieces, bent over, aggressive. As urgent as though they were landing helicopters at Camp David, they wave wave wave our car in!

I am a person who has wept in a rain-spattered Lutheran school parking lot . . . Who laid all my cards down before an implacable Mrs. Claus . . . Who sent a gift basket to Mrs. Carla Feninger, packed with free books, to no response.

I have broken tuna melts with Brenda, and taken notes for Joan Archer, of the tattered Parents Fools, the Patron Saint of Lost Causes, in Van Nuys.

I have kissed the asses of third-tier people, and below-tier people, and gotten only chapped lips.

But since the Frank Rich mention, it is as though a silent underground alarm has gone off. I am now an iron-clad folk hero, a Woody

Guthrie, a Rosa Parks, a . . . who is that lady? Rigoberto Menchú! The V.I.P. guest list—it's me and this group of Afghanistani doctor women. It happened overnight. Al Pacino requested to meet me PERSONALLY? What will be next? A Nobel Peace Prize?

I float through the party as if in a dream.

I am never left alone for a moment.

Never a back is turned to me. No, by contrast, conversational bouquets open to me . . .

Guests turn, with champagne flutes in hand, gasp, rush up to me.

I am introduced, "Here she is . . . the writer . . . who STOOD UP . . . to KCRW!"

People swoop on me not like crows but like royal falcons bearing gifts.

"I love Howard Stern!" an older man in a pinstripe suit says. "When he talked about you, I thought, I've gotta meet this woman!"

A fish-eyed younger fellow, more of a fallen-professor type, paisley tie:

"I confess to being surprised at your firing, Sandra. I wasn't even aware you were still on the air— And I'm certainly disturbed by the First Amendment implications of your case— But most of all . . ." The man's face suddenly turned red. He bends over double. His fists clench. "What I realize now is how much I HATE THAT WOMAN!!! The way she torments me on all those pledge drives! She's like a bad mother! A guilt-inducing, constantly berating Jewish mother! And I should know! I had one!"

"Well, thank you," I say . . .

But he is not done.

"Those PLEDGE DRIVES!" Spittle actually flies out of the man's mouth. "While some clock is always ticking down, it's like she's riding shotgun with me in my car as I crawl through L.A.'s choked, smoggy freeways, hectoring me that twenty-five dollars, fifty dollars, one thousand dollars . . . No matter how much I give the station, IT WILL NEVER BE ENOUGH!"

An older Hancock Park matron, platinum-white hair, perfect size-two yellow Nancy Reagan suit, comes up to me. She is holding a white poodle with bows. Puts it down.

"I have been a huge public radio fan for twenty years. I'm a Democrat, I'm a member of NOW, I know Gloria Steinem, I care about the Sierras, I care about what happens in Rwanda, I always want to hear what's on the BBC. I give and give and give every year. But then I read Frank's piece in *The New York Times*—it made me so mad!" She opens her Hermès satchel.

Takes out a KCRW mug. Carefully wraps it in a linen dinner napkin, takes out what appears to be an Emmy(?), and with an astonishing heft of strength smashes it!

"And look at this!" she says, pulling something else out of her purse.

"My KCRW Fringe Benefits cards! I've cut them all up! And I'm sending them to the station!"

More guests join us:

"Public radio's going to the pits!"

Why?

The complaints come hard and fast:

" 'Funny' news quizzes where radio stories used to be!"

"Precocious food shows! Whimsical Chardonnays! Sweepstakes involving Jaguars, where 'Ja-gu-ar' is pronounced with three syllables!"

A squat Wallace Shawn look-alike collars me:

"The bottom line? Nine words. 'Leonard Nimoy reading the work of Isaac Bashevis Singer.' "

"And John Tesh on PBS? Why is John Tesh on PBS?"

And now an Irish lawyer with muttonchop sideburns pushes me against the wall.

"Here is an e-mail I wrote to you that KCRW apparently never forwarded. I'm going to read it to you now.

" 'Dear Ms. Loh,' " he says.

" 'I do not fucking know if those fuckers at fucking KCRW are fucking going to forward this fucking e-mail to you, but—what the fuck!—I'll try, anyway.

" 'I fucking find it fucking outrageous that you should have been summarily fucking fired for having inadvertently used a 'naughty' fucking word on-the-fucking-air. To my mind, it's part and parcel of the Massive Wave of Fucking Stupidity that seems, once again, to be washing over this fucking country. FUCK! Just because fucking Middle America saw a black woman's tit during a fucking football game. Who gives a fuck?' "

God, I think. In a weird Los Angeles way, my life FINALLY MAKES SENSE.

I am not Amy Tan, I'm simply a conduit through which liberal people can express ugly thoughts. I'm just kind of a topsy-turvy MESS. Like society!

Celeste squeezes my arm. She indicates that I should turn my gaze forward.

A windswept woman appears before me, wild mane of auburn hair, big geometric earrings, a kind of peach-colored sarong, very silky.

The woman catches me, grips me, holds me like a figure about to leap away from her off a cliff. She holds me close, like a lover.

Her voice is oddly low and mellifluous, on an entirely different wavelength from the rest of the room. She has a wonderfully ornate, almost foreign, way of speaking.

"I'm Reva Thon. Admissions director. Wonder Canyon. Celeste has given us the possibly wonderful news, at least for us, if we should be so lucky, that your daughter Hannah may not entirely be spoken for, for September? Might we entice you, for a kindergarten tour, at Wonder Canyon?"

She pulls out a card and writes down, on the back . . . *her cell*.

7
Wonder Canyon

We are now in a magical time when there is only more, more, more magic.

I hear my phone chirp, chirp, chirp, like it is doing so constantly these days. I run to the kitchen to grab it . . . only to hear the dial tone.

And realize . . . it was Mike's phone.

From the dining room, I hear the cadence of Mike's voice as he wanders through our tiny bungalow, picking up our girls' as-usual scattered clothes. Socks, shorts, a tutu, a teddy wearing a tutu, a monkey wearing a tutu . . .

Instead of a jovial "Hey, brother, how're you doing?" (I always find it quaint how musicians call each other "brother"), I hear more of a measured, professional tone—"Yes, uh-huh, yes, I COULD . . ."

Then suddenly, "Today? You want me to come today? It's two already here, which must make it five over there . . ."

"What?" I cry out when he hangs up the phone.

He puts it down on the cradle, dazed.

Then puts up his hands.

"I didn't say yes for sure. I said I'd call them back. I said I needed to think about it."

"WHAT? WHAT? WHAT?" I yell.

His hands remain up:

"I did promise you I would not go out on the road anymore."

I'm stunned.

"Why did you promise that?"

"You made me, remember? Now that we're parents? You said my being away from the kids is too hard?"

"I don't recall saying that. I must have been hallucinating. WHAT?"

He suddenly dimples, boyish, at fifty-one.

"Bette Midler!"

"Aieeeeeeeeeeeeeeeeeeee!!!" I scream.

"They've just fired the guitarist!"

"Fired!!! Yipppppppppppppppeeeeeee!!!" I howl.

"They want me to fly to New York TODAY!"

"Woo-hooooooooooooooooooo!"

"Well?" he says shyly.

I look at my husband, surrounded by socks, skirts, tutus. This tiny, cluttered bungalow of females—this is no place for a man.

I shout, "Well, honey, what are you waiting for? You'd better get going!"

He comes and puts his hands on my arms. His tone is amazed. "So you're letting me go on tour? Really? You would do that?"

"What are you smoking? GO! It's Bette Midler!"

"I just . . . I also know I promised to follow through on Hannah's school stuff. Which I know you've been worried about. But I know it's going to work out."

He puts his hand on his temple, massaging the familiar migraine—
the familiar swooping crows—of his own family duties. "I made up
a calendar. The magnet letters come out in May. Then you can do
open enrollment . . . I started a list. I hate to dump it on you."

I put my head down, close my eyes, then tilt my chin up, channeling, I don't know, Diana Ross in *Mahogany,* forging bravely ON, in
this business of show, without a man.

"No worries. Just give the stuff to me. I'll handle it."

"What a great wife I have!" he says, in glee.

"Not that you haven't been doing a great job," the Great Wife
replies, lying through her teeth. "The great foundation you've laid
will make it super-easy." It's amazing what outrageous lies you can
still pull off after eighteen years of cohabitation. I guess that's the
beauty of men and women. I could not pull off such hilarious cork-
ers with my sister. "What I appreciate is your patience," I said to
Kaitlin one day on the phone, and she laughed hysterically for five
minutes. Three days later we talked again, and I murmured, "And I
love how nonjudgmental you are—" "Oh no!" she screamed, howling, as she dropped the phone.

"I'll call them back!" Mike exults . . . and all at once we're in a
flurry of activity, suitcases exploding open, iPod attachments, twisting wires, headphones, pants, socks, guitars, wawa pedals . . . !

I wave my fist in a victory salute.

"Better a musician far away working than home and unemployed!"

It is only when the excitement of Bette Midler! New York! Five-
month tour! subsides that I realize . . . Mike is going to miss the
Wonder Canyon tour.

I feel a stab of disappointment. It's so like missing the opening of
Christmas gifts on Christmas Day.

Then again, he will see the school eventually . . . and maybe it's a
good thing.

First of all, in this competitive town we live in, it's always MUCH more glamorous to have the husband AWAY.

Second of all, although Wonder Canyon is a done deal, we've basically been offered a slot . . . (I carry Reva Thon's card in my pocket at all times, which I rub like a lucky rabbit's foot.) Look, it's not that I don't think he presents well, but after the great Bobblement that was the Luther Hall kindergarten assessment, it's just much simpler to have the dad AWAY! Bette Midler! New York! Working!

And thirdly . . .

There is a person I know who deserves to actually see the inside of Wonder Canyon, the school where NO ONE gets a tour.

When Hannah and I get to Pane Simple, a track-lit French espresso/pastry joint on Ventura, Aimee is already there, in a dark suit, pacing. No BlackBerry, no earpiece, nothing. She is simply pacing and pacing, in preparation for meeting . . . Her maker? Her master? Her what?

I pull up, roll down the window. "Hey!"

Aimee's face, behind large oval sunglasses, is blank. Her voice sounds thin, papery.

"I'm nervous."

"It's a Play Encounter!" I say. "What could be less foreboding than that?"

"I know." Arms crossed, as though hugging herself, she turns away. Her voice becomes meditative. "It's just . . . After all the reading I've done . . . I've waited so long to see the inside of Wonder Canyon."

She doesn't make a move toward the dented white Toyota minivan.

"Shall we?" I ask.

There is a brief, humming pause.

"I've got a car seat," she says, jerking her thumb left. With relief Hannah and I climb out of the fetid minivan and mount stairs into Aimee's cool, clean, steel-and-leather Lexus SUV-thingy.

I'm actually quite happy to be going up the hill in a Lexus. Even though I know, what with my X person/Rigoberta Menchú/ Afghanistani women status, this is the rare L.A. occasion when I could literally drive up to Wonder Canyon in anything. The saying of "Fuck!" on public radio has somehow bought me that. ("She drove up in a Pinto! Isn't that cool? A Pinto." "What sangfroid! I wish I had the sangfroid to drive a Pinto.")

And besides, the Lexus does seem to be a delectable treat for Hannah.

"Ooh!" she croons, in the sheer pleasure of being surrounded by smooth leather rather than by such customary bad smells as rancid McDonald's fries and her sister's crumpled socks. Down pops Hannah's viewing screen. I hear a *beeeep,* then the cheerful theme from *Little Einsteins:* "We're going on a trip on a little rocketship!"

"Pick up the headphones, honey," Aimee instructs. "You see them?"

"Ooh!" Hannah says, with ill-masked pleasure.

"And there's a sippy cup of cold water back there, and sliced apples and rice cakes if you're hungry."

"Thank you," says Hannah, with sudden eerie good manners. "These apples are delicious and your car is so . . . so . . ." She leans forward to deliver the ultimate compliment, the most outlandishly high praise she, in her four-year-old world, can bestow. ". . . clean! Your car is so clean!" She puts the headphones on, takes in her surroundings. I can see the wheels and dials clicking in Hannah's brain. Hannah is making a mental note to search the seat pocket for tiny child-sized handcuffs, the better to handcuff herself to Seth's post in the Lexus in the same way I wanted to handcuff myself to the infinity pool at Auberge. (That's what I just call it now: Auberge.)

"I'm almost afraid to see it," Aimee observes as we twist and turn up toward Mulholland. "I have been studying Baz Ligiero ever since I was in graduate school."

"Baz Ligiero?"

" 'Baz Ligiero?' " Aimee repeats, lightly mocking my tone. Turning right on Mulholland, she shakes her head. She is almost talking more to herself than to me. "Who is Baz Ligiero! Ah!" She throws up her hands, as if in pain. As if it's all too much.

She recites the painfully good news almost dully, educational pearls to the swine.

"Wonder Canyon is the only gifted children's school—actually, school PERIOD—in the world whose curriculum is based on the cognitive developmental methods of Baz Ligiero. Before Piaget . . . before Reggio . . . there was Baz Ligiero. People think of Piaget as the first Swiss constructivist in child psychology, but the main part of Piaget's work, if you read it, is all based . . . ?"

"On Baz Ligiero."

"Yes!"

I hear the contented chomp of apples behind us. I feel that Hannah is accumulating ever more brain cells simply riding in this car. I wonder if dirt and bad smells can actually retard kids' cognitive and emotional development. Probably. And ants. Probably truly gifted children typically do not need to deal with ants in their car seats.

Aimee's voice drops lower. Within the hum of the Lexus, I feel as though I am in a James Bond movie and Q is giving me top-secret British Intelligence information.

"Baz Ligiero was a former Geneva armorer who taught at the Binet Boys' School in France at Grange aux Belles at the same time Piaget began. Ligiero was ALREADY teaching music via a method he invented based on his boyhood experiences in Geneva lying in the park and watching sparrow flight patterns. It was basically the Orff-Schulwerk method, and this was ten years . . . pre-Orff!"

I am now picturing portly bespectacled Swiss men in cardigans, shooting silent cutting looks at one another in the university cafeteria, over trays of IKEA-like meatballs and lingonberries . . . And I'm thinking, I'm sure a gothic purple writer like Ann Rice could make intrigue between battling Swiss child psychologists mesmerizing.

For my money, I would need at least a Swiss vampire in the mix, an internationally known chef, or a castrati.

But I have mocked Aimee before and been wrong. This information is clearly of high, high importance when it comes to our four-year-old American children.

"So is Baz Ligiero there, at Wonder Canyon?" I ask. "He must be at least a hundred!"

"Not Baz, but his son Dracul!" I hear Aimee literally say.

"Dracul?" I ask, a little hysterically.

And Aimee pulls up to an unmarked corrugated steel gate half hidden by a nest of trees. It has only a number on it, 6669. Oh my God, so that's the secret of the extraordinary power of Wonder Canyon! Undead Swiss vampire child psychologists! Played Count Dracula–like, in white twin buns, by Gary Oldman!

"No no no no," Aimee says, suddenly normal again. "Racul. Racul Ligiero. He and his wife, Lisalotte, are the only living disciples of his father, who of course after the war was blacklisted."

Wonder Canyon contains an Upper Campus, a Lower Campus, and a central complex of K–2 classrooms called The Glen. Because of all the construction on the Upper Campus, Play Encounter families park in a dirt lot and mount white hybrid SUV's that will take us down into the central Glen area. I see a bumper sticker: POWERED BY 100% VEGETABLE OIL.

We bump down the winding road past several large buildings with soaring steel frames. Nestled in the hills, they look like great birds about to take flight. They are painted in soothing watercolor hues of salmon, lavender, and celadon. Beyond are several other great-birds-in-progress. There is the faint whine of a bulldozer, a crane lifting.

I lean in toward Aimee.

"I know nothing about architecture, and yet I very much want to use the word *constructivist*. Can I say *constructivist*?"

"This is so exciting," Aimee whispers, giddy.

She points left to what appears to be a giant gazebo of weathered gray wood. Fairly simple, really, just a somewhat rambling gray wooden structure. "That's the tanzhaus. That's got to be the tanzhaus!" She points to squares of bright color lying here and there on the grass around it. "The tanztillen!"

"Their arrangement seems rather haphazard," I observe.

Aimee shakes her head, again, at my ignorance. "Logarithms," she murmurs, turning her face to the window. "Logarithms. The nautilus spiral."

As we continue to drop down into the canyon, the whine of bulldozers fades, and there are no more great steel birds. There are mostly trees, rocks, and the occasional stone sculpture, which you have to look really hard to find, so cunningly do their rough-hewn forms blend into the landscape.

Our SUV bounces to a stop.

Here we are: The Glen.

I am, frankly, underwhelmed.

The Glen looks less like an elementary school than a pre–World War II French village of perhaps eight small, plain wooden cottages. They are huddled together in a circle.

Coming closer, you can see that each cottage bears, on its front door, a simple wooden placard that announces its name. They are all names of trees: "Cypress," "Mulberry," "Aspen," "Birch."

To the left of "Birch," we duck into a low arch, stepping through a tunnel of cool stone for just a moment, and suddenly our world opens up again into a dappled arbor.

Our heads are literally crowned with green. The peaty, earthy, spicy scents about us are intoxicating.

"Lavender!" Aimee whispers.

"Rosemary!" I whisper.

"Sage!"

And now we hear, quietly but quite clearly, as though from some distant magical glen, the sparkling, ribbon-like musical intertwinings of Ravel. A string quartet. The music is so quiet but crystal-Bose-clear I wonder if it is actually playing in my head . . . if the Ravel is something I am thinking rather than hearing.

No matter. The point is, here we are in a lush, real-life Ravelscape. Because now that we're actually inside the ring of cottages, you can see they are simply exquisite. Through invitingly open Dutch doors and charming latticed windows, you can see that each wooden cottage is like a dream unfolding. There are colored rag rugs, pools of sunlight kissing rough-hewn pine floors, children's art brightening every wall. If anything, the cottages looked a little odd, to my eye, at first glance because they are . . .

Well, everything seems to be built to some slightly-smaller-than-normal proportion. What is that? Three-quarter size. It's like a special . . . dwarf French village.

It's like a very, very special . . . Auberge des Enfants!

"Welcome, Hannah! My name is Gretel!" says a smiling young beauty with smoothly upswept blond hair. If Uma Thurman had a sylph-like young cousin from the country, this could be she. Gretel bends down on one knee and waggles an adorable stuffed frog, who is wearing a white T-shirt that says WONDER! on it. The sylvan creature opens her arms.

"Hannah!" she says. "Would you like to meet Gary Grenouille?"

Hannah is the sort of person who would run to a smiling young blonde waving a real frog, even a dead one. Gretel could basically be waving a sock of poo. Off Hannah flies.

"Well, I'll never see HER again," I say.

"Do you want to come play with us, Hannah?" says Gretel. "Come on! We're making a village . . ." And here she stops, humorously quizzical. "From hats?"

Gretel makes a comical expression, as though wondering if she has gone just a bit batty. She looks at Hannah, questioning if Hannah can help her, in her momentary insanity.

"Hannah—have you ever made a village . . . from hats?"

"No, but I CAN," says Hannah, slipping her hand confidently in Gretel's. Why can Hannah trust her? Because she's the young Uma Thurman! "I've made a village from boxes. I've built New York!"

The blonde stops. Leans down again, amazed.

"New York?"

"The skyscrapers. Like in Gershwin!"

"Hannah! I think I know what music you're thinking of! Have you ever heard of the music *Rhapsody in . . . in . . .* ?"

Hannah listens intently, interested.

"It's a color?" the blonde says. "Like the sky? *Rhapsody in . . .* ?"

"*Blue?*"

"Gershwin! Wow!" The blonde shoots me a quick look, mouths: "Amazing!"

I jab Aimee in the ribs, in a paroxysm of glee: "That's the one thing their good-for-nothing father does with them, in that Clampett-like backyard of ours! They build things, out of cardboard boxes, to music! I thought they were just weird nests, kind of nasty, but apparently . . ." I lift my arms up. "Genius!"

"I like your hair clip," says Hannah, reaching up. "Is that a butterfly?"

"Here—take a look," Gretel says, reaching back and, in one deft motion, she releases the clip and hands it to Hannah. Her long blond hair swings into the air, free, full, like a fan of spun gold.

"Can I touch your hair?" asks Hannah.

"Of course!" Gretel exclaims, laughing . . . And shoots me a warm look, placing a quick hand over her heart to indicate she is in love with my daughter . . . Who now pulls her forward by the hand. And Gretel's attention is instantly back on Hannah. "Where did you say Gary Grenouille wants to go?" And off they trot to yon cottage of Mulberry.

"And look how the teacher draws her out," Aimee says. She looks physically sick. "I hate my sons' school." She hisses the word: *"Cole-man.* I want to kill myself."

We gather with other parents in what appears to be a small wooden chapel—which is to say it's laid out like a chapel, although there's no cross or anything. The chapel just smells fucking great, like sun-kissed maple or teak or something. In the corner is an antique glass barrel of water, with cut-up lemon and mint in it. We are each given linen-covered folders, tied up in twine. When you untie the twine, a few casual eucalyptus leaves fall out.

The smell hits. It's fantastic.

"Eucalyptus!" I exclaim.

Aimee repeats: "I want to kill myself."

"Imagine the killing Wonder Canyon would make if they sold their own line of spa products. I wonder if they give massages here, wraps, treatments."

Other parents are quietly taking their seats next to us, undressing their own linen folders. They are affluent Los Angeles people, clearly, but of the enlightened type, devoid of gold or baubles or anything tacky, cordial, thoughtful, clad in neutral natural fibers, and is that . . . Bishop from *Alien*? Do your remember? The kindly robot?

I jab Aimee in the ribs. "Bishop!"

"Don't look," she hisses. "Read your folder."

I do. I learn that five-year-olds at Wonder Canyon technically begin not in kindergarten but in a place, a state of being almost, called The Little Bungalow.

The Little Bungalow

The Little Bungalow is the first pod of a small, nurturing, pro-gressive, developmental K–5 learning environment whose educa-tional values include:
  - *Honoring diversity*
  - *Peaceful conflict resolution*

> • *Respecting the individual student's right to grow at his or her own unique academic pace*
>
> *Other features include:*
> • *Musical instruction via the Orff-Schulwerk method*
> • *An open-air dance and movement studio (tanzhaus)*
> • *Trips to the Getty, with Ph.D.-level art docents*
> • *Beginning Mandarin, including basic pictographs . . .*

The list goes on and on. But they protest too much. They had us at the frog. We want in!

We are instructed to write our child's name on an enclosed name tag, along with "the preschool your child is matriculating from."

I write on my name tag "Hannah—Valley Co-Op, VAN NUYS," which is akin to saying, "Hi! I'm from *Pluto*!" But no matter. I'm untouchable. I've got the Rigoberta Manchú "Get Out of Jail Free!" card. I paste my tag on, smile and look around at the other parents, who, reborn through the naming of their children, also now smile and look around. Who are we? We are . . . "Ethan—Little Dolphins." "Lennon—All Children Great and Small." "Sequoiah—Little Red Wheelbarrow School." "Iztzak—Brentwood Temple Beth Something or Another." "Ariel—The Nurtury." "Tuolomne—Maggie Haves."

"Now, that I haven't seen," I whisper to Aimee. "Tuolomne!"

Aimee doesn't reply.

I look at her to see if she has heard me . . .

And I see she is in a dream of her own. It's a very painful dream. She is reading an attached handout on the philosophy of Baz Ligiero, pictured, smoking a pipe, in a brownish daguerreotype.

Aimee's expression is naked, vulnerable, with a longing that's terrible to see. She looks like the Little Match Girl, pressing her face against the window. I'd never noticed before how small her hands are, almost like a child's.

And woken out of my self-involved reverie, of celebrating my own good fortune, I realize that I have completely forgotten that when Aimee even jokingly says, "I want to kill myself," she is bearing witness to the reality that while my daughter is going to come here . . . her son is not.

And it really doesn't seem fair. Aimee has been studying Baz Ligiero half her life, and I couldn't care less. I just want to be done with the trauma of finding a school.

It seems so unfair.

Then again . . .

Look at the way it went down at Luther Hall.

It IS unfair. Fuck it! Such is life!

The folder also contains "Bungalow Days," a newsletter apparently published by the parents of the K–2 students at Wonder Canyon. One of the headlines reveals the alarming news that apparently there is a new thing happening right now called Global Warming! Google it! Global Warming!

"Oh, well," I say, discovering the one tiny flaw that, as in a sacred Islamic mosaic, makes the overall design just even more breathtaking and exquisite. With all the help Aimee has given me, it is now my turn to toss her back a bone. "Okay—so it's not necessarily the parents who are the geniuses."

"Racul and Lisalotte Ligiero," a man announces and, all at once, as though meeting heads of state, we parents automatically stand.

"No! No! No!" cries out a short seventy-something man with black I. M. Pei glasses and a shock of white hair, shuffling out energetically before us. He is indeed wearing not the cardigan I imagined but something very close, a beige sweater vest that ducks fly across, accessorized with a comical green bow tie. He looks like a kindly elf, or a magical Gepetto person, perhaps, from a fairy tale. He is followed by a beaming, extraordinarily beautiful older woman with a waist-length white braid. While Lisalotte has the classic cheekbones and regal bearing of a Geraldine Page, she exudes warmth, sparkle,

and everything deeply good about earthy Scandinavian women—
clay-firing, pot-throwing, bread-making . . .

"Please sit! Sitting! Sit! My goodness!" Racul crows, with grand
amusement. "I'm not the Dalai Lama. Although I have met him and
I have to tell you . . . I'm no Dalai Lama!

"My father . . ." he continues, putting his hands in prayer position.
He thinks about going one way with it? Then goes another way. He
opens his hands. "Well! Much has been written about my father,
book after book. There has been lab work, research work, observa-
tion work— There are conferences in Geneva, in Bern, in Tokyo—
Do we put the children in pods, do we give them objects of wood, do
we split them at two, from the mother, so they can learn autonomy,
and independence—

"But this all is nothing," Racul says. "Nothing. At the end of the
day, my father said, 'One word, Racul . . .' "

The pause hangs.

And hangs.

And hangs.

Racul's gaze floats upward, toward a skylight.

My gaze also automatically floats upward and I see dust motes,
hanging, in a column of sunlight.

" 'Wonder. What we do here is about wonder. A child is born into
a state . . . of wonder. And the child herself . . . wonders.' "

A dream-like hush has fallen over the room. Even Aimee seems
becalmed.

"Lisalotte laughs at me when I say this . . ."

"Ach—zeah he gaws aGAIN!" Lisalotte exclaims, throwing her
hands up, in a charming Franco-Germo-Belgio accent that I just
knew she would have!

"Lisalotte mocks me—" Racul repeats, clearly enjoying this
comedic beat.

As do we all. We all laugh as Lisalotte, Racul's straight man, waves
her hands above her head. She pretends to push him.

"Ach! To me all ziss tooking, tooking, tooking is ze boring pohrt! I choost make clay. I choost make zings viss clay. Enoof viss zis tooking. Choost giff me kinder und clay!"

"Lisalotte mocks me and it sounds so sentimental, but the learning, and the wonder, begins with love. The gifted child . . . Life is not easy for the gifted child . . . I love this country—I have lived here forty years—I believe, barring some recent unfortunate government policy—"

There are murmurs of approbation among the group. We, too, feel some recent government policy is unfortunate, and we very much would like to funfer about it . . . !

With amazing speed—I think of that TV dog trainer, Cesar Millan—the old man flies a firm and shushing hand up. We are not going there.

Obedient, we fall quiet again.

"I believe the US of A is still the best hope, on this globe, for John Lennon's eventual, transcendental dream of world peace but . . ." Here Racul leans forward, shaggy eyebrows up, shaking his finger, amused. This much he WILL admit—! "Your America is not the most welcoming place for gifted children! The traditional American educational style is like a machine, marching, crushing! It's very hard—with all that noise, that drilling, that testing—

"Why do we test our children? Over and over again! This U.S. mania for testing, testing, testing! We do not test at Wonder Canyon. It's a cruel practice—I think of child labor, whipping, torture! And some American parents, competitive American parents, want Ligiero for all the tricks, tricks, tricks— Like monkeys they love to trot them out, like our math in pictures . . . How to teach a five-year-old square roots! Ah, ah, ah!" he exclaims angrily, as though fighting off an army. "Here!"

He whips a scarf off an easel . . .

And lo and behold, there it is!

The square root in pictures!

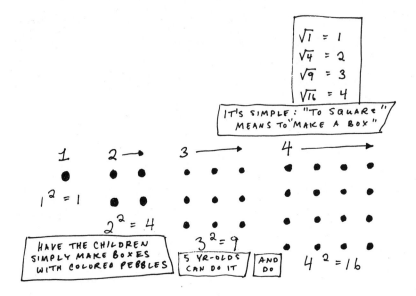

Ah! To have been given an actual quaff of the magic elixer, and so soon . . . we parents are stunned.

"Oh my God." I turn to Aimee. "This is Ligiero?"

She holds her hands up. Shakes her head in misery, a Cassandra who will never be listened to.

"Feh! They call Wonder Canyon children Wonder Children, wunderkinds, because in kindergarten already they have such a 'natural' feel for higher math. Ooh, the IQ scores! Ooh, the academic acceleration! But these are but monkey tricks. Yes, our graduates easily matriculate to L.A.'s best private middle schools and high schools, Marlborough, Harvard-Westlake . . . Yes, they get 1600 SAT's and AP5's." Racul seems exhausted to even have to recite the tawdry, the trivial, the obvious. "Yes, our Wonder Children go on to Harvard, Yale, Princeton, and Brown—" The words spill out quickly, Harvard, Yale, and Princeton being window dressing, beside the point. He waves his hand, sincerely angry.

"My father, Baz, did not even believe in college, in formal instruction after the age of sixteen. He thought higher education was a plot, devised by the elites, to separate the classes! *My father was a socialist!*

Why not the farmer's son, he said, to learn Latin! To learn physics, the beautiful laws of Newton, the daughter of the *koch* ... I mean the cook!" he rails, correcting a sudden slip into German!

I look over at Lisalotte, who, as per her word, does seem to be in a bit of a glaze. Her mouth looks a little slack, even irritated. And I must say, I love how authentic she is. She really would rather be working with *kinder und clay*!

"Anyway," he says, "in this capitalistic machine that is America, that makes ever more"—he hammers one fist brutally on another— "workers workers workers workers! In U.S. public schools, when funding is tight, the first thing they cut is art. I would say if you have to cut anything, cut everything BUT art! And public schools, with what is it—one teacher for every forty children, fifty? This is inhuman! What are children? Cattle? At Wonder Canyon your child will NEVER be in a classroom ... of more than six."

Aimee's head drops on my shoulder. A gutteral yet almost sound-less moan escapes her, as though she were a deaf-mute who had just been stabbed, between the shoulder blades, with a shiv.

"In such a factory-belt atmosphere as the U.S. educational system, it is impossible for the truly gifted child to be seen, to be understood, to be heard. You know your children—they are on a different vibration!" His face relaxes now that he is turning back to his favorite topic. "Here at Wonder Canyon, we give our small curious souls— who may do strange things—" Here he twinkles, like the elf again, the once-choppy dark Atlantic waters turned back now to calm blue Pacific. "They may wear a skirt on the head or make a trumpet from stones— Living with your children, I'm sure you know what I'm talking about—"

We all laugh. I think of Hannah bathing her stuffed animals. P.S. ... *To Gershwin piano preludes!*

"We give our small, curious souls a school—a home—of love. A love of learning, a love of wonder, a love of love ... Lisalotte and I greet every child in the morning by first name."

Lisalotte snaps back into consciousness.

"I vill heff ze names ze first day . . . Him? Zree!"

"But I will have them!" He laughs.

"But we want to go further, to illustrate our teaching method," our gentle gnome continues. "We want to split you into dyads. We want you to describe to your partners the hopes each of you has for your child's schooling. You may learn some things very interesting."

Aimee sits across from a handsome man with a shock of gray through his dark wavy hair. He is still in surgical scrubs—he has clearly hurried over from Cedars-Sinai to make the tour at Wonder Canyon. He looks like George Clooney—a very tired George Clooney. With kind of a fat neck. Already he is pouring his heart out to her.

"I drove by our corner public elementary and the grass . . . made me sad. It was so bare. There was no shade. It looked like a death camp."

I sit across from a painfully thin woman named Roan, with a mane of streaky blond hair, whose son is Ezekiel. She is very beautiful and fragile-looking, like a skinny Catherine Deneuve on crank.

"I am divorced. Horribly divorced. This divorce has shattered us. I am a corporate attorney who has seventy-hour work weeks. So Ezekiel needs a school that is like a second home. Because my money-manager ex is such a dick, Ezekiel needs father figures in his life, strong father figures, men, old-fashioned men, masculine men . . ."

Under "Ezekiel," her tag reads "Little Willows." How unfortunate that she was forced to send her in-need-of-a-strong-father-figure son with surely his already tiny penis to a place called Little Willows.

But that's the paradox. On paper, Roan would look like a full-on top-three-percent-tax-bracket ball-buster. But as she tells me her story, Roan conveys such nervousness, such extraordinary fragility. Like she herself is a Little Willow. Like she and Ezekiel are absolutely helpless in this world, adrift and alone. Some children in this world survive without shoes; Ezekiel will not survive if he has to take second-grade French from a nonnative speaker.

My mind awash in pictograms, I suddenly imagine the planet's top quintile sitting at the very tip of humanity's rowboat, but instead of looking backward and seeing how much better off they are than 80 percent of the world's population, they're gazing transfixed over the edge:

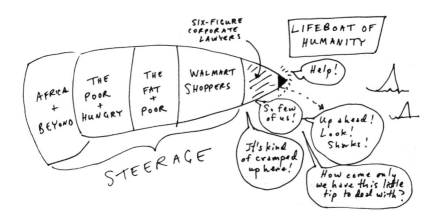

"I am against testing," Roan goes on. "Absolutely, it's cruel, it's inhuman, that's why we would never consider a public school of any kind—Ezekiel needs constant stimulation, constant stimulation, he needs to be stimulated! That's what I love about Wonder Canyon, it's never boring. Apparently the children RUN to class in the morning, they RUN— And besides, have you seen LAUSD math and reading scores?" Roan says, suddenly running a shaking hand through her hair. "Through the toilet!"

Reva Thon arrives, her auburn mane brilliant against a scarf of peacock blue. She walks us to The Orchard. It is tucked away in another corner of the Wonder Canyon property, which all told unfolds across about twenty-five acres. The Orchard is another small gathering of old wooden bungalows built around 1900.

The Orchard is a hidden piece of Los Angeles history. For many years, The Orchard served as a secret informal Los Angeles gathering place for traveling and expatriate painters and writers. Hemingway came here, Gertrude Stein, Salvador Dali . . . Briefly it served as a haven for the Hollywood Blacklist.

"Jack London had dinner with members of the Socialist Party in this room . . ." Reva says. "And here it is . . . our Picasso."

We gather around. It's but a simple dashed-off sketch, but highly forceful, very charming, and definitely Picasso.

"Do you recognize it?" says Reva. "It's this room! Pablo sketched here. He particularly loved the light in this west room. And oh—" She opens another door.

"Here is the room where Steinbeck is rumored to have written an early draft for the first chapter of *The Grapes of Wrath.*"

It is such a simple room, of washed-pine floors and walls, containing but a small rickety bed and a tiny wooden writing table, with a beat-up old black typewriter on it.

"Is that his typewriter?" I ask.

"He wrote longhand. That is Dalton Trumbo's typewriter," says Reva. "Steinbeck returned here several years later, after *The Grapes of Wrath* was published. Said he found such comfort, sitting right here on the porch. He said sitting in this rocking chair, for three days, he was healed."

"Can—can I—?" I motion to the chair. There is no rope across it or anything.

"Please," Reva says, motioning toward it.

I drop down into the giant wooden rocking chair. It's large, and carved, and smooth, and throne-like. Solid. I look out onto a painterly, non-Southern-California-like meadow of long grasses, cattails, and old-growth elms.

"The Orchard has always been a haven for artists under fire," Reva says.

"Why did Steinbeck need healing after *Grapes of Wrath*?" big-necked George Clooney asks.

"Well," says Reva. "Can you imagine? He had created a master-piece of literature and felt vilified for his progressive political views. Vilified! The man was forty-two."

And it hits me.

I see it.

Like the artists of The Orchard, I, too, have at best been an awkward fit in this world.

And now I see, through the power of history, that my best creative work may well be AHEAD of me. This motherhood thing, that New York thing, this Los Angeles thing, that debris of my twenties and thirties, all the broken flotsam and jetsam of my career efforts . . .

These have been merely my Pre–*Grapes of Wrath* Years.

The second half of my life may well be the shining future I have always been moving toward. Like a large-hipped Phoenix with a few gray hairs and a forehead wrinkle, I may well rise again.

"Hopefully, that's not the Plath oven," I murmur, indicating the potbellied stove in the corner.

"The Plath oven!" Roan chuckles. "And I hope those aren't the Virginia Woolf drowning stones!" she exclaims, pointing to a Zen pile of stones.

And suddenly I find the relief that comes of having your references finally understood!

My God! I'm so relieved not to have to *explain my cultural references anymore.*

I am home!

Just beyond in the garden, I can see Hannah animatedly telling a semicircle of other children a story. She waves her arms, jumps up and down, twirls. She is so in her element.

How could I ever have doubted her ability to shine?

I can't resist. I open up to Roan:

"I'm afraid to admit I took my daughter to a Lutheran school where they gave her the Gesell Kindergarten Readiness Test. I would never subject her to that again."

"The Gesell?" Roan spits. "That's to test how well a child can OBEY. How well he can sit STILL. That's for future accountants!"

And I realize I love Roan.

Roan leans in. "We need Wonder Canyon. I've had Ezekiel tested, by Dr. Frederick Sterns? The child psychologist? And Ezekiel may have Asperger's."

I feel my usual stab of anxiety when other families possess an exotic item we don't. Parents report this disease with such an evident . . . thrill of pride.

"My friend Aimee's son has a diagnosis of Asperger's—" I counter.

"At the very least, we're pretty sure he's ADD—"

"ADD?" I'm tempted to yell. "I'll go you one better! My daughter is NINE-DD!"

The blonde waves as she leads Hannah's small group the other way.

"Now we're going to see the bunny!"

Hannah is rapturous. She skips by.

"The bunny!" she exclaims. "The bunny!"

I want to give her this.

Because I suddenly see Hannah twenty years from now . . .

Harvard law degree in hand, cum laude, being flown to an East Coast think tank to head up the drafting of a new plan for international human rights with . . . some Kennedys. The better Kennedys. I don't know who the better Kennedys are now, but . . . you know the ones I mean. Not the chinless Hoosier frat-boy ones who get drunk at Spring Break and fall over a football. You know who I mean—the really, really good Kennedys.

And the beauty is, now I can give that to her! I can guarantee Hannah that! The key—the first step—to that glorious future is right here in our hands! There is no chance my darling will flop now, that she will be bored, fail out of school, or end up in mournful obscurity somewhere, like all those sad, empty young people you hear about who never find their inner spark. What a stab of luck, to be sitting here with the forty last families in Los Angeles, to be escaping from the flaming education-in-collapse Saigon apocalypse below . . . To be the last families airlifted up onto the helicopter!

But now comes a lady with blond button hair whose nametag reads "Clare Coughlin, Admissions Coordinator."

"This concludes the tour," Clare Coughlin says, distributing final white eight-by-ten folders, our door prizes. She is not rude, exactly, but her smile is guarded, businesslike. She lacks the magical dreamy quality of Racul, Lisalotte, Reva . . . who are . . . Where are they? They've disappeared.

"If you are interested in September kindergarten, please fill out an 'Intent to Apply' and leave it with me. Our office will follow up, if appropriate, with the full application. Your children are waiting for you beside Birch. Thank you so much! It was a pleasure having you. If you have questions . . ."

Big Neck George Clooney (BNGC) raises his hand.

"When will acceptance letters go out?"

"Acceptance letters go out next month on the fourteenth."

I circle my fingers around Reva's card. Thank goodness I hold this magic talisman and don't have to sweat this part of the process.

Roan's hand goes up.

"Can you tell us . . . The acceptance rate? How many kindergarten slots are open?"

"Due to a great number of siblings, unfortunately, very few this year. Just one out of every twenty new touring families will get a child in."

The crowd stiffens.

My bowels turn a little icey.

I thought being ON the tour was enough. I thought going on the tour meant you were IN.

But I shouldn't even worry! Reva did personally tell me Hannah was in. Didn't she?

Clare Coughlan continues:

"You are all exceptional families, and your children are all children we would love to have. But for Little Bungalow . . . In accordance with Baz Ligiero's guidelines, the children are served best if each classroom maintains the proper balance of genders, ages, personalities, learning styles . . ."

"What do you mean, 'learning styles'?" asks BNGC.

"Group versus individual learning styles," Clare Coughlan replies pertly. "In Ligiero, you have to maintain the proper balance."

Roan shoots a dark look at me and mouths, "Group versus individual learning styles? What the *fuck?*"

Just beyond, I see Hannah hug Uma Thurman good-bye, then skip happily off with her frog. Still smiling, Uma Thurman joins another sylph . . . and, faces still pleasant, they both pull out small notebooks. They are talking and writing . . . notes? About our children, NOTES?

I feel like Mia Farrow in that last scene in *Rosemary's Baby.* Oh no! That adorable Ruth Gordon, with her odd if refreshing milkshakes! You work for . . . the devil?

No. Besides, I know Uma Thurman *loves* my daughter and I *love* this school.

Even when I look down at the folder and see the annual tuition for The Little Bungalow.

$22,500.

Plus fees!

Grimly, I think, I'll find a way.

Clare Coughlin sets the "Intent to Apply" forms down before us parents and . . .

As frenzied as eels in that horse's head in Volker Schlöndorff's *The Tin Drum,* we attack.

The Wonder Canyon administration is housed in one of those giant sculptural bird edifices. Aimee and I actually have to split from the group in the parking lot, dart through the trees, and hike secretively down. It's not easy to find. Apparently, spontaneous dropping in at the administration building is not encouraged.

But Aimee seems to have a sixth sense about how the place is laid out.

Even though once inside the giant bird building . . . Well, it's a maze of spiral staircases, ramps, and polished rosewood floors that rake away from one, that threaten to spill one out onto enigmatic balconies with great 270-degree views but no actual entrances.

"Aha!" Aimee exclaims, noticing a frosted-glass door upon which are but faintly legible the letters, chilly as an Ingmar Bergman winterscape: ADMISSIONS.

Clare Coughlan blocks our way.

"May I help you?" she asks.

I feel just the slightest hesitation.

Aimee jabs me sharply in the ribs, makes a "You go, girl!" fist, hissing: "Celebrity Mom! Celebrity Mom!"

"Um—I am Sandra Tsing Loh?" I say. "I was fired by KCRW . . . ? Al Pacino's people . . . Through my friend Celeste Walden, as in Bran Walden?" I gesture at the window, in the vague direction of one of the new giant birds going up. "As in the Walden Mandarin Center? They said just come see Reva? That there should be no problem?"

"Do you have an appointment?" says Clare.

"Oh!" I exclaim, holding up my cell phone. "Just watch me dial!"

Triumphantly holding up Reva Thon's business card, I dial!

Damn.

No signal in Mulholland!

Fuck!

Aimee holds up her BlackBerry like an avenging angel, dials Reva's cell.

A moment later, the frosted-glass door opens.

"Sandra!" Reva sings out, emerging from her atelier. "Come in, come in, come in! Did you love the tour? I hoped you would!"

She catches me in her arms like a lover, and suddenly things are right back to normal. She leads us into her office, a sky-lit glass hexagon.

"Can I give you this?" I hand her our "Intent to Apply."

"Of course!" She tosses it to one side as if it's not even necessary.

"This is Aimee Lindberg," I say.

"Pleasure," says Aimee.

"Welcome," Reva says warmly, then turns to me. "Can we talk? I forgot to tell you the other day what a huge fan I am of *This American Life*!"

"You are!" I exclaim.

"Ira Glass," Reva purrs. "I could listen all day to his voice. What's he like?"

I jump into my Ira Glass material, which, except for a few meetings here and there in L.A. and Chicago, is, frankly, not really that substantial.

But I stretch:

Blah blah blah . . . Ira Glass!

Blah blah blah . . . Ira Glass!

Soon I am MAKING UP Ira Glass stories.

"I remember when I was with Ira Glass in Paris. We were doing a story on French World War II widows who had many cats. We were recording the sounds of the cats."

"Och," Reva says. "You know, some of our biggest donors are Ira Glass fans. The younger ones. Filmmakers. And I think they could be *bigger* donors."

I hear her, loud and clear. I proceed to butter myself, bend over and promise Reva—and Wonder Canyon—the most outrageous public radio favors. "I can get Ira Glass to fly out to L.A. for brunch! Sure I can! Feel free to auction off a footbath *personally given by Ira Glass* to raise funds for your new Second-grade Steven Spielberg Japanese Language Center!"

"Financial aid . . . ?" I float.

Reva smiles. Gives a quick shake of the head. "Not this year, what with all the new building. This year is full freight."

I telephone Mike with the stunning news that Hannah has been offered a slot for Wonder Canyon.

"That's terrific!" he yells from his cell phone in Manhattan.

"Isn't it?" I say. "Steinbeck wrote there!"

"That's very cool!" he says. "It's not too expensive, is it? The road manager here sends his two kids to private school and says the tuition's through the roof."

"It's . . . a chunk," I say.

"How much?"

"There's quite a bit of construction going on," I say. "The facilities are astounding."

"How much?"

"The price is steep but I still think we have to consider it because Hannah is so unique, she is such a unique style of learner—" I hope he won't ask me what style, because I frankly can't remember.

"What's the number?"

"Twenty-two five."

"Twenty-two five what? Twenty-two fifty a week? A month? A day? An hour?"

"Twenty-two thousand five hundred. A year."

There is a beat.

Matter-of-factly, he says, "Yi."

I lash out. In a flash, I feel vicious.

"I make a good part of the money in this family"—"Mr. *Little Willows*!" I suddenly want to add—"and I want this! I am making that this year at Marymount College!"

"But what about next year?"

"What about Bette Midler?"

"It's a five-month tour. I thought you said Wonder Canyon is K through five."

"Which makes it a very important FEEDER school!"

"To what? A middle school that's forty thousand dollars? I think you need to sit down with a calculator, honey, is all."

"This is not a time for penny-pinching," I say. "It's Hannah's whole future."

"Well," he observes, "bankruptcy isn't so great, either. That's the trouble with our bohemian lifestyles . . . bohemian income."

"No one gets into this school," I hiss. "No one. Aimee would kill to get Seth into this school."

"Well, LET her kill someone, then. Perhaps with Paxil."

"Do not take this from me."

"I'm just saying give yourself a night to sleep on it. It's kindergarten."

He doesn't understand about the Orff-Schulwerk method for music, and the patterns of sparrows.

Yes, he is a professional musician—!

Still, he doesn't understand.

And then the evil mind-manipulator says, those chilling words:

"Well, sweetie. I see you're really passionate about this. You do what you want. I'll stick by you."

Because he knows I am weak.

The money does gnaw at me.

It sits on my chest at night, like a weight. I can feel it slowly strangling me.

Oh, God—$22,500.

If it were one time only, we could do it.

But with the Squid coming up . . . that's $45,000 a year. The money seems so substantial, immovable, like a granite pyramid. And Wonder Canyon feels so playful, and translucent, and natural as the wind riffling wheat.

Yes, "I AM a Celebrity Mom!"

But now my Grrrrl Power–like battle cry has devolved to the far less glamorous "I AM a Celebrity Mom . . . who needs financial aid."

I don't know how attractive I am as a celebrity fund-raiser when I . . . can't actually afford the school.

And I realize that to get into the really good L.A. private schools, you have to be not just a celebrity but the right kind of celebrity. Look at Courtney Love—I'll never forget that *L.A. Times* piece I saw about her many years ago . . .

Where Courtney Love was crying because she couldn't get her little Frances Bean into the Lycée. If even the spawn of Cobain isn't just waved in, for free—

And I'm thinking, "Is this how dark my world has become? That the mother I most identify with is . . . Courtney Love?"

Celeste is on the phone.

Things have gone dark.

There is no way to put it elegantly. The words are like poison, but I have to say them.

"Celeste . . . Wonder Canyon . . . I simply don't think . . ." I form the horrible, awkward, ugly words. ". . . that we can . . . afford . . . it."

There is a beat.

Celeste's voice is soft, sympathetic, cajoling.

"The tuition is . . . out of this world. I know. And when we were young, our parents paid nothing. It's absurd. I know."

I'm practically sniffling.

I am Lara watching Dr. Zhivago pull out of the station.

I am Meryl Streep watching Clint Eastwood irrevocably leave town in *The Bridges of Madison County*.

It is all I want in the world, but in fact . . . we just can't do it.

Celeste continues, with empathy.

"You know how much it tears my heart out to see that fabulous school, which I'm on the board of, and to know that, yes, quite often the Wonder Canyons of the world are wasted on . . . the rich. Those who can afford it. The system is unfair! Look at my stepdaughter, Skyler! Poor Skyler. She struggles at Wonder Canyon. She lacks imagination. You've heard me say it—she's a pony girl. A horse girl. She likes animals.

"But Hannah . . ." Celeste's voice goes lower, deeper. "She's JUST the sort of kid who DESERVES a Wonder Canyon. Hannah is clearly gifted, special, extraordinary—"

And because I am a weak, terrible person, I ask, pathetically, "Is that what they said?" I long with every yearning molecule to hear a fabulous evaluation, news of her top one-percent-ness, her genius. "Is that what they said in the evaluation?"

Celeste wisely presses on. "And giftedness needs nurturing. I didn't say anything at the time, but . . . You don't *want* Hannah in a Luther Hall. Good Lord. The daughter of two amazing artists like you?"

I blort the words out. It's like vomiting out my intestines. "It's just . . . We are just in a different *class* than you are. We just don't . . . make that much. MONEY."

"But surely there's something you can do?" Celeste wonders. "Something you haven't thought of?"

She doesn't finish the thought.

She knows better than to say, "Just liquidate some stock!" That much, in our friendship, we have learned.

I dream that night that I am swimming, clutching Hannah to my chest, through an Ocean of Money.

And the bills are wet, heavy, dragging us down.

Just around this time, Joan Archer writes me, from the sad little co-op school of the fleas.

> Hey, Sandra!
>
> Because we haven't seen you in a while, I presume you're not continuing with the Spring Jamboree Committee, that you're wrapped up in writing deadlines and all. No worries. Since I know you were looking for a kindergarten, thought I'd just drop you a note to say it looks like Kester, which is a very good LAUSD school, may have a few open enrollment slots this year, and I know it's near you.

The Spring Jamboree Committee! My God! I am the world's worst—and shallowest—person. Lying, cheating, inconsistent. For some idiotic reason, I actually write back:

> Joan,
>
> Thanks so much for the note and 100 apologies for dropping out of sight. Our household has been in a bit of a frenzy. Unbelievably enough, Hannah just won an acceptance into the Wonder Canyon School for Gifted Children, and what with the tuition and Ligiero math and all that wacky German talk about socialism, it has thrown us into a bit of a quandary.

And then Joan actually writes back, completely misinterpreting my note:

> Oh does that take me back! I know what you mean. I remember when we first starting looking for schools for Jimmy, and I was simply this crazed mother. I remember reading about Wonder Canyon and thinking Ligiero math was wonderful, but if it's so super and so much based in socialism, why can't every child get it for free? Just yesterday I saw a Hispanic maid sitting at the bus stop trying to help her son with his math homework—and giving him all wrong

answers—and I thought, "Well, THERE'S someone who needs Ligiero!" So I know what you mean about feeling flattered and drawn into a whirling eye of private school evil.

Well, THAT was helpful!
FUCK HER!!!

I now go to the next Kübler-Ross stage: Bargaining.

Now that I have an acceptance from Wonder Canyon, the big Kahuna of private schools, maybe I can parlay that into an acceptance for . . . a still excellent but somewhat cheaper school, which might like a semi-celebrity?

Frantically, I buy the *Los Angeles Guide to Private Schools*. Deadlines are flying by. I'll have to work fast. Fingers trembling, I go through every page . . .

And here's what I find . . . That all the good schools, all the progressive schools, all the recommended schools, basically start . . .

At $10,000.

If the brochure says the children are taught:

INDEPENDENT THINKING, add $1,000.

PEACEFUL CONFLICT RESOLUTION, add $1,000.

HONORING DIVERSITY—oh, that's a big one—add $2,000.

Then there are the extras. For Spanish, add $750. French, $1,500. Japanese, $2,500. Music taught by the Orff-Schulwerk method, $1,000. Actual science labs, vague but important connection with UCLA, $2,000. Award-winning arts program, any mention of the Getty, Disney Hall, $2,000 . . .

Celeste calls me again, for an emergency lunch at some hip new place called Pax. I bounce queasily down La Brea in the dented Toyota minivan, whose Check Engine light is now mysteriously permanently on.

Celeste is waiting for me in her work clothes, a pale green suit.

"I'm a wreck," I say.

"I know, sweetie, I know," she says, hugging me. "But you will get through this."

"I have such indigestion!" I say.

"Take a deep breath . . . and relax," she replies, pressing me down into a cushioned chair. "We're going to take our time. The chef here is the same as at Auberge. The food is fabulous."

I flop open the menu and for the first time see prices. Oh my God. The lunch entrees are thirty-eight dollars! And they come with nothing! Is that what we paid at Auberge? Of course, I never saw a menu at Auberge. Celeste kept airily waving them away.

"The monkfish is very interesting," Celeste says. "And we'll definitely have wine. Remember?" She squeezes my hand, grins. "Mandatory wine . . . with . . . lunch! Women Getting On to the Next Page!"

And then there are the wine prices. Oh my God.

"Remember that Viognier we had in Napa?" she says warmly. "You loved it."

I'd kill for a glass of wine but it's sixty dollars . . . for a split! Is that $120 a bottle? Holy fuck.

"I'll just have water," I murmur. "My stomach."

"Are you sure, honey?" Celeste asks.

"Sure."

"Gas or no gas?" asks our waitress, who, with her tight French braids and tiny steel-rimmed glasses, looks like a chemical engineering Ph.D. with a minor in gassy water.

God, look at that—even the water I don't even want is fourteen dollars a bottle!

"Tap water," I croak. "Just tap."

Everyone looks at me.

"Because of the fluoride . . ." I add. "My . . . ah . . . my orthodontist says in these, my perimenopausal years, due to my . . . caps, I . . . really need the fluoride."

"Oh!" everyone murmurs, with relief.

Celeste and I—we both know we are on the eleventh shoal of our friendship. We are at the farthest reaches, battling for it. It's Greg Louganis, having hit his head on the diving board, trying to wrench his body back, midair, into a graceful swan dive.

"Here is some great news," Celeste says, leaning forward, taking my hand. "I know private-school tuition is tough, so I've been calling around for you. And it turns out that Radcliffe-Holyoke for Girls? In Brentwood? An amazing school, just amazing, I toured it the other day. And because they have great taste, if you can believe it . . ." She squeezes my hand. "They actually teach your style of NPR essay writing to their eighth graders! They're huge fans! Irate over the KCRW thing! 'Just send her over!' they said."

Unapologetic, I plop the *Private Schools* handbook onto the table—the handbook I now carry with me at all times. I page through it. "But Radcliffe-Holyoke," I say dully, pointing. "The annual tuition for that school is twenty-seven thousand dollars."

"Oh God—I know," sighs Celeste, running a hand through her hair. "Which can probably feed an entire village for a year in Rwanda."

"I guess that's what they mean when they say 'It takes a village . . .'"

"But think ahead," says Celeste. And I remember how often she used to say this to me, when we were twenty-five. "Think ahead. Where will your writing be in five years, in ten years? Think ahead." And clearly the time has come to think that way for Hannah. Who is four. "The wait list for Radcliffe-Holyoke is at least five years long . . . In fact, as it starts in sixth grade, it wouldn't be a bad idea to get Hannah on the wait list now. And they said—good news—they would LOVE you to come in, do maybe a couple of guest lectures!"

"What will that get us?" I wail.

"Not just admission," Celeste answers smartly. "Financial aid. Major financial aid. They're very big on diversity."

"But Hannah is white."

"And a quarter Chinese!" Celeste answers. "And you guys are not just boring industry types . . . You're artists. With you and your writing, and Mike working with Bette Midler . . . You should have seen their eyes open!"

"I cannot get Bette Midler to go anywhere," I warn. "She is my husband's EMPLOYER."

"No matter!" Celeste laughs. She goes into cheerful barter mode. "So you can tell Mike—Salt of the Earth—bite the bullet for a few years at Wonder Canyon, then come middle school, you'll be PRINTIN' money!"

Yes, I'll lead writing seminars at Radcliffe-Holyoke, yes . . . But what will I tell them—?

"That's right, girls—master my literary style and you'll end up like me, living in Van Nuys"?

It doesn't sound very fist raised (à la Ruth, my therapist), very "Fuck you!"

Although it seems all the original "Fuck you!" got me is a crumpled kind of "Fuck me."

I think of Marymount College for Women, and its cinnamon-bun lactose intolerance.

Instead of self-esteem, we are teaching our girls to be sensitive, demanding, experimental, impractical . . .

Thank God they're rich, as all we're grooming them for is to be useless . . .

Trophy wives!

Anna Kareninas!

YES, MORE MR. DARCY!

In the mornings, after dropping the kids off at school, I cry and cry and cry. My days are horrible.

Receiving another mailing from Luther Hall, and looking at its neat blue-and-gold stationery, I think back to Aimee's suggestion that we simply retest . . . at Luther Hall.

Or no, not at Luther Hall, but maybe a similar school?

But then I look at parochial schools and new formulas emerge . . .

Annual tuition still starts at $10,000. But if the religion is:

CATHOLIC, subtract $1,000.

LUTHERAN, subtract $3,000.

BAPTIST, subtract $5,000!

QUAKER . . . For some reason, that's PLUS $5,000. If the school is in an old wooden Quaker meetinghouse, the price skyrockets, I don't know why. Add Shaker furniture—and the word *Friends* in the title? Unaffordable.

Then there's JEWISH, but there are two types of Jewish. High Temple Jewish and low JCC Jewish . . . But it's a moot point, as I can't seem to find any Jews in Van Nuys, anyway.

And then there's chapel. Chapel required? MINUS $1,500! Chapel OPTIONAL? Well, that relative religious freedom is going to cost you . . . $1,500!

But look at this! Classes "taught from a Biblical perspective" . . . MINUS two thousand dollars! THAT'S a really great deal!

Now Bruce sends me his thousandth moveon.org petition, saying I need to FIGHT THE RELIGIOUS RIGHT and STAND UP FOR THE DEMOCRATS!!!

And for once in my life I type him back!

> Dear Bruce,
> You want me to help the Democratic party? Why doesn't the Democratic party fucking HELP ME? Where are they in my search for KINDERGARTEN?

In fact, our family is thinking of actually LEAVING Blue State Land, because progressive educational values cost too much! To save money, we're thinking of switching sides, going over to the Big Red Planet. I wonder what the God People could offer our family? Big tuition discounts at the very least!

Indeed, instead of all that peaceful conflict resolution, I wonder what price breaks we could get for settling disputes the old-fashioned way, aka:

Bullying: subtract $500! Name-calling: subtract $500! Melvins: subtract $750!

And what if we go even more religious, not just sitting first row in chapel, but . . .

Paying tuition in Old Testament currency, like shekels? Subtract $300? Home snake-handling? Subtract $1,000? Father to wear golden codpiece at all times? Tuition free perhaps, and 100 acres in Utah given! I love Utah! Sign us up!

Right now, I'm actually seriously considering a Baptist school in Panorama City. That's right—best friend to the poor? Baptists!

The school is a mere $3,000 a year, AND they offer not just discounts, but "classes taught from a Biblical perspective."

And I'm thinking:

How bad can Creationism really be? Or Intelligent Design?

Having our kids taught evolution is clearly an economic luxury. We have to be realistic. In this day and age, perhaps Darwinism is not a theory our family can actually afford . . .

And perhaps evolution science is over-rated anyway. Look at the Big Bang. Stephen Hawking . . . 30 years later he says oops, I was wrong. Now suddenly he's back in favor, for this week, but with all of science's flip-flopping, who really knows?

For once in his life, there is a stunned radio silence. I cannot believe this is all it took to get Bruce to stop e-mailing me.

So I continue:

> So fuck your Democratic party, Bruce.
> I don't know if you've noticed, but it's an entirely online party now!
> TIVO-ing the Daily Show is not actual political action!

He finally shoots back:

> I don't know if you've noticed, but the U.S. faces some urgent problems in the international debacle that has been the Bush administration. If you check the following links to huffingtonpost.com and truthdig.org—

And I shoot back:

> Fuck you, Bruce. Arianna Huffington and Robert Scheer and all your heroes . . . Did THEY put their kids through public school?

He shoots back:

> The Democrats are the party of women. The moveon.org founders have started this website: momsrising.org. Check it out.

And I type back:

> Right. Non-violent afterschool television. Non-sugary cereals. Flex time. Universal daycare. That's all Political Women ever talk about. Universal daycare. And guess what—daycare is over by age five . . . Followed by 13 YEARS OF PUBLIC SCHOOL. What about public school? Why do not Democratic women care about public school? Is it because they don't SEND their kids to public school?
> I believe we have a bunch of very fucking rich women who run everything now!

Naomi Wolf . . . Are her kids in public school?
Gloria Steinem . . . Does she have any kids in public school?

And Bruce types back:

Gloria Steinem does not have any children in public school as she does not have any children.

And I type back, lamely but defiantly:

See!

8
Malibu

I stand in the lobby of Disney Hall, a soaring golden cathedral of arches, waves, rivulets, angles, arcs, bishop's hats, all conspiring together as if to yell . . .

Frank Gehry! Frank Gehry! Frank Gehry!

It's yet another great soaring bird of a building, where wings fly you *up* to the third floor, then swoop you *down* into the underground parking. Disney Hall and all the other great flapping-bird buildings. They are Los Angeles, and I am but a flea on their backs. But I am grimly hanging on.

Held aloft by the second-level balcony, I look down twin ribbons of escalator into the maw of incoming concertgoers. Who look, to my increasingly rheumy eyes, to be white, white, white. Leavened through with Asians.

And finally, there they are, I can tell them by their painfully slow gait alone, like stunned insects, and a certain tattered shabbiness. My eleventh-hour Hail Mary pass. The guy who's going to save our ass.

My eighty-five-year-old retired Chinese engineer father, with his third Chinese wife—a sixty-five-year-old Manchurian lady named Alice.

Although technically Asian, like so many other rabid classical music fans, my father still sticks out in this crowd. Even though he has been in America for fifty years, he's still 100 percent immigrant. He doesn't blend with the beautiful porcelain Asians, properly be-suited and be-spectacled, the highlanders, the professionals, in their Lexuses. They are not like us, the lowlanders, hearty and tanned and roughed up from all that walking! And all that bus riding!

Which is to say, yes, my dad and Alice have taken public transportation, here, to Disney Hall. From Malibu. I know from experience that it will have taken them twelve transfers, four days, and at least five tattered paper bags of food scavenged from grocery store Dumpsters. You need to carry groceries with you, as you never know when a bus might be two hours late, or when there might be a Ralphs produce workers strike (aka poor harvest in the Dumpster).

In addition to the grocery bags on his back, my father is carrying his customary old wrinkled white plastic UCLA bag of what appear to be toiletries. He attaches it to himself by means of a yellow-and-blue bungee cord he found on the beach. Straining forward with the bungee cord around his neck, he looks like Jack LaLanne pulling a tugboat, except that the UCLA bag he is carrying is no larger than the size of a small airline pillow and is about as heavy as a bag filled with used Kleenex. Which it may well be. My father hates to waste paper by blowing his nose into a tissue just once.

As they ride up the escalator toward me, ever closer, I am relieved to see my father is at least wearing a turtleneck, jacket, and slacks. However, his dentures . . . appear to be wandering. Oh no! My father has exactly one tooth left. We've pled with him to get a new set of

dentures, but he always raises one gnarled hand, dismissively . . .
"Bah!" But last time he PROMISED . . . ! Argh!

His dentures are just one of many unresolved medical issues, like
the pacemaker the doctor insisted he get or he could fall over dead at
any moment. That was two years ago. Yes, he frequently passes out
and is unrousable. Then six minutes later he pops awake and starts
yelling at us. His resting pulse rate is already a subbasement-like 48.
What can you do? The man is barely alive as it is.

I guess the bottom line is, he's eighty-five and stuff is just falling
off him. It's just going to fall off until all there is left is a shoe. An
orthopedic shoe. Yells the shoe, waving a strap: "Leave me alone!"
Speaking of which, the bunions. The bunions are so frightening, I
close my eyes at night and picture them and I scream . . . knowing
that if I am lucky enough to make it another forty years, my reward
is that . . . these will be my feet.

Of course, when my Nightmare on Dad Street meets me at the top
of the Disney Hall escalator, he says, "You put on too much
makeup—I can smell it!"

Alice, by contrast, is excited by the rare specter of me in actual lipstick. Alice excitedly points her flash camera at me, to commemorate
the rare phenomenon—

And my dad angrily pushes the camera down and snaps at her in
Chinese—something like: "Da da da da da David Robertson!" Aka:
Don't waste film on anything not David Robertson!

"Now I have to go to the bathroom!" he exclaims angrily. And off
the two of them shuffle, lost again in the crowd of the giant bird.
Great. Another wait.

David Robertson. David Robertson is the reason I was able to get
my dad out of the house. David Robertson is the card I'm playing.
David Robertson, the world-renowned conductor. My father's long-
lost son. Not that David Robertson is aware of it.

Because it turns out my born-in-a-Shanghai-gutter father, falling-
out-dentures and all . . . is a snob. From his tooth to his bunions.

Understand that my father is not the sort of Chinese immigrant who has ever suffered low expectations for his children. Ever since I was little, it was clear that if we girls could not actually bring home the Nobel Prize in physics, then becoming head of NASA or president of Harvard College would do. Or if we had to feed a wild, artsy, creative urge . . . conductor of the London Philharmonic.

He favored professions, for his spawn, where one sits at a vast 757-sized board of controls, commanding at least two hundred people at a time, and convening frequently with heads of state. In Stockholm.

I used to laugh this off, but unfortunately, the older you get, the likelier it is that kids you grew up with may actually start becoming . . . these impossible-sounding things. Which is to say David Robertson, who attended Santa Monica High School, at the same time as my sister, Kaitlin? He has won the universal career lottery.

First of all, conducting. As opposed to, say, female desperate-buttons comedy performance, conducting seems to be the sort of career where conductors keep moving higher and higher, from Minneapolis, to Phoenix, to Lyons, to Grange aux Belles, then suddenly, at fifty-two, there you are, named head of the Chicago Philharmonic! An overnight success! You're like their youngest conductor ever! At fifty-two! All you need is one grayish lock of foppish hair and now you're a heartthrob!

Meanwhile, understand that 90 percent of my father's waking hours are spent watching PBS . . . which I realize might not be saying much, what with my father's resting pulse of 48 and all the naps taken literally in the middle of sentences. Anyhoo, the other 10 percent of my father's waking hours, aside from gobbling spoiled food, involves leaving frantic phone messages on my machine about what I am missing THAT VERY MINUTE, on PBS—! His voice is always garbled, distorted, hysterical . . . "Channel Eight!" he'll exclaim. "It just started! A four-hour biography of Arthur Rubenstein!! Rubenstein!!" Or sometimes he'll just bellow, in a cryptic verbal semaphore, "Firebird! Firebird! Firebird!"

To PBS, I just want to send out the good news that you're a hit with the eighty-five-year-olds. Some forty years younger, a mother who has to get up in the morning, I myself am unable to keep up with my dad's insanely demanding PBS-viewing schedule. (Although recently I did catch a show called *The Cheese Nun*. Because, as you know, nuns are a little edgy, and the topic of soft cheese is highly controversial, not at all comforting. But when you put them together— Oh, now I feel better . . . "CHEESE Nun!")

But this time, the frantic SOS-you're-missing-it-on-PBS! message was: "David Robertson! David Robertson! David Robertson!"

My dad taped it for me, on a battered VHS tape that looked as though it had itself been to Shanghai.

The tale told, about David Robertson's meteoric ascension, was mesmerizing. It was a pushy Chinese parents' wet dream.

Picture Carnegie Hall, sold out, the old famous conductor suddenly becomes ill, topples off the podium, kidney thing, twang of cellos, blat of trumpets. Who hops on the red-eye but this unknown young ringer—a mere boy!—with but twenty-four hours to learn this terrifyingly complicated modern score, the sort of score that toppled that guy in *Shine* and sent him to a mental institution. Basically, classical music is such an intense world, people are always popping too many pain pills and toppling. Nadja Salerno-Salonjo, didn't she topple? Or was it that female cellist who slept naked with her cello, toppling? I keep getting all my Fox October Searchlight films mixed up.

Anyway, point is, the young boy ringer—he does not crumple weeping and get hauled off to the looney bin. No, in twenty-four hours, he doesn't just deliver the score, he nails it— The audience is electrified—! He gets four standing O's—

Next, on camera? Beverly Sills. Her hand is over her heart. Her voice is husky.

She is blown away by this brilliant young conductor, who is . . .

"David Robertson," she murmurs. "David."

And sitting there in front of PBS at possibly midnight, my dad, gallon of long-expired mint-chip ice cream in hand, may well have had an aneurysm.

So now David Robertson is in town, conducting the L.A. Philharmonic at Disney Hall. And my dad calls me with the wildly illogical, poorly though-out idea that we should actually go. He lives in Malibu; I live in Van Nuys. Disney Hall is completely sold out— However, although I work in theater, which counts as nothing, lower than the gypsies, I do have my PR friend Kenny—my secret connection— my dealer, if you will, in fame, connections, and house seats.

And this will give me a nice occasion to let my dad know the happy news that Mike and I and the kids are moving in. Because that way, come September, gas bill in hand, Hannah can attend the local Malibu elementary. Hands down adorable, green lawns, fluttering American flag . . . API = 842! One hundred percent free! And legal!

My dad and Alice appear in the mob again.

"We're lost!" he exclaims. "We're lost!"

"No you're not!" I yell. "Come *this* way! Walk toward me!"

It's true that moving to Malibu is a last resort. Plenty of work lies ahead. My father bought his house in Malibu in 1963. Five bedrooms, with fireplace and peek of the ocean, just one block from the beach. For this house he paid $47,000, and since then, into remodeling, he has put about ten dollars. And those were hard to part with, what with the great lumber and plumbing parts you find . . . in Dumpsters!

Which is to say this is a 1960s tract house that has not been updated. It has all the original sparkling cottage-cheese ceilings, sixties shag carpeting, and sixties starburst linoleum. In true engineer style, cracked glass shower doors have been patched with duct tape; bathroom mildew has been gently spackled over . . . and over. The lawn is actually, horror of horrors, fertilized with my dad's own pee. The David Lynch House, is what I used to call it.

Never mind. It's still worth a zillion dollars now. And we are set to eventually inherit it but . . . not in time for kindergarten. Unless I'm prepared to commit a murder, I'll have to . . . speed the process up. Share the communal space.

"I have the tickets!" I yell. And, grabbing both my dad's and Alice's frail arms, I gingerly guide them down into the orchestra section, into the belly of the soaring bird, trying not to slide down one of the hidden chutes in the bird that will spill us suddenly, as if through a warp hole, into some dingy pocket in San Pedro, some dark underground cellar beneath a Thai restaurant, with air ducts and leaky pipes and snapping fluorescent non–Frank Gehry lighting.

"So," I say as we settle ourselves into our—I must say—excellent and cozy orchestra seats. "Remember how I was telling you about our problems finding a kindergarten for Hannah? About all of L.A. Unified like a Saigon, collapsing, in flames, the plunging API scores, the soaring La Cañada real estate— Remember Jonathan? From Caltech? And his gifted children? With the violin?" I throw in, to get a rise out of my Asian dad.

I should mention that one of the problems with my eighty-five-year-old father is sporadic, sometimes it seems to me almost selective, deafness.

"What?" he stabs out suddenly in alarm.

"Kindergarten!" I hiss. "Hannah! In kindergarten!"

"No!" he replies. "The Dvořák!" He taps his program in agitation. "We've lost the Dvořák! Look! We've lost the Dvořák! We've lost the Dvořák! We've lost half the concert! Tonight—it stops with the Beethoven!"

"That's the point of Casual Friday!" I explain, my voice swooping upward like a perky airline hostess trying to calm passengers on a nose-diving plane. "At Disney Hall! Casual Friday! Casual Friday is a somewhat shorter and more CASUAL program. To give working Los Angeles professionals a chance, after their busy week, to get home early . . ."

I look into my dad's horrified face, a retired senior who has nothing BUT time. This is an eighty-five-year-old man who will ride three hours to avoid using a single first-class stamp, a man who rode approximately five thousand hours to get here. I realize this description makes it sound like we, the classical music lovers, are getting gypped by the lazy, laconic, too-tired-on-Friday-night, BlackBerry-wielding professionals. And I suppose we are. What else is new?

I amend my clearly upsetting tale.

"Casual Friday. It's a shorter concert so that afterward we can mingle with the L.A. Philharmonic. In the café."

"In the café? WHAT?" my dad asks.

"That's the great thing about the Casualness," I press on, with my sunny sales pitch. "Today's classical musicians are not the standoffish ones of yore. Pshaw. Look at this flier"—I pull out a brochure I picked up in the lobby—"of the people in this orchestra in turtlenecks, doing high kicks, flying through the air, juggling . . . Isn't it funny? A clarinetist? Juggling!" Today's new kinder, gentler classical musicians . . . They're clearly a *hell* of a lot of fun. I wonder what will be next. "For just a small fee you can take a French-horn player Rollerblading, or a bassoonist for a skydive!"

"Why is the symphony wearing jeans?" my father asks, waving his hand in dismay, as the L.A. Philharmonic files onto the stage in their Casualware—Hawaiian shirts, clogs, sandals . . . Is that a tank top?

I pat his arm soothingly. I lower my voice, in hopes he'll get the idea to lower his.

"It's because they yearn to meet us, to mingle with us, afterward in the café," I repeat. "And hey, you know who I bet will be there?"

"Who?" my dad says suspiciously.

I take a beat.

"David Robertson!"

His body stiffens with the blow. This is his weak spot. He knows I have him.

"All right," he says resignedly, even bitterly.

Alice is bent over her Ralphs bag, and pulling out . . . a bruised banana. She waggles it at me. "Hungry?"

"Food is not allowed in Disney Hall and— Oh my God," I say. "Is that from the Dumpster?"

"Very clean!" Alice insists.

"Very clean," my father agrees, lifting out of his bag a not-so-fresh-looking Starbucks cup. "Today we have hazelnut," he says like some demon barrista. "It is a hazelnut-vanilla combination. This morning at the Malibu Starbucks, I poured together two cups people left behind."

"Oh my God," I moan.

"*L.A. Times,*" he says, pulling out a grease-stained newspaper. "Also I took from Starbucks. Very clean!" He taps it. "That's where it lists what we lost. The Dvořák!"

"The Dvořák, he's just not very . . . CASUAL," I flail.

He grunts.

"How much were the tickets for this Casual concert show?"

"You . . . don't have to pay me back now," I murmur, looking around.

It seems gauche to talk about money in this setting, Frank Gehry's swooping bird. I'm actually afraid the bird is going to hear me, bringing down a tsunami of more birds—The Birds.

"No," he snaps irritably. "I want to find out now before I forget."

I lean in to whisper.

"Ninety-six dollars."

My father lets out a bellow reminiscent of a bull being gored:

"Ninety-six dollars!!!!!!!!!!!!!!!!!!!"

At least six people in the row in front of us, all old white people with white hair, lean forward in dismay. One man bearing a stark resemblance to the late Eddie Albert, in an elegant dark blue sort of yachtsman's jacket, with red cravat, puts a startled finger on his whining hearing aid.

"Ninety-six dollars!!!!!!!!!!!!!!!!!!!!! And no DVOŘÁK!"

I find myself losing it.

"Yes," I hiss. "That's what art costs now. You need to throw down a hundred dollars, two hundred dollars, ten thousand dollars! Art is expensive now! It's not like the loosey-goosey days of yore when just ANYONE could have some!"

"All right," my dad replies, prickly.

He reaches down into his grocery bag, begins to rattle around in it.

"You don't have to pay me back now," I hiss.

"Ach," he grunts, "you're giving me a headache!"

And right there, in the middle of the orchestra section, in front of the ENTIRE CITY OF LOS ANGELES, my dad counts out $192 cash for me for two L.A. Philharmonic tickets in arduous twenties, tens, fives, even ones!!!!!!!!!

I try to snatch the cash quickly from him so we are not sitting so exposed in Frank Gehry's soaring cathedral of Art, with the many small, crumpled, immigrant bills flapping around us—

But our hands hit each other midair and the cash goes flying.

A cascade of crumpled twenties, tens, fives, ones blows about the yachtsman's head!

And due to some strange laws of circulation in the bird, it's as though the bills are eerily held aloft, circling, circling, circling . . .

It's a blizzard of crumpled little ones, blowing around Disney Hall!

Oh my GOD, I think:

We are SUCH IMMIGRANTS!!!

My father is buoyed by David Robertson's short but brilliant and not at all casual performance—

Four standing O's . . . !

I want to try to bring up kindergarten again, to reveal the happy news that our whole family is moving in with him, and that we will be commuting back and forth between Malibu and Van Nuys . . . and how we have to do it by August 15 . . . but the applause for David Robertson is literally too deafening.

Or it could be more "selective" deafness—

Well, I know my dad is eager to meet David Robertson, practically in a panic about it, and certainly after he does that he will relax . . .

So now, in search of David, the three of us hustle, with all the grocery bags of rotted food, downstairs to the café.

We find three steel chairs, sit, and wait, as do a small passel of other audience members, trying to look Casual, as though we are not in fact stalkers waiting to meet the clarinetist who we hope, as in the brochures, will be juggling! What will we speak of, Casually, to one another. "How about those Mets?" "Do you get gassy after eating cherry tomatoes, or is that just me?"

Members of the L.A. Phil start drifting down, but they are not really the A list. There is a trombonist, timpanist, viola player . . .

There's not even the first violinist, the concert master . . .

Oh, look! The guy who played the . . . triangle.

Three times. *Ting, ting, ting.*

And looking over . . .

I have to say I feel for my dad, in his little red V-neck sweater. His entire body betrays utter gouged-out gloom. Conductors and Nobel Prize laureates: These are the people my dad lives for. He is their biggest fan. To him, when the Nobel Prizes in physics are announced—it's more heady than the Oscars. He devours every word about them, in his stolen-from-Starbucks *New York Times.*

How many more years does the man have to live?

He's so small and crushed. And Disney Hall is so vast and wingy, almost threatening to engulf him!

So to cheer my dad up, I give a sense of Event, to the Casualness.

I say, "Oh, look, it's cellist Barry Gold, who gave that wonderful opening speech!"

And I kid you not, my dad prods Barry Gold in the chest and bellows four words:

"Where is David Robertson?"

The L.A. Phil musicians are very kind. Perhaps, they suggest, the security guard will take a note to David Robertson for us. To give to him . . . sometime. The fact is, famous conductors rarely stick around after concerts. They're not part of the oh-so-Casual program.

Indeed, observes the security guard, knowing David Robertson, after the concert, as is his usual habit, he has probably immediately gone out to dinner with his wife, Orli . . .

And I don't know how this happens, but with perfect twenty-twenty stalkerazzi vision, I know, in my bones, that our elusive quarry is AT THAT MOMENT DINING next door at Patina!

Off go the three of us—me, Alice, and my dad, complete with Ralph's grocery bags, and UCLA sac, with bungee cord, doggedly pushing forward like Jack Lalanne—

I locate my inner "Fuck you." I push open the glass doors of Patina and, with enormous flair, Rigoberta Menchú–like, armed with my own small colorful natives, I sweep past the maître d'.

"I'm looking for a friend!" I breezily tell the startled maître d'. (I have a backup line prepared, in case of trouble: "We are the newest Nobel Prize winners in peace—from a tiny village in Laos called Pnom Thnak! With the Richard Gere Foundation? Surely you heard about us on NPR.") I hunt table after table after table, of L.A. Phil subscribers with their tiny canape plates and twin flutes of bubbling refreshment, finding nothing, but then, just beyond, there is a wall of frosted glass! The private room!

I boldly push the frosted-glass doors open. Fifteen surprised white heads look up, swirl of diamonds, at the head of the table: David Robertson! GRACIOUS AS PIE!!!

My father barrels in, holds David Robertson in a death grip!

We obtain our half-dozen flash photos before I gently extricate my gurgling father and drive him home to Zuma Beach.

Success!

I have slain a bear . . . for my father!

And during the drive back to Malibu, in the pleasant dim glow of the minivan, I go into a warm, bubbly litany. I am my own magic flute, my own magic flute of champagne. "Wasn't that fun? Isn't it nice to be driven home and not have to take the bus? If we lived together, all the fun we could have! We could go to concerts together! Mike and I could give you rides all the time! Everywhere! For free!"

No response.

I press on: "What fun that would be if our family moved in with you! And then, like I said, our girls could go to the Malibu schools."

And of his five-bedroom house, my dad says flatly, "I don't have enough room."

"What are you talking about?" I exclaim.

"My boarders."

The boarders. For the last decade, to make extra cash on the side, my father has been renting out our childhood bedrooms to Malibu hippie followers of the local guru.

But what does he make? Two hundred dollars a room?

"Four hundred fifty," he corrects. "I raised it."

"Well, how many boarders do you have now?"

"Three—and a new one is moving in. Says he's an old friend of yours."

Since I've been fired from KCRW and been on *Real Time with Bill Maher,* everyone and his cousin is a friend of mine. Particularly when it comes to the sort of washed-up fifty-something hippie men who want to rent a moldering room from my father. "Hey!" one Vietnam-stare-eyed guy said to me once. He appeared to be sitting in his boxer shorts on a sleeping bag, clipping his toenails. "Your dad says you're a writer! I'm a writer, too! Screenplays! Thriller screen-plays!" A toenail went flying.

"Well, get rid of the boarders!" I cry out. "It's your granddaugh-ter! Kindergarten! She has nowhere to go! Your boarders can't be more important than—"

"But I like my boarders!" he says. "And they bring in good money."

"But you have to think of your . . . your health!" Here I throw the gauntlet down, the veins practically popping out on my temples. I go for the jugular. I hit below the belt. "You're an old man. Stuff is falling off you. Malibu is far, far, far away . . . You and Alice could start experiencing mysterious new medical problems." I gesture wildly around the car. "And if so, THIS . . . is your ride to the emer-gency room!"

"But the Malibu paramedics—they're very good!" he protests. "They always come right away!" Damn California and the high property taxes that result in such phenomenal city services! Actually, no, wait a minute: Thanks to Proposition 13, in Malibu, my father is still basically assessed on the home price he paid forty years ago . . . $47,000! While meanwhile in Van Nuys, my child is going to Mexi-can kindergarten. Thanks a lot!

And still the paramedics zoom to his aid!

"The danger!" I exclaim, through my teeth. "What with no . . . pacemaker! Without me to drive you—"

"Well, your car's engine light is on," he adds with broad good humor. "I don't know if I could trust this vehicle. Maybe YOU are the one who needs help!"

On the minivan floor, I see one of Hannah's stuffed unicorns, which due to the constant shampooing has a mane sculpted into a bit of a lopsided Mohawk.

I feel a dark rage coming over me.

"And you call yourself a Chinese father! You used to pull your weight! What happened to you? You were the one manic about edu-cation! Don't you remember all your flash cards at the dinner table, the calculus tutoring, the endless wild diagrams of ions and pions? Have you offered to teach Hannah conversational Mandarin, a little trigonometry? No! Now that you're a grandparent, you're just some kind of PBS-watching slacker on the beach! Maybe she'll just go to *clown* school for all you care!

"Or maybe I have myself to blame!" I rail on, my voice hitting a shrapnel tone of fury. In the rearview mirror, I see Alice's eyes widen in surprise. "I took my Caltech physics education and went into the liberal arts, which to a Chinese father is like pole-dancing! Guess you're paying me back now, huh?"

This car is hot, so hot!

My shout reverberates!

And in that moment we all stare at one another. My father, Alice, and myself.

We digest, in one shocking moment, the information that *I am shouting*!

In my childhood, it was my father who shouted!

Back when he was the sole wage earner for a family of five, it was he who had the temper. Now, waiting for rides to Disney Hall, oh, he is quite calm! He has quite the eternal patience. Consuming his moldy bananas, he has all the time in the world.

Perhaps realizing the irony, the switched places, that now it is I who am manic, my dad says something to Alice in Mandarin and they point at me and they . . .

They *laugh*!

I wake up the next morning in my father's house in Malibu.

There is bottom, there is below bottom, and now this is, well, the flapping left mud-covered cheek of the bottom.

At forty-two, 9:03 A.M. on a Saturday morning—as indicated on the 1970s Panasonic clock radio that used to sit in my sister's room—I am actually BEHIND where I was as a kid.

At twelve, I actually had my own bedroom. Now some hirsute strange bearded homeless hippie guy flops his hairy balls all over a wrinkled sleeping bag in my room. Meanwhile, I'm sleeping on a cot in a corner of the dining room, behind a ragged curtain of beach towels.

That's right: I am actually sleeping on beach towels, in lieu of pillows.

I can actually feel the terry-cloth imprint on my cheek.

I am humiliated.

The sting of it is, my dad had invited us to live with him many years ago. His third marriage—to his second Chinese wife—was collapsing, he was seventy-something, it was just him rattling around in his lonely five-bedroom Malibu house.

He had just the one boarder at the time, a three-hundred-pound elderly Greek woman, who was very depressed. Even though she spoke no English, she would always rush right to the phone, stabbing out, "Allo!" half in fear. And I would say, "Can you hang up so I can call back and leave a message on the machine?" "Okay!" she would reply. I'd dial the number again, and again she would rush to the phone, and grab it again: "Allo! Allo! Allo!" Repeat forty times.

The point being that neither Chinese Wives Number One or Number Two had taken. They came full of verve but ended up being flummoxed by the collapsing suburban house. They didn't know how to make it work. They wanted to update it, but as my dad gave them no actual money, they ended up merely scavenging shiny, peachy Hong Kong–like tiles from their more settled immigrant friends in Monterey Park, and setting them down at various odd places in the house, without grout.

But Alice is of a different sort.

Look at her.

Without even moving on my beach towel pallet, I am aware of Alice's constant movements, all around the house, as though practically pacing the perimeters of her bailiwick, patrolling the castle.

In the fluttering shadows beyond, on the back walkway, she pins up laundry. Next she is padding about in the kitchen, in a clattering of pans and dishes, boiling rice, stir-frying vegetables.

Good Lord—that is how the woman has always been, always on restless move in this house . . . because like so many immigrants, she's ridiculously overqualified for the job of Chinese Wife. She was head of a staff of two hundred nurses in Manchuria . . . ! When baby Hannah first came, Alice was a whirlwind, cooking seven-dish meals, doing all the laundry, massaging Hannah's chubby little legs, doing these kinds of healthful calisthenic, Chairman Mao marching exercises with them—

It was as if Mike and I suddenly had our own Chinese Wife! It was heaven!

At one point, I remember looking out the window and seeing Alice, with Hannah strapped on her back in a BabyBjörn, calmly hosing down our Toyota minivan, including hubcaps—which literally hadn't been done in years!

And that's the way Alice cares for my father. She cuts up his fruit, lotions his bunions . . . his bunions! Ai! In China, they're used to things like bunions, but as a lazy American, I have lost it. I cannot contend with my father's bunions. I can't . . . lotion the bunions. This would be like slow torture, like that scene in *The Silence of the Lambs.* "It takes the lotion out of the basket . . ."

I mean—I can't compete with that! What are my domestic skills? What do I cook? Peanut butter on toast? With raisins? And expired Danimals . . . ?!?

I feel like a female character in some kind of Pearl S. Buck novel . . . battling for a spot in the old master's house. But I'm like Wife Number Two or Three or Ten. I come with lots of baggage, lots of demands, no skills . . . and a passel of blond children!

I am the weak second generation in America. The immigrant-offspring generation. We have neither the money of our elders nor the skills. The bunion-lotioning skills.

And now, the final insult?

Because of the new boarder moving in, my father has set several boxes of my stuff before me.

Not only has he kicked me out of my room . . . he doesn't even want my stuff around. Boxes of my things sit in front of me waiting, like a small shantytown of failure.

With a sigh, I swing my legs down off the bed, lift the lid off the first box, and . . .

Oh! And here's the next insult!

This particular box is not even of my stuff. It's Kaitlin's old school stuff! I guess he can't tell his daughters apart anymore. We're just people who are NOT David Robertson.

It's a box of Kaitlin's old high-school papers . . .

I pick up the top one. It is on France. It's yellowed, crispy, thirty years old.

"A city of lights, and of sophistication, and of romance, Paris will forever glamorously remain."

Oh my God! The grammar! My mother's tortured German grammar!

And I realize that pushy parents didn't appear yesterday.

I remember now how my Danzig-born mother wrote all my sister's papers, which Kaitlin then dutifully copied as her own. But the result was less Ivy League early admissions than, as my sister will joke, "my strange German syntax, to shake, I have never quite been able."

Oh my gosh!

And now here is my old lab book from 1980, the time of my summer job in freshman year at college, the job my dad got me at his own place of employment, Hughes Aircraft.

Taped to the back?

My father's Hughes long-distance codes! Or at least the ones he stole.

Yes, my father was always professionally eccentric. He carried not a briefcase but a brown paper grocery bag filled with empty Frosted

Flakes boxes. Scientific papers would slip inside the Frosted Flakes boxes, pens would clip on the outside. To get to work sometimes, we'd hitchhike together on the Pacific Coast Highway. He'd push me forward and hide in the bushes, thinking that pitying motorists would stop sooner for a sad, lonely girl.

It all seemed so logical!

But this list of numbers reminds me of the strange habit my father actually practiced while at his desk at Hughes Aircraft. Dialing out long-distance in those days required punching in a special five-digit long-distance company code. Each employee had their own. Including my dad—

But what fun was using your own code? Sometimes, just out of curiosity—that was the brilliant scientific mind at work—my dad would amuse himself by sitting in his office trying different five-digit sequences at random to see which ones worked. He probably single-handedly held the U.S. missile program back five years. He'd write down the correct codes on the back of an envelope and, when we'd visit him in his office, grandly offer us the keys to his illicit telephone kingdom . . .

"Is there someone you want to call long-distance, Sandra? A boyfriend? In Alaska maybe? Pick a number! Any will work! I've triple-checked them!"

And to think, this free spirit was the same one who, during my senior year at Caltech, kept calling my dorm to shout, over the thumping ZZ Top, "SANDRA! APPLY TO ANY GRAD SCHOOL IN ANY ENGINEERING MAJOR!" Sadly, thanks to the freedom of the EZ student loan the great cheapskate himself had helped me secure, I was already off dating a rock bagpipe player and spectacularly bombing my physics GRE. (Out of a possible 99, my percentile was 07—a number so low, it inspires almost Talmudic awe in those who hear it.)

"Ah, Malibu," I say suddenly aloud, lifting out . . . what a treasure trove!

Because now, oh! My old yearbooks!

Oh my goodness!

Malibu Park Junior High. Nineteen seventy-six! The horror, the horror!

Look how pathetic!

Sandra Loh, Student of the Month . . . Well, it appears I am that every single month. In tiny photos. In fields no one else would even publicly admit to pursuing. Along with president of the Debate Club, treasurer of the French Club, and first viola, out of two. Oh my God. It was large acne-scarred me and my lonely achievements, against a groovy, much larger, much more cinematic background of Hang Ten T-shirts, puka shells, and drugs—which apparently, to hear my classmates tell it twenty years later, they all enjoyed very much!

Jeez.

Things were so much simpler in those days. No one expected school to be anything but horrible.

My mother never angsted over different schools, researched them, toured them, interviewed them. In her words, it was always: "There's the junior high school . . . good luck." And then of course: "Horribly miserable, try not to be, if you are able."

In those days, there was just one school in the town that everyone went to.

This was in California in the supposed golden years, pre–Prop 13. My high school had four thousand kids and no one said boo about it.

And God, look at these teachers, I think, leafing through. Mrs. Dean, Mr. Tucker, Mrs. Fonner . . .

Jesus. Thinking it over now, I realize my own schooling included good teachers, bad teachers, medium teachers, in-retrospect-what-we-all-realize-now-were drunk teachers, and of course, the rheumy-eyed PE/driver's ed teacher who put his hand on all the girls' knees when we downshifted . . . which was widely regarded as, if not particularly pleasant, a known rite of passage.

I seem to recall a poetry teacher weeping under her desk (possibly drinking)? Drunk and weeping. Very appropriate if you're teaching middle-school poetry. That's where I would be. It's sort of where I am now.

In fact, I recall now, in my own educational history, many crappy teachers. Never the solid field it had initially seemed, the aircraft industry actually provided for my father quite a few professional ups and downs. As a result, our family traveled a lot, and it seemed we were always running out of money. We didn't so much move away from places as flee, first to other cities, then to exotic countries, where my dad would score these strange little professorships (few Americans wanted to relocate so dramatically—this alone rocketed my dad to the top of the science talent heap). And so my own global education was dotted with the rare extraordinary academy amid a sea of crappy schools—for a spate my sister and I studied ballet in Sao Paolo with that crazy Brazilian with frighteningly bad hair named simply "Yolanda!" Hoop earrings, bell-bottoms!

God. And then my father scored that brief professorship in Egypt. In Cairo, with all those bored Russian expats around, my star-struck mother was able to hire Irina, a drunk ballet mistress from the Kirov. Who tried her best to ignore Kaitlin and me while she gossiped with our mother, chain-smoked, ate little tea cakes, and complained about her bunions.

And here is a photo of my dad holding—what? His degrees! From Caltech, Stanford, Purdue . . . In applied physics, applied math, metallurgy.

He never said, "At school, white people will laugh at you because you're part Asian." No. He said what all Asian parents say: "At college, people will laugh at you if you major in the liberal arts." My dad was obsessed with the great waste of time that was the liberal arts. Every bad thing in life was attributed to it.

"You'll starve on the street like animals if you major in the liberal arts."

"Forty thousand dollars they lost on a degree in the liberal arts."

Kids of other neighborhood families were held up as tragic examples. "Katie? The Andersons' eldest? Thirty years old. Waitress. New York. Four-hundred-square-foot apartment. No dental insurance. She majored in . . . the liberal arts."

And so of course I went off to college to major in physics.

I lift out the next yearbook—my Caltech one, and . . .

Oh, what flutters out? A funny article I wrote about Caltech in the *California Tech*. That's what I did at the great science school, wrote comedic articles.

That was my Caltech career—bombing my tests and writing funny pieces about it for our unread student paper!

To wit:

> *Academics at Caltech are admittedly complicated.*
>
> *Consider, as one example, that beloved academic tradition, the take-home open-book INFINITE TIME EXAM—*
>
> *That's right! Take all the time you want! Won't really help you because, PS, Problem Number Two? It's actually impossible. That's right! It's a famous impossible conundrum! Even Descartes couldn't solve it, after working on it . . . for 37 years. Then he went insane. Had a fight with Foucault, bar in Lyons, few drinks, argument, duel . . . Funny story, we thought it would be amusing to give this unsolvable drove-Descartes-mad paradox to you freshmen . . . In Math 1 . . . your very first week at Caltech!"*
>
> *But rest assured that Caltech students do learn to fight back, in this intellectual hazing process. Even the mediocre ones. I know, because I am not just one of them, I believe I'm on the short list of candidates for patron saint of those lost at Caltech. Junior year, I have been assigned as physics lab partner classmate Sekhar Chivukula, widely renowned as a genius. Of our pairing it is said: "Sekhar will do the calculations, Sandra will handle the radioactive samples."*

Never mind— By senior year, I have developed my own law of quantum mechanics that has nothing to do with Wigner-Eckhart's Theorem or Clebsch-Gordon Coefficients—

No, Sandra's Theory is: "On any Phys 106 exam involving the spin of an atom, the answer is at least 60% likely to be −1." I don't know why but you'd be amazed how often it works: To skip the calculations and just boldly put down −1 and then scrawl next to it an illegible snarl of curlicues that vaguely resemble any of the Greek symbols—lambda, iota, zeta, tau, ampersand— With any luck a tired Pakistani TA might just look at it, get a headache and throw you a point—!

So now that I am graduating, I am proud to say I have a diploma entirely MADE of . . . partial credit. My degree is glued together, faintly pulsing with radioactivity, graded less on a curve than on a kind of wild hyperbola asymptotically approaching some imaginary actual answer . . .

Ha-ha-ha. What a screw-up. The grand sum of $150,000 wasted. Good times, good times.

And here, my own red *Feynman Lectures on Physics*!

Oh, the memories this brings back!

I myself met Feynman, when I was an undergrad, in 1979.

We were freshmen in Page House, in a glaze from our first "INFINITE TIME" exam . . . which has triggered our first series of "all-nighters"—known as "borrowing from tomorrow to pay for yesterday today." And in walked our first after-dinner guest—author of those great red Bibles: *The Feynman Lectures on Physics*. Richard Feynman. Feynman. We were sitting there stunned, our mouths hanging open as he spoke. And Feynman, a brilliant anecdotalist who's used to going into a room and just killing—

He sees us glazed freshmen for what we are, a dead audience.

And so, to perk things up, in describing electromagnetic induction via the standard magnetic coil pulling a needle in, out, in, out . . .

Feynman suddenly stops, and erupts comedically, in his thick Bronx accent: "Look at that! It's little like f&*—!"

And he says the word I got fired for!

Great.

I have had the best schooling in the world.

And what happened? I started as an overachiever. Pushed by my parents, I earned an 800 Math SAT in high school and a perfect score on AP calculus, and then I . . . somehow lost it. Over the years, all my math gradually drained out of me.

Today, at forty-two, I can barely complete a basic sudoku puzzle without garnering a massive headache. And I don't mean the hard sudokus. Oh, I start strong, sprinting confidently out the gate with my No. 2 pencil, smugly filling in all those little boxes—3! 3! 7! 4! . . . And then the whole thing unravels. It all seems to work except for this line in the north and two murky southern mysteriously "3-heavy" patches.

I myself did not fix on a career until the age of thirty-four. At the time I was living in a spider-filled bungalow, with health insurance being paid for by VISA—which is to say my sister's VISA.

All I have become by my forties is nervous. The only math I do now is shading in little pie charts on airline magazines to keep the plane from falling out of the sky.

And I had a GOOD education!!!

What are my children going to face?

9
Guavatorina

The dented white Toyota minivan is being serviced. I am without wheels.

And perhaps it is appropriate that, at long last, now that I'm finally going to bite the bullet and enroll my daughter at Guavatorina Elementary, the thrumming central vortex, the literal lair of the L.A. Unified dragon, I will be doing so . . . on foot.

It's just three blocks, and it's a mild Los Angeles day, sunny yet hazy, about seventy-two. So I figure, yes, I can do this.

I push open the front door, pad down the driveway, turn left.

The sidewalk seems . . . in fairly good shape. Check it out! Pretty flat.

It's so peculiar, this walking. The houses and lawns drift by so slowly.

And ach! There's a dog! He runs along the chain-link fence: *Arf! Arf! Arf! Arf!*

By the second block, I feel chafing in my left heel. Good heavens, if I plan to keep it up, all this walking, I really must get different shoes.

Another left turn and there 'tis, bobbing toward me. The familiar block of low, putty-colored buildings, ringed by chain-linked fence.

And there's the familiar marquee, where the announcements on the marquee are . . .

In . . . English. WHAT? Is that ENGLISH? Yes! It says . . . "Registration"!

But I think . . . Wait a minute! I cross to the back of the sign. This is the way I always approach it, from the south, on my driving route, and yes . . . The other side is in Spanish, as per usual. But hey, this I never noticed, the NORTH side is in English!

So it's bilingual, this sign! Bilingual!

I feel like lifting my arms, with this small victory. "All right! So they've got some English here! At Guavatorina Elementary, of the concept of English they are not completely uncognizant! Someone inside that building may even speak it!"

So I turn now and stand before Guavatorina. I take a moment to actually gaze upon it, from the front. It is a humble fifties-era building, concrete stairs leading up into a tan alcove framing two brown double doors. The grass isn't emerald-green lush, but it's not actually dead. Nor is it the type of CRAZY grass one sees around far-flung Chatsworth methamphetamine flophouses—you know, that hairy, weedy, leathery crabgrass that is much like Don King's hair . . . C-c-c-razy!!!!!!

Really, I have to say that studying the front of Guavatorina, I find nothing violently wrong so far. Overall, the impression one gets is that of a government building in a small, not insanely prosperous—but not horribly destitute—country. There is no royal circle of dwarf palms royally sweeping you in, nor are there homeless people camped out in front, in tatters. Guavatorina would be perhaps in a small, slightly tropical country . . . the Department of Motor Vehicles.

So if Guavatorina is not a First World or a Third World country, it is perhaps like a . . . Second World country.

Coming closer, I notice the signage.

On the left double door is taped a poster, with a picture of a smiling yellow sun:

START YOUR DAY WITH A GOOD BREAKFAST! Ditto in Spanish.

Well, I cannot fault the thought expressed here. One *should* start the day with a good breakfast.

A poster to the right, with a picture of a green book with a happy face in it, reads:

READ TO YOUR CHILD EVERY DAY! Ditto in Spanish, I presume.

Attached to the chain-link fence is a bilingual banner depicting a "BOOK DRIVE!" Another reads: JUMP ROPE FOR HEART HEALTH DAY.

None of these bulletins sing to me. None of these notions cause my spirit to soar within me like a great lifting bird. I don't hear Ravel, either in reality or in my mind. However, at the same time, one must admit there is nothing here that technically violates the concept of an elementary school. There are no posters that say:

GOLD JEWELRY AND GUNS PAWNED HERE FOR GANG HOS, INQUIRE WITHIN.

TODAY IS 20% OFF ON ALL CRACK!

Or simply:

SYRINGES, SYRINGES, SYRINGES! And then again, *en español*!

The signs express an intent, at least, that within the building, conventional schoolish-type things should happen.

I push open the double doors to the hallway inside (ceiling fan, beige walls with kids' drawings pasted up, white linoleum). I push open another door and there is the front office, containing a wooden counter, a small hive of desks, and—what can I tell you—sitting in the middle is . . . ?

Oh, please God, no.

The sullen-faced, round-shouldered nightmare government employee. We are talking big curls of oddly colored dark hair with some streaks of purple, some of gray, Bride of Frankenstein–ish, a silky aqua Boogie shirt, chunky gold jewelry, plucked eyebrows, and strange, faintly apricot-hued makeup. She is the woman at the DMV who tells you to stand in yet a fourth line after you've already stood in three for a total of five hours.

Sitting quietly on two chairs, waiting, as if for Godot, are what appear to be two Mexican *abuelitas,* in country dresses. Grandmothers.

I slip into the open chair next to them.

Ah yes. I remember this from the DMV. Waiting. And waiting. And waiting . . .

While the Bride of Frankenstein chews gum and continues to type.

I look at the clock. I look at the flag. I am half transported to my own public-school days in California, waiting to see the principal . . .

When it occurs to me maybe the *abuelitas* aren't actually waiting for anything.

"Are you—?" I ask them, waving toward the Bride of Frankenstein.

They put up their hands, in polite surprise: "Oh no no no no no!" Either they have been helped already or—in this Second which I am now considering downgrading to Third World country—they have accepted the fact that waiting is a futile act.

Either way, I now have license to approach the counter.

"Uh, excuse me?" I murmur to the Bride of the DMV.

She continues typing. Behind her I now notice the Bear Flag of California.

A bit louder, I say, "Hello?"

More typing.

The Bride stops typing for a moment . . .

Looks down to recheck her pad . . .

Then continues typing.

My heart sinks. How far I have fallen! We are back at Square One, not just at Square One but Square Minus One.

I have been swept into the V.I.P. rooms of Hancock Park mansions, where velvet ropes parted. At frickin' Wonder Canyon I was waved into the frosted-glass inner sanctum. Even at Luther Hall, I got immediate service. It was cheerfully hateful service, but I was at least SEEN.

You know, even walk into a McDonald's and you get a "How may I help you?" Even at Target, ask a question, "Where would I find Swiffer pads?" and red-vested stock people, however disenchanted they may be with their lot, will at least respond.

Now I am standing at an LAUSD counter in Van Nuys and no one is even acknowledging my presence. I feel the first whiff of hysteria grip me, the validation of the forgone conclusion. That's the way it is in U.S. public education! It is a factory! Worse than Detroit. It's *Guavatorina*. API = 683. It's a fuckin' 3! Why did I even come?

"EXCUSE ME!" I half yell.

The Bride jumps. Takes something out of her ear. Turns to me, startled, a bit amazed.

"I'm here to register my daughter for kindergarten for the fall?" I say. "And to . . . inquire about a tour?"

"A what?" the Bride queries, in a strange nasal Persian (?) voice. What is that accent? Is it Russian? It's very thick.

"A tour?"

"I don't understand."

"You know, a tour. To . . . look into the classroom. See what it's like."

"You want a tour?" the Bride repeats.

This is becoming a bit like a "Who's on first?" routine, but without the wit.

"Yes, a tour!"

"What?"

"A tour!"

"Tour?"

"Yes! Tour!"

The Bride gets up slowly, fishes a thick registration packet out of a stack, and slides it across the counter. "You can register her but . . . If she is coming to Guavatorina, anyway? Why would you . . . ? No one has ever asked for a tour," she finishes, baffled.

"But I can't send her here if I can't even see what the inside of a classroom looks like!" I exclaim, starting to lose it.

She presses an intercom button: "Martin." I hear a staticky voice: "Yes, Kokik." That's what her name sounds like—Kokik. "A lady here says she wants a tour?"

A door beyond flies open and out shoots a balding white fifty-something man, with a clipped beard, khaki pants, a red tie and blue button-down shirt, and a nest of tags hanging off him.

"Yes?" he says. His attitude is brisk, wide-eyed, efficient. "I'm Martin Byrnes, assistant principal here at Guavatorina. How may I help you?"

I feel tearful. There is a lump in my throat. But I've dragged myself this far across this hell pit called Los Angeles . . . The last three hundred feet on foot! Literally on foot! I am like a dog with barely the strength to sink his aching yellowed jaws into his last bone. My voice is a tiny squeak: "I'm registering my daughter for September and I would like a tour."

"We don't typically have those this month, but if you'd like to come with me now for a few minutes, I can show you around."

"Really? I would like that," I admit.

"Mm." Martin turns. "Kokik, did you call Building and Safety? There's still that smell."

The Bride's expression does not change. "I called twice, left a message. They just sent an e-mail, will be here by two."

"Good," Martin says, a tad fretfully. "'Cause there's still that smell. It's giving me a migraine." He reaches into a jar of M&M's and pops a small handful into his mouth, turns back to me.

"Kindergarten?" he asks.

"Yes," I say, and . . . I notice an amazing thing then, in this vast dark land of L.A. Unified, the lair of the dragon. When Martin Byrnes fixes his bright blue eyes on me . . . I see it, unmistakable, his magical talisman. A secret totemic marker, a small lighthouse in the wasteland of this blasted *Lord of the Rings* world.

Which is to say, under the left ear of Martin Byrnes, I see a very, very tiny, very, very discreet . . . gold earring.

Oh my God, is he gay? The assistant principal of Guavatorina, is he a gay?

And the tie . . . Are those . . . little yellow school buses flying across it? With little wings?

"Thank heavens!" I want to scream. "Inside Guavatorina . . . The mark of civilization. Praise the Lord, IT'S A GAY!"

Martin picks up a second set of papers, clips them neatly together with—he takes just a second to select the perfect one—a color-coordinated paper clip, and hands them to me. But as he does, something in his manner exhorts me . . . to comport myself. To maintain a certain decorum. To not throw up my hands and shriek, "Oh my GAWD—this whole crazy plan just MAY work out! I am going to be your new best friend because I see that you are gay!" To not immediately assume that Martin Byrnes and I are going to be singing old Culture Club tunes together, doubled over laughing like girlfriends in twenty-something club-kid mode.

And it vaguely dawns on me, in a public-school setting, with the two old Latina *abuelitas* behind me, that in fact Martin Byrnes, assistant LAUSD principal, may not appreciate my shrieking out: "OH MY GOD—YOU'RE A GAY!!!!"

"We're very excited about what's going on in kindergarten," Martin says, trotting down the hall. Without breaking stride he corrects things he sees—picks up a piece of litter, flicks off a water fountain that's dripping. "We have a new literacy coordinator, Rita, who is terrific. She has managed, just this year, to raise our API score seventy-two points—"

"It's 683, isn't it?" I say, before stopping myself.

"That was last year," he replies. "The new results just came in . . . Our current API is 755."

I'm stunned. I didn't know it was possible to actually improve an API score. I'd never factored that in as a possibility. I had considered a school's API score a fixed destiny, which immediately tarred all children who came in contact with it with the destiny of being someone's gang bitch in prison. A prison in . . . in Fresno.

"Well, that's very good!" I say.

"We could crack 800 next year," he says. "Well . . . That's a bit optimistic. Let's say two years at most. Our instruction is FINALLY meshing together. It takes a while."

I feel a sudden stab of exultation. You mean Hannah could be at an 800 school? Just down the block? For free? My God! I'm still reeling from the concept. Who knew API scores could go up? Without divine intervention of some kind by the . . . the Gates Foundation? Or Oprah?

I hear . . . is that . . . music? From one room beyond, I hear violins. Scrapey, squeaky, it's a familiar sound—that of a bad elementary-school orchestra.

"Is that . . . the kids playing?"

"That is our string program."

"You have a STRING program?"

"Hm," he says. "K through 2 is vocal, and then come third grade the kids can choose strings or recorders. I myself like the RECORDER," he adds suddenly. "I think it's a better home base for kids to start from, there's more commonality there. Of course, I myself was a wind player, so my bias is for—"

"And there—there are still slots for kindergarten?" I ask, anxious all at once. I feel the familiar panic closing in. Oh no. Guavatorina—it's actually an undiscovered jewel—and we are exactly two steps behind the wave.

"This is your LAUSD school?" he asks.

"Yes," I say.

"Well . . ." He pushes open another double door.

"Yes?" I ask, exhausted. I really cannot drag this project any further without help. If I'm thrown any more obstacles, even at my free corner 96 percent Hispanic public school, I will really be at my wit's end.

"Will your daughter be five by December second?"

"Yes!" I cry out. "Hannah's birthday's in September!"

"Okay, then," Martin replies, as though it's all so obvious. "Ach, there's still that smell. Can you smell it?"

I shake my head. I can't.

"Maybe it's my sinuses."

Hannah's admittance to Guavatorina—did he just say it was a given? I need to double-check. I look for the loophole.

"You don't . . . You don't have to keep an . . . an even number of boys and girls, do you?"

"Well, we like to if we can, sure . . ." He turns his head back to me, quizzical. "But you can't always predict, can you?"

"But do you try?" I persist. "Do you use some kind of . . ." I wave my hand in the air, to imply wheels and dials, to let him know I know how sometimes you have to . . . fudge things, to get the best result. So all the kids can . . . succeed. Better. Together.

I persist. "Do you maybe admit some kids FIRST, ones you think are going to be more successful, see how many you have, and then . . . ?"

He stares at me.

"You know," I continue, "to balance individual versus group learning styles? Do you place them in kindergarten based on, you know . . . informal assessments?"

"Well, that would be illegal, wouldn't it? By law, we have to educate every child who comes to us. This is PUBLIC SCHOOL."

Martin stops, puts his hand on the knob of a chipped beige door brightened with a giant yellow sunflower.

"And here's the library. The librarian is Mrs. Lewis. A forty-year veteran, she still likes to go by 'Mrs.' " There is the faintest arch of a brow . . . But then it's gone. There is not quite enough of a brow lift to provide a giant gap for me to drive my Mack truck of personality through the curtain to scream: "OH MY GOD, MARTIN, YOU'RE GAY AND I LOVE THAT!"

"She likes to go by 'Mrs.' and at Guavatorina we honor that," Martin says. "Does Hannah like stories?"

"She loves stories!"

"Ooh boy! Then she'll lo-o-ove Mrs. Lewis!"

He pushes open the door.

And there it is. An ordinary classroom with a chalkboard, desks, chairs, posters. Perhaps a dozen Hispanic children sit cross-legged on a rug of colored squares. On the walls around them are sunflowers with names handlettered on them. Not Cody, Cole, Coley, Colin, but RAMON, TERESA, AMY, PIERO, JOHNNY, AMIK.

And I have to admit I am . . . surprised.

This possibility literally never occurred to me.

I never imagined there were actual children inside these plain-brown-wrapper walls.

Every time I've spat out "Guavatorina," as when other parents would spit out "Grant," it never occurred to me that any of us was talking about actual children. I had always assumed we were talking about the Bush administration, an evil government torture institution, twin office towers full of bureaucrats, a bunch of smoky, sky-fouling oil derricks.

I had actually assumed, I don't know . . .

If you sacrifice your kids to public school, the Republicans . . . win!

But no—that is not so at all.

My God. It is like that moment when Charlton Heston yells, "Soylent green . . . is people!" Oh my God, I think. The horrible truth is . . .

Guavatorina . . . is children!

The LAUSD . . . is children!

L.A. Unified . . . is children!

The hopelessly broken U.S. public-school system . . . is children! Acckkkkkkkkkkk!!!!!!!!!

And seated before the Guavatorina students is an hourglass-shaped sixty-something-year-old teacher. She has a gray, sensible, somewhat bowl-shaped haircut, oval-shaped glasses. She is moving . . . very little. All she's doing is reading in a pleasant, measured voice. For my taste, her reading style is plain. I like more theatrical flair. But the children gathered around her are rapt.

The children . . . who are not the children of famous people, of rich people, they are not beautiful, they are not un-wiggly, they are not necessarily frighteningly gifted. They are thin and fat and tall and short and clear-complexioned and pimply. Even though they are all brown-skinned children, yes, Hispanic with perhaps one or two Armenians, in truth, they seem the full spectrum of everything children are.

It seems a miracle that such ordinary children have been invited in.

It seems unbelievable that my own to-be five-year-old, warts and all, is also welcome here.

Around the group is a ring of bookshelves. I see familiar covers turned to us: *Where the Wild Things Are. Hop on Pop. Madeline.*

And what is the book Mrs. Lewis is reading?

Charlotte's Web.

And then Mrs. Lewis reads the familiar, if long forgotten, words:

" 'It is not often that someone comes along who is a true friend and a good writer. Charlotte was both.' "

And then Mrs. Lewis closes the book, the children crowd around her, and her hands move together over the tops of their heads like birds building a nest.

And I realize she is their quiet, web-spinning Charlotte.

And at that moment, two Hispanic moms working in the corner

lift up the project they are working on. The whole room exclaims, claps hands together in delight. It is a painstakingly crafted yarn web, which reads:

SOME PIG

Stumbling out of that school, I am swept up with euphoria.

I'm higher than I would be on any of Aimee's company's pharmaceuticals. I realize I will never be like the sad women in her company's mournful TV commercials, sad women in V-neck sweaters staring tragically out misty windows.

Perhaps it is the wonder of periomenopause, but my days are suddenly shot through with luminous, almost hallucinogenic magic.

All at once, I see the meaning of my whole year.

I thought I had failed my family by not being tough enough to bite the debt bullet. I was not strong enough to commit to borrowing the hundreds of thousands needed to acquire, for our children, years of top-notch schools like Wonder Canyon.

One foot already on the last helicopter lifting out of Saigon, my family strapped safely on board . . . I fatally looked back down, saw the weight of the money . . . and let go of the life rope.

The unthinkable happened: I failed to save Hannah . . . to insulate her future from the horrors of a bad—or at least mediocre—or at least obscure and undistinguished—education.

But while I plummeted through space, full of grief, here was the wildest revelation of my unmedicated, premenopausal fever-dream: I suddenly saw what had been hitherto invisible to me, an astonishingly beautiful universe, a shimmering web made of millions of gossamer threads, tended, day by day, hour by hour, patiently, by the stubborn and unsung force . . . of women.

Everywhere around me, in the city, the whole time, there had been Charlottes, spinning their webs.

Brenda, Joan, Aimee, Celeste . . .

Even that damned Doris at Luther Hall. Who so loved her Gesell. This was what the world was made of.

Women!

Bossy women . . . PTA women . . . Church women . . . Neighborhood Watch block captains who walk their dogs at six A.M. and stand on people's lawns and yell at them about their trash . . . Women who you can *tell* are those captains, by the mere forward tilt of their heads, the angles of their visors, as they briskly step off the curb in front of you . . .

Women—who all at once I start to see everywhere, all over Los Angeles.

Brown women, white women, young women, old women . . .

Behind the Trader Joe's I've always rushed to as though in a tunnel, my lens widens to notice a special-ed school . . . into which special-ed kids roll down via ramps in wheelchairs with their twisted necks and wide, liquid eyes.

They are all THE WRONG ethnicity. Some are fat. Some are ugly. Some wear Wal-Mart Bratz T-shirts.

In a universe darker than ours, no one would give two figs for these kids. These children would be the discards.

I watch with amazement as they roar in on yellow school buses. As bus drivers carefully help lower them out. As a bearded security guy in a pressed blue dress shirt helps them in. And, at the open gates, every single morning, women with smooth faces and lined faces and skinny asses and fat asses wave in these to-them-precious children.

"Welcome! Welcome! Welcome!"

People love these children! This is a miracle. Humanity . . . The human race. It is a miracle.

Waiting at bus stops in the morning, too, I begin to notice masses of brown children waiting, with backpacks, their *abuelitas* tweaking their already exquisitely braided hair. I see that they are loved, too.

There is grace all around me. The universe hums—the invisible web.

In a daze, I go to an ATM in Sherman Oaks, get cash, get back into my car, and there she is, a black woman in Chanel sunglasses tapping at my window. "You left your card in the machine," she exclaims, a little angry at my inattention. "Here it is!"

At the stoplight, an Armenian woman—a Kokik—gestures at me. "Your tire is flat!" she yells. "Stop! Tire! Flat!"

I'm in the Van Nuys Ralphs and there's a new checker. Middle-aged, been around the block, and yet wearing a fairly exciting blouse, for Ralphs, in a wild Pucci-like print. Checking the sad condiments of the dour male computroll in front of me, with a demon twinkle in her eye the checker suddenly sasses him with:

"So . . . What's for dinner?"

I love checkers who ask that—I find it hilarious! It reminds me of a time in the West Village when I saw a gay checker in a deli whimsically remark to a mournful three-hundred-pound Middle Eastern immigrant, regarding his T-shirt: "Taurus—who knew?"

All around me, the city is literally vibrating, shot through with light.

I am so at peace with the world, it doesn't even phase me when a letter on official-looking LAUSD stationery flops through the mail slot.

I open it. Call Mike.

"Hannah got in . . . the magnet school!"

"Hurray!" he says.

"Oh my God. I thought the odds were like one in twenty-four hundred!"

"I know," Mike admits cheerfully. "Woo! You're telling me! That was a close one!"

"Right!"

"But I told you to trust me," he said. "Didn't I? And now that she's in the magnet, instead of going to the one hundred percent Mexican school, she can go to the fifty percent Mexican, fifty percent Armenian school."

"It's all good!" I reply. Is it?

10

Therapy Graduation, or My Dinner with Sandre

I am finally actually sitting in the cliffside home of my long-suffering therapist, Ruth. I am suspended in her glass box overhanging the rocks, while the Pacific Ocean crashes in thundering sprays below. Between sprays, you can hear the musical tinkle of the Zen fountain in the foyer just beyond.

I do not know if it is because I have been coming here for almost twenty years now, or because it is my last session, literally my therapy graduation, my final time here. But her house has already, oddly, started to feel like a memory to me. The gold-framed poster of Cezanne dancers, the African masks, the books by Jung . . .

It's as though it's a memory of a different time entirely. A time of my youth. When these totems of art, sculpture, literature held magic, a fond magic.

Or maybe this house just feels like a memory because so many of the artifacts are now literally in boxes. Stacks of books, crates, and

half-packed-up art stand around us, a Forest of Stuff we have nego-
tiated our way through to get to the familiar tan leather couches,
with the familiar white sheeps-ruggy things over the backs.

"These movers!" Ruth cries out, waving her hands and shaking
her head with a humorous look of wild exasperation. In person, she
is still the statuesque Grecian vase of a woman she has always been,
in beige caftan, with turquoise rings and silver bracelets and big geometric earrings, her wiry hair only slightly shot through at this point
with leonine streaks of white and gray. If anything, her skin seems
fixed in time, smooth, marble, yet elastic.

"Moving INTO Los Angeles, that costs practically nothing. But
moving out . . ." She gestures to a sculpture of a Native American
woman holding a baby in the cowl of a blanket. "Do you know how
much moving Manda alone will cost me?" Ruth refers to all her sculptures by first name. "Simply getting her to ferry to the island . . ."

The island she is referring to is in the San Juan Islands. After practicing therapy for several decades in Los Angeles, Ruth is finally
cashing out her giant Pacific Coast Highway "box of light"—that's
what she has always called it, her "box of light"—and moving to a
forty-acre compound up in a remote, forested area in Washington
State. It's part of a multimillion-dollar investment she has made with
several other baby boomers, a consortium made up of two other therapists, a restaurateur, an investment banker, a lawyer, a woman who
made her fortune in herbal muscle relaxation products . . .

"Herbal muscle relaxation?" I ask.

"Something like that," Ruth says, waving a hand. "There was
sadly a negative ruling by the FDA, completely unfair, totally on a
technicality . . ."

"What was the—the technicality?"

"Lab tests in Belgium had completely supported her company's
claims, but the Fed got different numbers . . . Fortunately, Dani has
been able to keep most of her money, but the whole experience left

her feeling very tired of the corporate world and of our government, which is so narrow-mindedly Western and anti-holistic."

Ruth shows me the white tabletop model for their compound, called Sanyassin.

"Sanyassin?" I ask.

"Yogic term for spiritual seeker. In your middle years, your 'householder' years, you are consumed with the duties of marriage, raising a family, and maintaining a household. But when that's done, after sixty, you move into the Sanyassin years. In Sanyassin, you meditate, you pursue your spiritual practice. If need be, you become a tribal elder, give advice. We will be blogging our political thoughts, poems, stories, and prayers for world peace on our Web site."

The plan for Sanyassin looks absolutely stunning. It is all waterfront, forest, skylights, decking, and dramatic angles. There is a movie theater, a steam room, a yoga studio, a greenhouse . . .

"And best of all . . ." Ruth says, flopping open a photo album of backup visuals. "Let's see, where is it?" The page falls open to a photo of what appears to be a terrifyingly fit sixty-something-year-old man with flowing white hair, a red bandana, and little tiny buckskin shorts standing arms and legs akimbo before what appears to be a bank of windmills. He is kind of like the cowboy, the outlaw, the pirate captain of wind energy.

"Oh, that's Thor," Ruth laughs. "He's our designer. He has already built a whole wind energy system in Sedona . . . Which is to say, Sanyassin will be ninety percent solar- and wind-energy-powered. Within two years, we will be ecologically self-sufficient. A surprisingly small carbon footprint."

She taps a spot on the map.

"And we've just started planting in this area. There is an experimental type of grape Renard—the restaurateur, he started Shallots in Berkeley—is planning to plant for the cultivation of our own wines. A Merlot, a Cabernet, and maybe, depending on moisture levels, a Pinot Noir." She taps another spot on the map. "This is already built. A small dairy farm, with cows and goats Renard has personally selected, to make our own cheeses.

"In fact," she says, "as it will be our last session together . . . Actually, until you ever come up to the San Juan Islands—and you must bring your children up! All that nature! They'll go crazy!

"Anyway, forget the tea. Let's drink some of this."

And she lifts out of a crate a bottle, with little pieces of straw falling off of it.

"It's—what? A 1984 Chateau de la Roi du Rhône . . ."

"Oh!" I exclaim. "A big nose, hints of chocolate and vanilla, very tanniny. With a giant caboose at the end."

"Yes!" she says in surprise.

"Pair with lamb. Aging potential of ten to fifteen years."

"Yes, yes . . ." she agrees.

"In short," I finish triumphantly, "the chateau is still reeling from it. It's a fruit bomb!"

"How did you know?" she marvels, sticking what appears to be a surgical instrument into the top of the wine. There is a muscular pop, a glug, and out she pours it, into large, twin pear-shape-bowled glasses.

"That's what I've been wanting to tell you," I say. "This is but one wine of eight I had at a wine tasting at some friends' of mine, Kent and Maria, like two years ago. I used to be so confused and slow-minded! I couldn't even put a to-do list together! But my memory for detail now—my recall—is incredible. Now I remember everything!"

"Wonderful!" she exclaims. "So it must be going well, then? Your new project? What is it—a book, a novel, a play? And oh, here's to being offered your job back at KCRW and not taking it—good for you," she exhorts, clanking her glass with mine. "I'll never get over what happened at KCRW. Really! In this time where Bush and his

Supreme Court are already clamping down on free speech, the last thing we need is for public radio to—"

I feel a weary glaze coming on and I hurriedly say, "Yes, thank goodness THAT'S over with—"

"Which leaves room for you to focus. To go back into your artistic zone. So . . . what's next?" She puts her glass down and leans forward, palms pressed together.

And once AGAIN I fear a weariness coming on. "I—I guess, well, I have a TV writing project I got called about. It's about obscenity, and the First Amendment . . ."

"Network?" She proffers a palm.

"Cable," I say.

"Cable." She proffers the same palm, implying no difference.

"Uh-huh," I say.

The other palm goes up. Now there are two palms. "Which you're conflicted about because I know how much you're bothered by the collaborative process—"

"No—"

"Aha. Something has changed. You are now COMFORTABLE with the collaborative—"

"I mean— I guess the thing is—" My voice is shrill. "I guess I don't really care that much about my Art anymore!"

Ruth stops. She reclines back into her tan leather armchair, ever so slowly, like a canny charmer backing away from a weaving cobra.

"I mean I care," I rush in, to mitigate the blow. "I guess I just don't feel like talking about it anymore. I'm forty-three years old, I've been at this creativity game now for twenty years, and . . . I guess I no longer consider it a tragedy to have a day when I don't create, nor some kind of stunning miracle to have a day when I do. You know? I'm a writer. I write. Some days are better, some days are worse, my career goes up, my career goes down, but if it's not working out at this point, I'd better just SHUT UP ABOUT IT ALREADY!"

I hone in on the poster behind Ruth, on Frida Kahlo—oy, there she is again! "I'm moving toward fifty!" I blurt out, feeling suddenly angry, and not sure quite at what. "Good Lord! I just want to GROW UP ALREADY!"

"Mm-hm," says Ruth, closing her eyes and putting her face into clasped-together hands. She slows down her breathing, and our conversation. "Tell me," she intones. "I'm listening."

There is a beat, during which the waves crash.

I take a harsh short breath.

I hate moments like this.

To calm myself, I reach into my bag and take out my knitting. Just touching the fluffy sapphire-colored wool, with its little red and violet spots, like hidden jewels, and unfolding the cascading foot-and-a-half length of my muffler, and its many satisfyingly even stitches . . . I instantly feel a lift.

I sit back on my chair and begin to absorbingly clack my needles.

"I certainly saw what a personal breakthrough you had via the whole KCRW incident," Ruth prompts. She waves a fist with a thumb in it. "Good for you!"

"I guess the main thing I have to report is that for once in my life I am incredibly happy," I reply. I have moved to the end of my row, which was almost finished, and now flip over the muffler and begin a new row. This new row picks up a little more of the violet, within the sapphire. The whole effect is very pleasing. It's such a kick-ass scarf.

"Really? How have you been sleeping?" Ruth asks, a bit pointedly.

"Much better now that I knit," I reply. "And if I do pop awake at two A.M., well, these days, I always have some kind of enjoyable project going—"

"NOT ON THE COMPUTER!" we say together, her warningly, me triumphantly.

"Exactly!" I say. "Only manual projects. Only working with my hands. No screen. And I must say, I'm so into knitting now. Oh my GOD, do I love my knitting. It's almost obscene how much I look forward to it. It makes me happy. Look at this scarf! Just looking at it makes me really, really happy. That's why I'm graduating from therapy after two decades. I'm just pretty . . . damn . . . happy."

"Well, hallelujah!" Ruth laughs, clapping her hands together, suddenly merry, pouring us each a second glass of wine. "Happy graduation! Marta? Can you bring out the—you know, the . . ."

"Yes, Mum," I hear the call.

And in a moment we are surprised with the most delectable cheeseboard. Ruth points. "This is a Triple Crème, this is Humboldt Fog, this appears to be a shingle of—"

"Ooh, a shingle," I say.

"Marta? I want to say a Gruyère. But aged. Very mellow."

"Oh!" I exclaim, feeling a stab of pleasure as I taste it. "With the wine—!"

"So tell me, my dear?" Ruth asks. "You have been coming to me since you were twenty-three. We've been together through the single phase, the married phase, the breaking-away-to-do-your-art phase, the now-you-are-blocked phase, then you wrote, then you had children, you came in with Mike, there were all those big sleep problems, then you were fired, now you are forty-three, what I call a midland journeyer . . . Why so happy now?"

She tilts her chin on her hand. I know I have the fullness of her attention, and the joy of being listened to rises within me. I have wine, I have cheese, I have my knitting—there is nothing not perfect in my universe.

"Well, because . . . Actually, it's rather Oprah-esque," I reply. "I have finally had my mid-forties . . . Al-Gore-standing-on-a-dune-in-his-shirtsleeves moment."

"I LOVE him!" Ruth groans, hugging herself as she falls backward into her chair. "Now, now, now THIS is the Al Gore I always knew was WITHIN. The twenty-first-century Al Gore is like Atlas . . . unleashed! If only I had been his therapist when he was running for president! Remember what we talked about when you were fired?

And I told you about the—" Here she balls her fist up. "The fuck you! Did you see *An Inconvenient*—"

"No, I didn't, but I heard it's very good," I say quickly, not wanting to lose the thread. As much as I deeply admire Al Gore for his bold breaking-away/standing-on-a-dune-in-his-shirtsleeves moment, I do not wish to share my therapy session with Al Gore. Or global warming.

Ruth makes a note. *"Inconvenient Truth.* I'll give you the DVD—"

I wrench the conversation back to my point: "Anyway, the point is I ADMIRE Al Gore because of his dune-in-shirtsleeves moment."

"Because—?" she asks. "What does that moment mean to you?"

"Well? It is the moment when you stand on a shore and you confront your humanity. It is the moment you turn your life to . . . service. Is that possible? Does that make sense? SERVICE."

"Go on."

"I have . . . I have . . . Well, my happiness has come from thinking of myself less as a competitive individual in a footrace I can never win, and more as part of a beautiful mass social undertaking, like building a cathedral that will live on after me."

"Cathedral?"

"Okay, well, here it goes." I put my knitting in my lap, to focus. "It's like the cathedral is democracy. Which looks beautiful from a distance, say one hundred years later. But on a day-by-day basis, building the cathedral of democracy isn't pretty. Feh! Democracy—when you really experience it—can be tedious, poorly lit, and not always charismatic. It's about getting one hundred little raffle tickets in on time, because democracy is made not with one big check but with many small nickels. It's—well—about waiting in line at the DMV."

"The spiritual 'aha,'" Ruth continues, picking up the thread. "That's very medieval. Very archetypal. Many of the female Catholic saints . . . You know how much I love . . ." And here she gestures to a tiny wooden gold-embossed painting above her. "Catherine of Thiels."

"Catherine of Thiels?" I ask.

"A very obscure saint," Ruth says. "Some even argue Catherine of Thiels was never properly canonized. The Belgians—!" She puts her hands up. "Anyway."

"Where IS Thiels?"

Ruth nods, with the anger of it.

"Exactly!"

"No, I mean I really don't know."

"Thiels was a very, very small medieval town that had only, like, limited flax production. Maybe some herring. Some wool dying. That was the problem. It wasn't really an important town."

"But for her witchcraft they burned her!" I exclaim, anticipating the story, making my "Fuck you!" fist.

"Noooo," Ruth answers, draining her wineglass. "Catherine didn't die. She lived to a ripe old age, which in those days was thirty-seven. But she was known for doing countless good works— ministering to orphans, teaching them the domestic crafts, bringing food to the poor . . . Catherine was known widely for her exquisite needlework—"

"I guess it's true that that doesn't sound very—"

"But the point is, an angel came to her. She had a transformative experience. Before she was simply a merchant's wife—she was count-ing his money and supplies, in a tower in Thiels. But then—as the story goes—the angel comes to Catherine and tells her to put down her coins in the counting house and to SERVE THE WORLD— And hundreds of other people SAW the angel, apparently there were witnesses—"

"I guess it's still a kind of borderline . . . I thought to be a saint you had to be burned at the stake—"

Ruth puts her palms up. "Like I said. There's still a debate."

I place my knitting in my basket and stand up to study Catherine. But my attention keeps getting pulled away to the burning eyes of Frida.

"Ruth? Frida Kahlo— For me, she has become kind of the Coca-Cola sign of— Can I—?" I make a twirling motion with my hands.

"Of course," Ruth replies. "It's just a reproduction. Put her face down on the couch if you want. The movers will anyway."

I carefully lift Frida off a hook, balance her on my hip to give her one last close look . . . and suddenly I'm yelling.

"I guess I'm just tired of Frida Kahlo's crazy-ass buggy eyes lookin' at me from every espresso bar and museum calendar and drink coaster! You had some responsibility for your own happiness too, Frida!" I am holding her before me and yelling right at her! "Diego Rivera—that old drunkard you stood by, he has shit to answer for! Not ME!" My words are a little slurry, but I feel I'm in an utterly safe space.

"I'm going to use the loo," Ruth says. "Have a look at Catherine. Take your time. If you look closely, you'll see she's really quite wonderful."

I tilt Frida against the wall and pick up Catherine instead, the small would-be Catholic saint, a quiet package, medieval, weathered old oils, gold-embossed. I have come to this office for twenty years. How is it I have come here for so many years and never seen this?

The small painting, not more than a ten-by-ten box, shows a tiny woman, in a fluttery white head veil, kneeling before an altar in her small green, red, and blue medieval bedroom. Around her knees, on the floor, are ordinary household items—baskets of fruit, loaves of bread, a jug of wine, spilled coins, possible needlework, and is that a satchel of knitting? Knitting!

It's either knitting or a set of slightly scary medieval dental instruments, perhaps for fixing the teeth of the poor, which in medieval times, you have to admit, would be a daunting prospect.

An angel of indeterminate gender, with brown pageboy haircut, is less leaping through the saint's twin open peaked medieval windows than sort of dancing forward to Catherine. In one hand, he/she holds a slender gold trumpet, which he/she blows, and in the other he/she proffers various items: a sceptre of some kind, a small booklet on a chain bearing ornate medieval letters, and some sort of . . . almost slightly military breastplate—

I look more carefully into the small white face of the angel, with her wide-set brown eyes, and small tipped nose, and realize, in a *2001: A Space Odyssey* hallucinogenic flash moment, the light around me smearing into tunnels, that, oh my God, it's—

"Joan from Valley Co-Op! Oh my God! The angel! It's Joan! It's Joan!" I exclaim in amazement. And Catherine—the face of Catherine also looks like Joan! And all those household objects around her . . . the needlework, the scissors . . . Probably in another basket around the bed are raffle tickets for the Spring Jamboree! Which Catherine/Joan was probably known for, in Thiels, and people were probably tired of the Jamboree . . . Which is why, no doubt, she didn't land the saint thing.

"Oh good Lord," the bishops probably said. "Do we have to give it to Joan? That's probably what she would love. Sainthood! Joan!"

And in an automatic move, to calm myself, I reach for my knitting, but looking at my own knitting basket, I realize . . .

I look back at the painting . . .

"Oh my God," I exhale, almost hyperventilating. "I literally feel like I'm plunging into some sort of a Hunter S. Thompson acid trip, where the room is hot, and forms and colors are unusually vivid—!"

"Which is very common in perimenopause," Ruth says sympathetically, returning. "Unless treated with medication."

"In this painting, I see myself! And I realize . . . I am also Joan!"

"Yes," Ruth says breathlessly, dropping back into her chair. "Yes? Joan of Arc?"

"Well, yes/no/I suppose/maybe!" I cry out. "I realize I, too, have knelt at a small medieval chapel in the middle of my life, in Thiels—"

"In Van Nuys," Ruth says.

"Exactly. An unremarkable town. We, too, are not known for anything. And anyway, in the echoing shallows of my forties—which in Catherine's case would have been the echoing shallows of her late twenties—"

"What with the speeded-up medieval hormonal—"

"Whatever. Exactly. I realized, in the middle of my life, I, too, have had the experience of the angel coming to me, blowing her trumpet, and calling me out of my regular life!"

"Who was that angel?" Ruth asks breathlessly.

"Well, unfortunately, the angel was Joan. Of the Parents for Public Schools. Who I call the Parents Fools. And also her husband, Walt, who looks like a kindly ferret and who came bearing a great many gloomy books by Jonathan Kozol."

Ruth puts her hand on her turquoise caftan chest.

"Oh, dear."

"That's right," I say bitterly. "Unfortunately, like Catherine, my angel was the Angel of Social Work. And that Jonathan Kozol . . . Good Lord—have you read his books? All those poor, black, inner-city children in their hopeless public schools. And the government not DOING anything about it, decade after decade. GOD, are his books depressing."

"Hm," Ruth says. "Not so good for the insomnia, I gather."

"Exactly," I say. "I sometimes think Pfizer should invent the antidepressant Zokol, for help after reading Kozol. At one point I was going to put all my Jonathan Kozol books into a wicker basket like orphaned kittens and I was going to bring them to you to help me drown them. I've felt at certain times, the Parents for Public Schools— my new cause, all those earnest people—have been this load I've been

CARRYING. It's like I'm CARRYING the Angel, who is so heavy, so heavy—"

Ruth leans forward excitedly. "That's another famous Catherine of Thiels image! Where she is shown walking from city to city CAR-RYING the Angel— Oh, where are my sacred art books—" She wheels about herself, looking. "Of course, they're all PACKED already— But where Catherine's CARRYING the Angel— In some versions, the Angel is literally riding on her back—"

"The Angel of Social Work," I repeat bitterly. "I call it the Way of the Flat Brown Shoes. Sometimes I wonder why I was assigned this Angel. Sometimes this Angel is an Angel I want to throw back. I live in Los Angeles, for crying out loud! I mean, I'd so rather be saddled with the Angel of Global Warming. The Angel of PETA! The Angel of Free Speech—"

"You DID carry that Angel—" Ruth points out.

"Ah yes, Freedom of Speech—in Los Angeles, it's among the most popular of our amendments. The First, that's the Jennifer Aniston of the amendents, whereas the Second Amendment—the right to bear arms—not so much. Well, at least I didn't get the Angel of the SEC-OND Amendment, which is probably more like a demon on a Harley. In my neck of the woods, the Second Amendment is almost as unpopular as public education."

"Well, you're the Freedom of Speech queen!"

"For five minutes I was. But that was a whole year ago. At a recent party I saw my old *Times* editor, Josh, who said, 'Now I hear you're a public-school activist. Good for you. Rah rah rah,' he finished, and then his wrist fell, desultorily, toward the sushi plate.

" 'Sandra's for the public schools?' said another editor. 'Yes, appar-ently she thinks we're all evil for having our kids in private school,' said this other NPR journalist and now they all descended on me in a mob, like a gang in *West Side Story,* looking for blood. They all jab their champagne flutes moralistically at me because I'm not writing enough about global warming! Oh sure, their kids may be sequestered from our ninety-eight percent Hispanic, free and reduced-lunch elementaries by going to the twenty-two-thousand-dollar a year Willowwood School—"

"Willowwood?"

"Yes, Willowwood is really into honoring diversity—they have to 'honor' it because they don't actually have it. Their 'diversity' looks like fourteen white kids and madly-tapping Savion Glover. The kids never see brown people because while Willowwood teens have ridden the Metro in Paris and the London Underground, they would never dare set foot on a bus in L.A. Last year the senior diversity 'retreat'—retreat *from* diversity, more like it—was going to Santa Barbara to see the movie *Crash*."

"Well—"

"And these journalists have no shame! They aren't embarrassed at all! Oh no, they're so proud that they gave canned food for the tsunami and that Willowwood School recycles! And I'm yelling, 'How dare you try to jump your hybrid Lexus SUV over my Mexican kindergarten ass!' "

Ruth moves us to the hot tub on the deck. Marta lays out plates and silverware, platters of Thai food appear.

"So now the charisma is draining out of me and I'm literally starting to feel hobbled by my cause, the Angel of Public School. Utter even the phrase 'public school' and rooms clear. This Angel is like a little social-working Blue Nun for whom I am merely her driver. I work for this Angel—I follow her dour instructions. The other week I was delivering a stack of old computer printers for her to an address some tired public-school teacher wrote down wrong, one digit off.

"And I'm screaming while trolling down Slausen, 'Shit, shit, shit! Someone ELSE should be helping the poor! They're called BOOTSTRAPS—ever HEARD of them? At forty-three I should be sampling Chardonnays in wine country!'

"My gift is charm, and the people you meet along the Way of the Flat Brown Shoes are impervious to charm. I got the wrong Angel! I'm so horribly ill-suited to be carrying around this Angel! I could have had the Angel of . . . of neutering puppies. I could have a cable show about puppies. Because I'm a type A person. I'm used to getting an idea, making a plan, and swiping the VISA card to make it happen. But no, in the public-school world you have to work with the system. I signed up to volunteer to teach reading at a Van Nuys elementary. I expect some kind of medal, because I'm so fabulous, and I've given up my whole glamorous former life and instead, this tired volunteer coordinator's first words out to me, as she tosses me a ten-page-long application to be a volunteer, are:

" 'YOU need to get a tetanus shot!' "

"There ARE all those rules and regulations," Ruth murmurs, heaping pad Thai on our plates. "I certainly remember those from when I did therapy in the women's prisons."

"And God!" I cry out, with my mouth full of pad Thai. "The fluorescent lighting in public schools! The linoleum. The putty-colored buildings! The chain-link fence! The crispy grass! *Queer Eye* or somebody really needs to come up and do a makeover!"

Ruth lifts her fork.

"Don't forget that in this corporate age, that 'third place,' 'the public square,' that place where we feel most comfortable is Starbucks. Starbucks!"

"Exactly!" I say. "My generation . . . our psyches, our aesthetics have become totally Starbucks-ized! I expect every space I enter to look like Starbucks. I walk into a room and expect to be immediately bathed in earth tones, track lighting, and a story on a chalkboard about how far organically grown Costa Rican beans have traveled to see me, me, me . . . Along with an adult contemporary remix of something jazzy with John Coltrane on the cover, to make me feel better about myself, like I am somehow consorting with Black History Month while slurping my hazelnut latte . . . That to me has become *normal.* By contrast, our humble and drab public schools cannot even expect to *compete* with such exquisitely honed, consumer-targeted architectural design. All the fluorescent lighting of our public schools! The drooping American flags! Such a cumbersome design, the American flag! The jangling primary colors, and that mess of stripes! It depresses! It harkens back to the dull school assemblies of one's childhood! It feels visually discordant! And wrong!"

Ruth is now pouring us two glasses of "a very dry rosé. It's the new rosé. Open your mind. Give it a try!"

"Oh my goodness," I exclaim. "That combined with the pad Thai. It's perfect."

"What to drink with Thai food has always been a puzzle for me. But Renard explained it to me . . . Never mind. Go ON. The point is . . . You began by saying . . . YOU WERE HAPPY."

"Yes, because in the meantime, I realize I've actually been on an extraordinary ADVENTURE. Through the clanking, integrational government machinery of my daughter's LAUSD magnet school—"

"Wait a minute. Didn't you tell me on the phone how much you loved the elementary down the street?"

"I did!" I said. "With the gay assistant principal! But the very next day we got a letter saying we also got into the magnet, which is K through 12, so Mike said we'd better go."

"Magnet? Hannah got into a magnet? Don't you have to test gifted to get into those?"

"No, no, no!" I exclaim. "Here's the beauty. In L.A., the magnet system was started in the seventies to kind of"—here I make a circular hand motion as though I am stirring a pot—*"swirl around* the races. It's about racial *swirling around.* Kids get assigned magnet points based on how heavily minority and overcrowded their home schools are, and then they mix *these* kids together in magnet schools— the kids from high-minority overcrowded schools, like so many of the ones we have in Van Nuys—"

"So your magnet school is more racially integrated than the one down the street?" Ruth asks, massaging her temples.

"Sort of," I say. "In Hannah's kindergarten class of twenty, she's still the only blonde. But instead of just Hispanic immigrants, our brown children come from many, many countries. Not that Mexico and Peru and El Salvador are the *same* country, but—"

"And . . ." Ruth waves her pen, trying to find a through line. "Growing up in Malibu in the sixties, you were the lone brown kid in a sea of white."

"Exactly!"

"But your magnet school is more affluent than—"

"No, no, no!" I retort. "It's poor! It's Title One! It's fifty-nine percent free and reduced lunch! It's practically all immigrants living in apartments, but instead of just poor Hispanic families, there are Hispanic mixed with Armenian, Middle-Eastern, Russian, Filipino . . . Often I don't know WHAT the hell they are . . . And one day I realized they don't know what I am, either—how could they? I look like the Third World nanny to my blond daughter, so it was up to me to be the welcome wagon! I would have to strap on my fear-of-rejection social armor! I would have to hurl myself across the cultural divide!"

"Very empowering," Ruth agrees, spreading sauce for the spring rolls.

"Which can at first be jarring. At Hannah's magnet school, for the first few months, I felt like I was continually crossing the parking lot behind a cabal of what seemed to be perpetually disapproving-looking mothers, who were always chattering almost secretively together in another language. So one day, just before getting to my car, I turned to the group and—as though hurling my body before bullets—asked them, point blank, 'So . . . What language are you speaking?'

"And the head disapproving mom—whom I called their union boss—stops, in surprise, then puts her hand on my arm and says,

'Oh, honey, it is Armenian!' And I realize Hasmik is actually very warm. She will give you the sweater off her generous meaty back. She just has . . . Anxious Armenian Face. And then we all went belly-dancing at the Y!"

"How marvelous!" Ruth exclaims. "I love belly-dancing!"

"And then there was the school bus incident." I put my rosé down to steady myself, at the traumatic memory. "We'd had our babysitter Nan over so Mike and I could get some work done and go out for dinner. We'd walked Nan to the bus twice, she knows where it is, it's three-fifteen, Nan says she'll go to the corner to pick up Hannah . . .

"And twenty minutes later, she calls us on her cell phone in a panic. 'Hannah did not get off the bus! Hannah has disappeared!' And now I freak out and jump into the minivan and go screaming through the neighborhood— And you remember our neighborhood, right? We're in Van Nuys! I'm screaming past the tattered pupuserias, ninety-nine-cent stores—"

Ruth puts her hand over her heart.

"And then it occurs to me to actually drive past the school bus stop, in front of Van Nuys Elementary. And catty-corner from the bus stop, I can see Nan running the wrong way up the street and weeping—I guess she got her directions confused—"

"Yes?" Ruth whispers, hand still over her heart.

"And right where she's supposed to be, on the steps of Van Nuys Elementary, I see Hannah sitting calmly with what I might previously have assumed to be a chunky gang girl, with a pierced nose, gold cross, and black tank top. They are sitting very quietly, chatting, holding hands.

"And I run up to this teen girl and scream, 'Thank YOU for waiting with my daughter!' And the Hispanic teen says in a high, soft voice, almost as though mildly insulted, 'This is what I *always* do. I *always* wait with the little kids.' And I drive this girl—her name is Monica—home and she lives just off Vanowen Boulevard in one of those teeny bungalow units, with the couch on the front porch, and a giant hanging carpet of the Virgin of Guatemala.

"And now her mother, Teresa, who speaks very limited English, invites us to a 'posada'! Meaning on Saturday night they will come to our house for ten minutes and sing, like, Mexican carols or something! They will play Joseph and Mary, and we will play the innkeepers who will deny them. Three times. In Spanish. And Saturday night sixty Hispanic people walked up to our porch, holding candles, singing— It's so very beautiful— And we all sing the printed lyrics together in Spanish, and even as the denying innkeeper—'Yo, Jose, even though you're a humble *carpinterio,* no *molestar'*—I couldn't help flashing a huge smile at everybody, as if to say, 'This is all really . . . so very, very fabulous!'

"Then we walked to Teresa's house, where she'd laid out a simple meal of tamales and pozole soup for seventy. And there in back is the giant, illegal iron springs pointing everywhere . . . Homer Simpson trampoline. And as if in a dream, I find myself jumping on it with eleven kids, five Chihuahuas, and three chickens.

"And then mariachis come, and they play 'Cielito Lindo,' and everyone dances and I think . . . The violin! I love the violin! Why in this competitive Western culture do we always have to sit around frozen while some eight-year-old gifted monkey prodigy, the son of lawyers, plays Suzuki for us? Music should be a group activity! And P.S.: Violins, we should have those in public school! Violins in the schools!

"And then I wrote a grant, I brought all these violins to our little fifty-nine percent free and reduced lunch school . . ."

"How marvelous!" Ruth exclaims, eyes wide. "Good for you!"

"Except that did you know violins come in different sizes?" I chatter on. "My mistake was that violins don't just come in full size, they come in three-quarters, one-half, one-fourth, one-eighth, one-tenth, one-sixteenth, and even, God help us, one-thirty-second.

Ahhhhh! For a second, I feared my Violins in the Schools project was going to culminate with me, a wild-eyed mother, staggering out onto a school campus, opening her tiny violin case, and taking out the world's teeniest Uzi—!

"But the point was, I fixed the problem, I re-ordered the violins in the right sizes, and I now feel very empowered that I can write a grant and fill out forms and that I am not afraid of bureaucracy!"

" 'Not afraid of bureaucracy'!"

"That's another thing! I've learned bureaucracy isn't necessarily boo! some evil thing. It's just paperwork. I'm a writer! I can fill out forms! I'm becoming a kind of paperwork *dominatrix*. In fact, I've come to believe that government—and laws—are really interesting! Sometimes when plant managers or similar cite 'bureaucracy' as an obstacle, that's just code for 'I don't feel like it.' 'Bureaucracy' is just a convenient metaphor for personal futility, like 'big'! I'm so into . . ." I throw out my arms in excitement, sending little glass noodles scattering. Marta kneels to scoop them up. "CITIZENSHIP!"

" 'Government is interesting,' " Ruth repeats wonderingly, writing another thing in her notepad.

"And in discovering ever new ways in which these wheels and dials fit together, from the personal to the political to—to the *community at large,* the big democratic *cathedral* . . . It's like I'm on some kind of high!"

"Why do you suppose that is?" Ruth asks, lifting some small pastries off a dessert tray.

"Because after four decades I have found myself."

"And who are you?" Ruth says, pouring limoncello into two perfect tiny glasses.

"Well, the answer goes back to the damn bra ball."

"Which you called me about. You couldn't burn your bra because you have too many . . ."

"Last year I went to this Auberge in Napa, which had this patio upon which the women would relax after their treatments. And what has stayed with me is the image of all of us women lying in our white robes, with cucumbers over our eyes, while wind chimes play. And it has occurred to me that for the past decade or so I've been asleep. I think so many women of my generation have. We've been lying in state, Sleeping Beauties, paraffin-wrapped on biers of three hundred-thread Percale sheets, ringed by eucalyptus aromatherapy candles and soporific fans of *Real Simple*. I actually had a four-handed massage! Did I tell you? A four-handed massage!"

I take a sip of the limoncello. "Wow! Fabulous!"

Ruth is writing: "You're lying on a bier of aromatherapy . . ."

"Yes—the bier!" I say. "Not that this is unpleasant, but in my mid-forties, old as the women's movement itself—I like to say I feel as old as Betty Friedan's hair—I realize I am bored to death with this life of *consuming*. I'm tired of being an obedient participant in this, the high-water period of feminism's Condé Nast–icization . . . a weird Island of Dr. Moreau–like union of feminism with capitalism where our Self-hood—or *Self* magazine-hood—boils down to two questions: One, how am I feeling? And two, what should I buy? You know? Instead of 'I think, therefore I am,' it's 'I feel, therefore I buy'—or in mothers' cases, 'I *fear*, therefore I buy.' So when we high-five each other, 'You go, girl!,' it's all about splurging on a fabulous pair of Jimmy Choos, chugging that third Cosmo, or shimmying onto the dance floor for some *sizzling salsa*. Which I'm not against, but I have to say so many decades in, I am bored to death with the frantic hamster-on-a-wheel cycles of losing weight! buying things! oh my God! eucalpytus candle! Several decades in, I am now thoroughly exfoliated. I have run out of product to spray into my hair!

"In this capito-feminist era, it seems there's no female desire that can't be granted by VISA . . . Be it the dream bra, dream sandal, dream lipstick, dream couch, dream neighborhood, dream kinder-garten, or even dream friends. But what we forget is that women are the very people who've always had the gift of being able to creatively imagine—and ingeniously fashion—their own lives, relations, and communities. Women used to impact not just sales but the world!

"And what I realize is that I'm tired of being a napping, well-creamed girl. I'm so bored of looking at myself in the mirror. It's been decades now. When will the tedium end? Fuck it! I want to paint on the big canvas now. To be a pioneer woman. To construct a log cabin with my own two hands. Maybe kill a bear. I smell the heady salt air of people unmet and sights unseen. I yearn to be, from my own bloated navel, Outward Bound. Because it appears that I am grown up now. I have tools. I have skills. I can pick up a telephone. I can paint a mural! I can do things!"

Ruth pumps a fist supportively in the air and madly writes in her notepad.

"Look at Anna Karenina," I say finally. "In the end, she was just bored. After she lands Vronsky, it's just four hundred pages of boredom. Four hundred pages of buying stuff. That is the true meaning of . . . her little red handbag. She jumps under the train, leaves the handbag."

"That so?" says Ruth.

"And even better," I say, "I have found my community."

"Your community!" she exclaims.

"Yes! Do you remember that old Woody Allen routine where a television hypnotist convinces a member of his studio audience that he is a fire engine? After pooh-poohing the bit, Woody Allen goes to sleep, only to wake up in the middle of the night with an irresistible urge to don red pajamas and bolt into the street. Block after block, he is joined by other equally excited men in red pajamas, running—they decide giddily to join forces, and off they sprint together to find the fire. This has been my experience—while much of my brown-shoe public-school journey has been unspeakably drab and vexing, over and over again, at the eleventh hour—what with the 'You need a tetanus shot!'—I'll meet a complete stranger consumed with the exact same fever dream. It's like reliving, over and over again, the adrenaline rush of your best-ever eHarmony/match.com, where thirty seconds into lunch you're literally screaming your mutual enthusiasm, grabbing each other's wrists like pincers while becoming instantly FRIENDS FOR LIFE."

Ruth does not recall the Woody Allen routine. "I can't quite follow—"

"It's like in the movie *Close Encounters,* where you keep coming across a new person, sitting in a diner, making that same tower-shaped pile of mashed potatoes."

"I still don't recall the Woody Allen—"

"Oh, forget Woody Allen. I used to love him, but now I feel so betrayed by him. He's just an elite Manhattanite pedophile whose children—what are their names, Satchel? Snatchel?—will never mix with the rest of us."

"It's true many of us feel betrayed by Woody Allen."

"If he lived in L.A., he'd probably send his kids to Campbell Hall. Episcopalian, ponies, like seventy percent Jewish. As I like to say, in Los Angeles we have three types of Jews, Orthodox, Reform, and Equestrian."

"Ha-ha," she notes. "I still don't understand the point about the fire engine."

I take another slug of limoncello and enjoy the burning. "Argh!"

"This cheesecake is fabulous," Ruth says, carefully lifting a slab onto my plate.

I press on: "What I mean is that, in my travels, I've discovered I'm far from alone in craving a more epic female life. Every day I've met a new woman waking up from her Sleeping Beauty bier. The experience has been tarot card–like, Middle Aged, Chaucerian, a veritable *Canterbury Tales.* There are all sorts of visions women are waking up to. In my case, on my particular journey, many of the women I've met along the way—Joan, Brenda, even Aimee—they all did not begin as but, after going through the fire, BECAME public-school mothers. Even Aimee, uptight Aimee, was so shattered and angry by seeing the inside of Wonder Canyon, she has quit her job to start her own gifted charter thingy . . ."

"Gifted charter wha—?" Ruth asks, lifting up her page to go back in her notebook. She is starting to look tired. I glance at her watch and with startlement realize we have been talking for three and a half hours. Thank God I'm not paying for this!

"And look what we're building!" I exclaim. "The cornerstone of democracy—it's Jeffersonian! Good public schools EVERYWHERE! Knowledge is for EVERYONE, not just for a precious few. And it's not a grim old Jonathan Kozol that's going to make it happen, it's the mothers! And it's so *counterintuitive*! Look at what we were up against!

"Surely, when historians look back on early-twenty-first-century America, they will see that educated mothers were overwhelmingly conditioned for fear. For us—they will note—daily life felt like a pulse-pounding jockeying for position in a fragile bubble floating slightly above a yawning maw of unsolvable ills, a senseless *Mad Max* movie of destruction. Down below, on the ground, there was no longer any village, of Hillary Clinton fame. No, the village was in smoking ruins, thanks to Bush's tax cuts and suburban sprawl and Proposition Thirteen and, you know, all that dependence on foreign oil. Foreign oil! Alone in the world as mothers, even our first breast-feeding crisis—"

"Which you even called me about—the engorgement—"

"Exactly. Engorgement. Too much milk—no place for it to go! What a metaphor! So you hit your first breast-feeding crisis, and instead of being able to place an emergency call to Grandma, it is all the VISA-wielding mother can do to place a call to an eighty-dollar-an-hour lactation consultant from the Booby Station! And after that first swipe of the VISA, it gets ever easier to parent that way, to have things FedExed up to the Parental Fear bubble—the *Baby Einstein* videos, the organic wheat-free crackers, the leafy-walled 'progressive' schools where the other bubble students are handpicked, to avoid infection from the down-there *Mad Max* feral children—who also, famously, bully. Which is not allowed in the bubble. Nor is puberty. Such is my generation's aversion to middle school that it's as though middle schoolers have become their own unwanted ethnicity. We only hope that with today's medical advances, the unsightliness of puberty is a kind of temporary allergy that CAN be nutritionally treated.

"But no. That's why these Mothers on Fire, running about together, chasing the fire engine? They are breaking the Darwinian mold. Breaking from the pack. They are doing the opposite of what statisticians would predict. Instead of cliché affluent lives of anxiety, paranoia, narcissism, and buying overpriced baby products online, modern motherhood has catapulted us atop a roaring new tsunami of optimism and oxytocin—old school, archetypal, biological! It is the ancient statue, the stone urn, the giant pair of Venus of Willendorf breasts shooting out milk to feed the entire planet! You haven't lived until you've seen a euphoric, seemingly forty-seven-week-pregnant mother wielding a sledgehammer to break ground on a new 'teaching garden' at the hideously scrubby L.A. Unified school she has determined her as-yet-unborn child will attend in five years, along with one thousand poor neighborhood immigrant children. 'Jesus—that's a sledgehammer!' you yell, but the cosmos always seems to protect them, the crazy and the pregnant . . ."

There is a slight glazed-over quality to Ruth's eyes, which may be the wine. For a second I feel I remember that glaze—the glaze in the eyes of the parents at Valley Co-Op Preschool, watching Joan as she first gave that *Lord of the Rings*/frantic troll speech. Before any of us became brave—or frankly desperate—enough to join.

Before I realized that *optimism* is the only *worldview* our family can afford.

"It's about trust," I implore. "Trust between humans. In all those private-school tours I took, they kept stressing how the head of the school said hello each morning to all the children, how the parents were all on a first-name basis, how it was like a small-town 'community.' At twenty thousand dollars a year. Community apparently being something we have to buy now. You have to pay twenty thousand dollars so a teacher will say hello. We've put a price tag on this. People no longer have the trust that *everyone* simply deserves this.

"Because that's what it feels like to live in the parenting fear bubble, which so afflicts my generation, where you have . . .

"Loss of trust in people.

"Loss of trust in children.

"Loss of trust in the universe.

"But the opposite pole of Fear is Love, I tell you! Love! Love is everywhere!" I spread my arms. "Community—LOVE—is everywhere! We can go from fear to love, from consumer to citizen, from a sense of scarcity to a sense of . . . abundance!

"Of course, we may just fear everything because we're so damn fragile. What happened to us? We're so high up on the pyramid of needs, we simply can't function anymore. We ask, 'How am I feeling about my job? Is it fulfilling me spiritually, mentally, physically?' as opposed to the Guatemalan person who is cleaning our house, thinking, 'Can I catch the eight o'clock bus home or the eight-thirty?' "

I draw a sketch on a napkin.

Parental anxieties: A timeline

Pre-1800s	Potato famine, death of entire villages
1900s	Trying to keep dad's job through depression so entire family does not starve or have to sell off children to agribusiness
2000	Infringement of Parenthood on sense of Personhood

"And at bottom of all this parental consumerism is a lack of hope. Mothers today, we must plan our three-year-old's K-through-12 future because my family is alone. There will be no help. Other families are only there to compete. Our boats sail alone. It's a time of apocalypse. Choked by money, people have literally lost their faith. But in fact, my child was never in kindergarten danger. Trying to save Hannah, trying to get her onto the last helicopter out of Saigon, I lost hold of the rope and fell. Not knowing there was a safety net below the whole time. There was a gossamer infinite spider's web of love, Charlotte's, stitched together by the hands of women, many invisible hands."

I finally stop talking.

We sit absolutely still before the darkened Pacific.

Ruth finally breaks the silence.

"Dear heart," she says, "it's called the manic defense against despair. I'm giving you a prescription for an antidepressant, and the name of an extraordinary Waldorf school in Pasadena run by my former Jungian colleague Rebecca. Not expensive."

Her words are like a record-needle scratch.

"Have you not understood even one word I've said!" I shriek.

Ruth grabs both my hands in hers. "Listen to me. You don't understand. Times have changed. I've lived in Los Angeles all my life. When I was a teenager I rode the bus all the time. But things are different today. No one rides the bus."

"Three hundred thousand ride the bus in Los Angeles every day!" I shoot back in disbelief. "Who are they? I guess the same ephemeral three thousand ghost shapes who go to high school at—at GRANT!"

"That's why I'm moving out of state, dear heart," Ruth says sadly. "Over the years I've been practicing, I've seen our society get much more crass than it was. In the sixties, people were idealistic. And we had great leadership. JFK, Martin Luther King! There was change in the air. But today . . . That's why we're moving up north. I don't know that there's any hope anymore. People are like animals. There's no decency. Look at Bush—with this No Child Left Behind!"

"We love our tattered little public school!" I shrieked.

"It's irresponsible to keep Hannah there," Ruth says. "You know how delicate YOU'VE been. It's only decades of therapy that has helped you. In a No Child Left Behind environment, your child will be crushed."

"I cannot even believe after over four hours this is where we've ended up!"

"Oh dear heart, don't beat yourself up," Ruth murmurs comfortingly, lifting up a prescription written on Glaxa stationery. "You're a mother. Of course you're obsessed with schools. Motherhood does narrow one's focus."

And at that moment my Fuck You comes out.

I sweep aside the wineglasses, the cheeses, the pastries, the pad Thai.

"You . . . You . . . You . . . You!" I say, getting up. I wave my arms wildly. I feel as though I could start smashing books, sculptures. I could take paintings and snap them in two, right over my leg.

"Oh my God!" Ruth exclaims at the violence of my movements. "Marta!"

Marta rushes over, but I have a brilliant light pouring off my head and I am unstoppable.

"THE BOOMERS ARE TO BLAME!!!!" I scream.

"It all started under your watch! All that busing—and fleeing—began in the seventies, when, excuse me, it was YOUR generation who were just becoming parents. Rosa Parks . . . Of course her grandchildren can sit anywhere on the bus now—they can have the whole damn bus . . . Because all you former Freedom Marchers just speed along on an entirely different freeway system in hybrid SUVs!

"You boomers have presided over the greatest decline, the greatest return to public-school segregation in U.S. history. Consumers rather than citizens—it is entirely your doing!

"You boomers have ALWAYS been in Sanyassin! When have you not been in Sanyassin? Even raising children you were in Sanyassin! Wake up and smell the Sanyassin!"

I lean over the tiny wooden model of Sanyassin. "Where is that fucking steam room? Where is that fucking meditation room? Where is that fucking yoga room? Stop doing yoga! I destroy your yoga room! We—the next generation—are poking our faces up against the windows of your yoga room, trying to get your attention to yell . . . FUUUUUCKKKK YOUUUUUUUUUUUUUUUUUUUUUU!"

"Ah!" Ruth screams, cowering with Marta.

I yell out: "Don't fucking medicate me with chamomile herbal tea packets . . . And FEAR!!!!!!!!!"

My whole body vibrating over the little white tabletop model of Sanyassin, I make the violent irreversible decision. Defiantly I—I . . . put my thumb through the thin Styrofoam walls of the yoga room!

"Aiiieee!!!!!!!" Ruth screams.

11
Surf's Up

So here we are, gathered as always near summer's end, on the beach in Malibu.

Our family and a ring of Malibu surf dudes, a melange of white-blond hair and wet suits twisting off their bodies, amputated arms and legs. We sit in a circle in the cooling sand, before the great cyclorama of the sky, which is fired with orange, purple, red, and blue, and a tumbling abundance of puffy clouds, a splendid coil of fantastical shapes.

The earth is cooling, in the evening of this day, the last gasps of balmy summer air simmering, in waves, across the dunes and ocean.

It's the after-burn.

The burn is gone.

The heat is off.

At the far edge of our circle is an old surfer guy, in a knit cap, so crusty he literally looks covered in fine powder. His whitened hair and skin look perhaps like what those Easter Island–like heads would look like after a yearlong sandstorm. He sits in a ragged beach chair and plays a beat-up guitar.

He appears to be playing an old Beach Boys tune, "Surfer Girl."

It sounds slightly mad and cacophonic, on his out-of-tune guitar. But it is as relaxing as a moldering-around-the-edges plant or crispy lawn, which is soothing because of the mere fact that it does not have an anxious army of white-shirted staff hovering over it.

We watch my father swim. Sort of.

My father is so old, he moves with almost Tai Chi slowness, like a prehistoric brown lizard. To us, he appears as but a single leathery brown arm rising and dropping, above and below the waves, which are wine-dark in the sunset. He rises and drops, rises and drops, breathes in and exhales, breathes in and exhales.

Grunting, he emerges from the waves, his black ladies' underpants like a wrinkled second skin about his boney hips.

A cry goes up from the circle.

Tecate beers rise, in salutation.

"Dr. Loh!"

He looks at the group in pleasure, and almost surprise, so focused was he on the arduous matter of his nightly swim, or at least his nightly flop, in the placid waters.

My father lifts a sinewy arm, yells out a throaty greeting.

"Hey!" he exclaims.

"Mr. Loh!" the surfers yell out, in camaraderie. "The Naked Handstand Man! How was your swim?"

"Oh, very nice," he replies. "No current today!"

"Yeah, the water was mellow. How about a beer?"

"Oh no," he replies. "I'll just take a sip of Cindy's."

Cindy is a somewhat blowsy fortyish frost-'n'-tip blonde with light pink lipstick. She raises meaty, welcoming arms. "Come sit here next to me, Dr. Loh."

"Soy beans?"

Proferring a Tupperware of soy beans is . . . my ex-boyfriend Bruce.

Bruce . . . the fourth boarder.

Bruce, the mystery man who now . . . lives in my room.

Over the decades, I've tried to introduce Bruce to so many of my single girlfriends. How wrong I was. It turns out, the soul mate who was waiting for him all along was . . . my dad.

Bruce's $450 a month includes, aside from my own tattered childhood bedroom, use of this private beach club, and of Malibu West's private tennis courts!

I'm glad at least somebody found their Mr. Darcy! The man with Malibu land!

It's funny, really . . .

And suddenly I hear myself murmuring to Mike, "You know what? I just realized something quite wonderful, quite relieving."

"What?" he says.

"I realized I don't hate white people."

"That's a good thing, because I am rather pale, as are your two daughters."

"I realize I don't hate any people."

"Smoked fish," he asks, opening the cooler.

I take a bite.

It is so moist and fleshy and sweet.

"Oh my God," I say.

"Fluffy are my pancakes," he says.

All around us, the surfers' wet suits flap on the fence, like immigrant laundry, or Tibetan prayer flags, or . . . Well, like Malibu surfers' wet suits.

And I realize, in my forties, I have had my exotic adventure.

As my father strips off his "swimsuit" to change into his pants, his brief nudity draws a chorus of approval, and indeed of marvel, from the throng.

"Go, Mr. Loh!" everyone yells.

"Your dad is so amazing," Cindy says, a little tearfully. "My dad would never have been so free."

"I've seen your dad do naked handstands since I was five," says another surf dude.

"I grew up with him."

So I realize, for many, my father IS, with his ball-flying nudity, a kind of spiritually freeing Paolo the Swordfisherman.

And I realize that I have lived my own *28 Beads.*

Without leaving my city, I have belly-danced with giant Bedouin women, jumped on trampolines with Chihuahuas, consorted with the Virgin of Guadalupe.

I have had the most exotic and life-changing adventure right here in town.

To our right is Broad Beach, of multimillion-dollar glass castles . . . no one is in.

No one lives there, called away with the pressing business of making money.

But here we sit on the beach.

Malibu's oldest residents. The VW van drivers. The perennials. The natives. The beach bums. The fixtures. The originals.

But this doesn't matter anymore.

There is no ocean of money before me—it is merely an ocean.

Los Angeles is merely land.

California is only a coast.

And finally, there are no castes or classes or divisions but only souls, some lost, some found, all trying to spawn up whatever river they are swimming. Trying to yellow-highlight, to MapQuest their way through the ever-shifting rapids.

It is a vast nirvanic vision, and only now, after this journey, do I finally feel large enough to contain it.

I lie back on my beach towel, a massive pulsing letter—an

omega—with my children on each side, my husband to my left, father to my right, in a ring that is my community, in the circle that is my city, in the heart that is my world.

Up above me, circling high up in the sky, higher and higher . . .

Birds.

12
Julie Andrews

I am impervious to the artificial cultural offerings that are supposed to give a stab of sentimental comfort to women of my own flabby upper-armed age. These include but are not limited to:

The rose-covered CDs of lite tenor opera classics

Surprise baskets of teddy bears and lotion

Ladies Only! night at Harrah's casinos

Six-ounce low-fat yogurt cups with decadent carob-like flavor sensuously *mixed in*

The glistening torso of Matthew McConaughey erupting out of a swimming pool as he targets us with a peppy "finger gun"

Then one day I flop open my newspaper's *Weekend Calendar* with its grim march of weekend listings and see something that makes me stop. And let me note that clearly some powerful, mysterious force beyond my control has drawn me to flop open the *L.A. Times Weekend Calendar* in the first place—

To begin with, its cover does indeed feature a laughing Matthew McConaughey erupting out of a swimming pool, and I fear hernia, because by my count Matthew McConaughey has been erupting out of swimming pools for so many decades, he must be as old as I feel, meaning about sixty-seven. I fear that right after that erupting-out-of-the-swimming-pool photo was taken, Matthew McConaughey immediately bent over in a cramp screaming, and that the series of full-color follow-up photos inside would be various shots of Matthew McConaughey lying in fetal position by the swimming pool, among knocked-over photography equipment, clutching his hamstring in his tiny white shorts, and howling.

If so, it would be the most interesting thing ever published in *L.A. Times Weekend,* which for years has been a notorious literary wasteland. (A wasteland in the T. S. Eliot sense in that it is a hideous entertainment-listing combination of both *The Wasteland* and *Cats.*) Clearly, as the weeks, months, years, and decades have ground on, the editors have fallen into a rut of quiet desperation, resulting in a kind of walled-off *Grey Gardens*–like paranoia about publishing anything that is NOT cheerful and NOT about the weekend! So all the articles go: "It's the weekend! What do you do on the weekend? Is there special, soft R&B music you play on the weekend? Why is it we feel so moved to barbecue on the weekend? Is there a delectable carob-like dessert you particularly savor on the weekend? What is your favorite day of the weekend? Favorite time of the weekend? Favorite moment? What is your favorite alternative spelling of *weekend*? Weekynd? Weakend? Wekeynd? Weikïynddh?"

And now come the Q&A's where Los Angeles celebrities are frantically interviewed about the weekend. They are very short—never more than thirty-seven words—in case foundering readers will get confused and lose the thread OF . . . The Weekend. *Knight Rider* is coming out with its eighty-ninth anniversary collector's edition

DVD, so there, capsized by the side of another pool, clutching his hamstring, is David Hasselhoff. "David Hasselhoff, do you like to BBQ on the weekend? Do you have a favorite dessert you savor on the weekend? Do you have a favorite song about the weekend? Is there something special about LOS ANGELES weekends? Provocative question: Have you ever weekended . . . in San Diego?"

And, clutching his hamstring, David Hasselhoff will grudgingly admit, "I like to barbecue on the weekend. I suppose I'm not one to turn away a carob-like dessert on the weekend . . ." And then he'll gradually fly into a rage. "I really have no idea about the weekend. Fuck off about the weekend. You're like some kind of freak of the weekend. Fuck off!"

Paging through this sorry end to an old-growth forest, this papering of the city's litter boxes, however . . .

That's when I see her.

Ageless, timeless, untouchable.

Julie Andrews.

Ringed off—protected from the riffraff—by the ornate borders of her own perfect ad.

Perfectly coiffed.

Perfectly cool, amid the hamstring-clutching debacle that has become modern civilization.

I see Julie Andrews and an urgent bell, inside me, goes off.

For me, Julie Andrews is not a celebrity, not an entertainer, not an actor, and possibly not even a person.

Julie Andrews is a force.

A wind.

A feeling.

An ache.

A vibration.

To say that for the past forty years Julie Andrews and I have had an extremely close personal relationship is a wretched understatement. When I drive over a hill and a vista of emerald-green valleys suddenly drops opens before me and the mad, shocking, bittersweet beauty of the world hits me like shock plugs to the chest, causing a song to spontaneously lift out of me like a soaring lark? That is Julie Andrews. I carry Julie Andrews internally, like an organ. Within my torso I have a heart, liver, lungs, and a Julie Andrews. On the back my driver's license, I signed a thing where in case of a car accident, they can transplant, to any young teen or old person who may be in need of it . . . my Julie Andrews.

My personal Julie Andrews is not so much the *Sound of Music* Julie Andrews. Yes, I've seen *The Sound of Music* more than a hundred times, but for my taste, that is the more corporate Julie Andrews. And when she comes back from her honeymoon with Captain Von Trapp in that telltale gold suit, it's clear she has a life now, and adult responsibilities, and dwells no more in the magical realm.

No, the moment I first really CONNECTED with Julie Andrews—when she leaned out of the movie screen and literally REACHED OUT to me—was in *Mary Poppins*. I was five. I remember the moment as though it were yesterday. Julie Andrews was singing to that bird in the mirror, her reflection sang back to her, and all at once, in a moment, Julie Andrews turned her head over her shoulder and shot me this sudden wry look . . . ! It was over in an instant. None of the other children watching saw it. It was a look just for me. I was the only child *with a heart and eyes OPEN enough to understand.*

And all at once—in that quick, humorous, frank look—I saw into the complexity of Mary Poppins's world. That she enjoys being Mary Poppins, she's a little bored with being Mary Poppins, but she knows the entire planet needs her to BE Mary Poppins, and so, while finding the job of Mary Poppins to be a little repetitive, she does always freshly thrill to her outrageous competence—the snapping of the fingers, the leaping of the clothes back into their drawers, the jig-like restacking of the blocks . . .

Julie Andrews/Mary Poppins can also be pretty saucy. She never vies or pleads for attention, but when, on a London rooftop, chimney sweeps beg and plead and press her to join them in their great chimney-sweep dance of kicking and leaping and self-slapping . . . of course, she is an effortless virtuoso, blows the roof off the place.

How I marveled over this because as a child, of course, I was the exact opposite. I would arduously battle to gain some narrow edge, some sliver, some narrow crescent-moon-shaped miniscus of the spotlight. I remember my deepest, most painful wish was to be in our kindergarten *Winnie the Pooh* play. I thrilled at the prospect of playing any of the roles: Pooh . . . Christopher Robin . . . Tigger . . . Piglet . . . Eeyore . . . Kanga . . . Roo . . . I knew all the lines, I chanted them on the schoolbus in preparation for the audition . . . in a room that I can still picture—as I can the audition spot, that mystical opening between pushed-back desks at the front of the classroom, the slightly worn spot on the beige linoleum floor that I giddily bound onto. I entered that space, I sang my three lines, the teachers politely smiled and applauded and pushed up their glasses to make notes.

And when the roles were announced, my name was not called. I was stunned. I suggested to my teacher, Mrs. Thompson, that if there were too many children, perhaps she and Mrs. Anderson could bend the rules a little and make up an animal, some obscure forest character no one had heard of—"Tiglet," say—so even if I had no lines in the play, I could at least have a name.

But no, come the play, there I sat on the sidelines with all the other Nobodies . . . in no distinct, special costume at all but my regular old black ballet leotard, in some strange mismatched ears my mother stitched for me on her sewing machine that resembled those of no recognizable animal.

It seemed, in my years of school life, some variation of this template would be repeated again and again. The humiliations, the disappointments, the cuttings . . . You would be herded like cattle into the slaughterhouse into a frighteningly lit junior-high-school locker room, given a swimsuit color-coded for SIZE (so instead of skinny orange or svelte green or even plumpish red, you were indelibly marked with whale-like blue), and now you were standing on a small platform at the edge of a vast, echoing Olympian pool . . . one hundred beady eyes on you in a terrifying unwanted spotlight, the coach shouting at you to dive one thousand feet down into the icy bottomless blue, and you would be so panicked, you would suddenly let loose a juicy nervous fart that would echo echo echo echo.

Which would NEVER OCCUR on Planet Julie Andrews. If, sitting up on that cloud, she saw such a scene unfolding, she would sweep down and forbid it. Spit spot! She'd drain all the water out of the pool. Snap fingers and my heckling teen peers would be turned to carousel horses. Pop open her umbrella and waltzing carousel music would begin, and pink cake would arrive . . . for my birthday party!

And now, some four decades later, my own six-year-old daughter has become infected with the Julie Andrews virus. Already she has seen *Mary Poppins* perhaps twelve, fifteen times. What with the colorful, perfectly preserved wide-screen DVD version, the virus has traveled to the next generation.

(I suppose I only have myself to blame. A visiting mother recently asked why I appear to allow my children to watch approximately twenty-nine hours of television a day. And I replied, in surprise, "That's not television. That's Julie Andrews!" Or, alternatively, "That's not television. That's *The Aristocats*!" For me, *The Aristocats* is art, possibly a more important experience for young people than four—or, as in my case, ten—years of college.)

When Hannah gets one look at the Julie-Andrews-at-the-book-festival ad I've clipped and pinned to my office corkboard . . .

"Mary Poppins!" she exhales. She taps the photo with her small hand. "Mary Poppins!"

And that's it.

While I myself might not have attempted to locate the children's stage in the northwest quadrant of the Target/Home Depot plaza in the middle of the vast 150,000-person *L.A. Times* Book Festival, for my daughter . . . ?

We were going to do it.

The sun was shining in Los Angeles, there was a joyous lark rising within us, Hannah and I clutched each other's hands because the dream was alive, hers and mine . . .

Julie Andrews!

Because I was a bit flummoxed over the colored, many-planed map to the Target/Home Depot/Staples/Bed Bath & Beyond plaza, which seems to fold out to a size of about twenty square feet, the plan was to get to UCLA on Sunday morning at least an hour early so we could even FIND Julie Andrews.

But of course, hampered by my two actual small children, and their confusion of little shoes and little skirts and little socks . . . which had to be color-coordinated exactly, as they were to be seen by Mary Poppins, who would probably, if they were mismatched, correct them . . . And with me, the harried mother, very much lacking Mary Poppins's crisp organization and flair, our family arrives at UCLA . . . merely ON TIME.

And when, after much confusion, we arrive at what turns out to be the Julie Andrews stage, I am struck with horror.

Certainly it was unrealistic to expect Julie Andrews to nestle coolly on a comfy Victorian chair while Hannah and I, and perhaps a handful of other children, sat patiently at her feet, gathered around what I knew would be Julie Andrews's tastefully fabulous shoes. Shoes that didn't draw attention, but when you looked closely at them, were discreetly fabulous.

And yet neither did I expect this—this Cecil B. DeMille–like vision, this vast, echoing Valley of Julie Andrews. In that moment, I see my fatal and naive miscalculation. Julie Andrews is not just my personal friend. Julie Andrews does not belong to me alone . . .

Oh no, I see myself and my naked Julie Andrews rabidity reflected in the eager faces of approximately ten thousand other premenopausal forty-something mothers. Flanked by their own children, their own demonspawn clutching their own Mary Poppins videos—which are identical to the wide-screen collector's edition we have—the mothers jostle one another with their identical-to-mine EZ-cut khakis, and T-shirts and tote bags bearing the logos of all the proper classical music and public radio stations that Mary Poppins would expect us to have at age forty. The mood is tense as we accidentally—or is it?—bang our healthy Mary Poppins–approved bottles of water and tubes of SPF-60 sunscreen against one another—

I see, with this throng of ten thousand competing rabid mothers, that even getting within shouting distance of that Target Julie Andrews stage is going to be ugly. Not only did these Julie Andrews–mad mothers get here early, they were clearly privy to the hidden capitalistic code that gets a human being close to Julie Andrews. The complicated passes from radio stations, the secret Internet clickings at all those hideous timed five-minute intervals . . . Or perhaps it was their much-better-than-ours airline miles that got them within a hundred feet of the stage, or they used their Platinum American Express cards, or they turned in their courtside Lakers seats . . . They parsed all the complicated bar codes of Western civilization, which, if punctured from a forty-five-degree angle just so, will magically open.

Fortunately, though, Brenda is here. All business and cinnamon Dentyne, she has staked out . . . the tree behind the sound mixer. If I perch Hannah on the top bar of the metal security fence, through a Y of tree branches . . . yes!

We can see Her head! We can see Her head!

We can see that Julie Andrews is wearing a white pantsuit!

She raises an arm!

She speaks!

She says, in her lilting, mellifluous, 100 percent real Julie Andrews voice, "Good afternoon, everyone!"

All at once, as though TORN from our ten thousand–plus throats, a howling scream rises!

And rises!

And rises!

We are Romans in a coliseum. It's almost scary, a little gladiatorial, because we are not just ordinary, schvitzing forty-something women, we are Julie Andrews–mad mothers with our Julie Andrews–mad children . . . The estrogen supernova is a dark whorling eye you could probably see from outer space . . . From where Julie Andrews may well wish she were sitting on a cloud and observing us—

Julie Andrews puts one perfect white sleeve up again—

We shush.

Julie Andrews mentions her latest book, *The Great American Mousical*—

We scream again—

She could mention anything.

A Julie Andrews clog—

A Julie Andrews *chapeau*—

A Julie Andrews low-fat Havarti—

And we would scream and buy it.

And now what happens is almost . . . too painful to relate.

It is perhaps the most painful of all the painful childhood moments I have previously tried—and failed—to shield my daughter from.

The under-attended birthday parties, on those weird cursed week-ends when at the last moment everyone suddenly gets sick . . . The face falling. "Perhaps James is coming? Kristy?" No, they are not.

The first morning Hannah rode the school bus. It had been her idea. She flew to the bus stop that morning in such excitement. While waiting in the semidarkness, she danced on the sidewalk, in her white-and-pink-striped sweater, a bit too jaunty, chattering confidently to all the older kids. These included her assigned school bus buddy, a third-grade girl named Rae, with a cloud of light brown hair, Princess Jasmine backpack, and a sweet, kind face. A face that went into a dumbfounded stare when the two of them stumbled onto the crowded school bus and there was only space for Rae to sit down, not Hannah . . .

And to my terror, I saw the white-and-pink-striped sweater . . . continue on down the aisle, deeper and deeper into the bus! I saw Hannah's very being crumple under her too-large backpack, her face stretch into a frightened, surprised wail of tears, and as she stumbled into the bowels of the back of the bus amongst impassive, iPod-wearing older teens . . .

I jumped into my car and screamed after the bus, the roots of my hair on fire for the entire 12.5-minute ride. While screaming along behind the bus, I dialed Kaitlin on my cell, chanting, "Remind me again why I should not pull next to that school bus at a stoplight, take out a tire iron, break the glass, and pull Hannah out of there. I vaguely sense there is a reason I should not do this, but I can't quite remember why."

Or there are the endless pill bugs and ladybugs that Hannah finds among the plants and leaves in the garden. Insects my daughter lovingly hugs to her breast . . . even as she is slowly suffocating them. With loving care, and such alertness her fingers tremble, Hannah fashions cunning little homes for her pets, adding water, and delicious leaves so they will be cozy. In slow motion I am forced to watch as, her face shining, her voice rising and falling in cadences of hope, Hannah describes all the happy plans she has for her and "Pilly," how they will wake up together each morning, the sights they'll see, the picnics they'll have . . . Even as I can see "Pilly" frantically trying to clamber up the slippery sides of his Dixie Cup deathtrap with too large a plop of water in the bottom, begging for air, legs flailing . . . What will be in an hour the caved-out defeat of my daughter's dreams, her crushed heart.

No no no no no no.

More painful than any of these things is the event that occurs now.

When Julie Andrews says . . . she will take live questions now FROM THE CHILDREN.

And all over the—the—the—southeast northwestern quadrant . . . the vast, rolling acreage . . . of the UCLA campus . . . Hopeful little hands go up!

I remind you that, in the leafy valley directly in front of the giant oak tree we're standing behind, the tree whose upper Y of branches frames Julie Andrews's coiffed head—which for us is about as big as a Tic Tac—we can't see Julie Andrews's body, only her head—

Who will GET to ask a question? Well, in that leafy valley that opens beyond, you can vaguely make out these ant-like figures who are the members of some kind of dreadfully perky young Target and Barnes & Noble youth team—

Which is to say they are pimply corporate summer job twenty-somethings with no sense of history, of fairness, of literary judgment . . . In this hideous, horrendous, nonmagical world we live in, these minimum-wage Target intern hooligans don't know from nineteenth-century London or pieces of letters that magically fly up through chimneys or the splaying legs of Dick Van Dyke (and how Bert would play, elbows flying, on his many clattering instruments in the park, and how no one would give him money, not even the copper, not even a *tuppence*)—

Yes, it is these pockmarked, white polo–shirted young people who now laconically thread, without any particular plan or focus, their faces entirely relaxed and unconcerned, each holding what appears to be a tiny, Mousical-sized mike, through the vast valley beyond the giant tree that is blocking our view of the Julie Andrews stage.

Yea, they are picking their way only through the close-to-the-stage families—! The organized ones, camped splendidly out in their matching beach chairs, with their coordinated visors, tennies, and water bottles—

As if to say, "Ooh, look at US! We arrived at the Target Children's stage at dawn! We breakfasted on power bars, then all together, in perfect tandem, legs pumping in unison, we had a family run!"

How helpless I am, in the wide sea of this world, to help my family, my tiny, bobbing lifeboat of a family!

"Hannah," I hiss. "Put your hand down."

She ignores me. The hand goes higher, held aloft in the purity of her perfect faith.

Because, you see, Hannah knows she is . . . a child. Mary Poppins has asked for questions from . . . the children. So Hannah is absolutely confident that if she quietly waits her turn, Mary Poppins will soon get to her, because that is the way things worked in Mary Poppins's perfectly ordered universe.

"Honey—!" I plead.

"I want to ASK Mary Poppins," she says simply, "how do you do your magic?"

Ai. My own late mother was a woman who would have tucked her daughter under her arm like a football, scissor-kicked over the fence, trampled ten, twenty, fifty families if needed, grabbed the Mousical-sized mike from one of the expressionless Target employees—the Nobodies—and she would have torn an answer from Julie Andrews if it was the last thing she did. Such was the incredible power my mother sucked, at the end of the day, from her one illicit cigarette.

But, a nonsmoker, I feel helpless, rooted to the ground. There would only be futility, only embarrassment . . . Which I could well soldier through except that then at the end Hannah would be sitting there, her face frozen in a silent, disbelieving wail.

"Put your hand down," I hiss.

Hannah knits her brow together, sticks her hand higher.

"No."

I read her like I read myself. I know she thinks her mother is getting in the way. Her mother doesn't believe in Mary Poppins's magic, very much like how parents were in the movie. Her mother doesn't understand! Her mother is wrong.

Because, of course, Mary Poppins has also sung to the bird and looked back at herself in the mirror and then turned to Hannah and given her the special Mary Poppins look that is Hannah's alone, a look that has nothing to do with her mother or any of these people . . .

And I do have to honor at least that idea, I suppose.

So I whisper to Hannah that another way for her to ask Mary Poppins her question is after the reading, at the official Julie Andrews "signing tent." To beat the system, we leave the reading right then and there, we leave while the tiny Tic Tac–sized head of Julie Andrews is still talking.

But I instantly see that there is another five hundred-person throng already waiting in line, snaking out over two city blocks, before the *Julie Andrews signing tent* . . . One mother, she and her two daughters in matching Costco sunbrella hats, says the three of them have been waiting in line already for four hours. The security guard dispassionately estimates that Julie Andrews will barely get through signing the first one hundred books, then they will cut the signing off and we will have waited, ninety minutes, for nothing.

Plus . . .

Five-year-olds do ask for many things, in a day. Candy, an ice cream . . . a thousand dollars' worth of American Girl dolls, complete with matching outfits and cutlery sets and jewelry.

(Indeed, after all that American Girl begging, a relative did finally take pity and send us two American Girl dolls. The day they arrived, I read my two daughters the elaborate, several-page-long care instructions, which sadly we could never find again. Swept away by the romance of it, Hannah gave her American Girl what she imagined was the fancy otherworldly name of "Sheisana," or sometimes "Sheislana." Which she may have come up with due to her mother's bad habit of yelling the poop-based Germanic "Sheise!" in traffic. Nor was it a good sign when Sheislana's historically accurate jacket appeared on the back of a Chuck E. Cheese monkey. But probably the nadir came when The Squid drew an indelible blue Bic pen mustache on the upper lip of Sheislana . . . the family heirloom we were planning to pawn for her college education. I'm pretty sure there will soon be a new American Girl doll who comes with a tiny scroll containing a moving narrative of her heroic and urgent campaign to escape from the clutches of our family—"Sheislana" starring in *Escape from Van Nuys*!)

I tell Hannah, "We will wait, but there is almost no chance we will get to meet . . . Mary Poppins."

"I want to wait, anyway," Hannah repeats, in the calm knowledge that she is standing with an unmagical idiot.

And I suppose one must forge forward, I don't even remember why anymore. That is the metaphor for what mothers do. Although it is HOPELESS, I will wait in line, for ninety minutes of poor-quality time, with my daughter.

Failure is probable, death certain.

So at the Barnes & Noble tent, among the Gifted Children's books and the Learn by Numbers and all the other crap . . . I purchase the only Julie Andrews book we could find in the clawed-over Target inventory . . . *The Last of the Really Great Whangdoodles.*

We take our place behind the *Dr. Zhivago*–style refugee mob.

We wait.

After five minutes, we move two inches forward. We wait again. In another twenty minutes, we may be able to enjoy the shade of a tree.

Hannah says nothing, her pert nose tilted optimistically ahead, toward Mary Poppins.

After another two minutes, she fidgets—just a tad.

I look down at our *Whangdoodles* book.

"Hannah, to pass the time, should I read this book . . . AS Julie Andrews?"

And it is a testament to her masked—if clearly slowly growing desperation—that Hannah curtly and unhappily nods. She absolutely LOATHES my doing an English accent, which I absolutely

LOVE. One of the greatest pleasures of being a parent is having an audience for my English accent while reading Captain Hook's lines in *Peter Pan,* which my children screamingly forbid, in the rare instances that they are awake when this moment occurs.

I open the book and begin, in my bad Julie Andrews accent.

" 'It was a crisp, sunny October afternoon and Benjamin, Thomas and Melinda Potter were visiting the Bramblewood Zoo . . .' "

And it is a testament to Julie Andrews's power that even though I am bent over my responseless daughter practically whispering and my Julie Andrews imitation is horrible—like secondhand Julie Andrews smoke—I'm actually starting to accumulate other children. They crowd forward in line and gather around us, glazed-eyed, practically shoving at one another. These five-year-olds are wordless and big-eyed, like Children of the Corn. Children of the Julie Andrews Corn.

And I realize I simply can't keep this up for ninety minutes.

Mike, who passes by, carrying Number Two over to the Barney tent, cheerfully tosses out the info that on the other end of the quad, through the trees, you can see two black town cars, and what do you know? A giant stretch limo. With a big TARGET logo on it. Target logo? Target stage? Julie Andrews? Oh yes . . .

Mike has a sixth sense for these things, having now toured copiously with Bette Midler. He knows where the divas are kept.

I murmur to Hannah that we are going to take "the shortcut." I take her by the arm and drag her out of line. By now she willingly complies. Her small body, in her coordinated blue-and-white pleated faux–Jane Banks outfit, is starting to droop in the sun.

We settle against the wall that's about twelve feet from the Target stretch limo, where two security men are waiting, on walkie-talkies.

"Well!" I exclaim loudly and airily, for their benefit. "Let's just rest HERE, honey, and look at our map!" Then I turn to Hannah and whisper, right into her ear, that "Mary Poppins may soon be getting into *that car.*"

Yes, we are going to waylay Julie Andrews at her limo!

After Julie Andrews has appeared before a gladiator-stadium-sized crowd, signed more than a hundred books for over an hour, and now, approaching the final blessed moment of escaping into her air-conditioned limo . . .

One more sweaty mother and child will startlingly pop out of the bushes!

Although . . .

Hm . . .

While I do not brook anything bad ever being said about Julie Andrews . . . If truth be told, a Book Festival worker had let slip that, what with five hundred people in line, Julie Andrews had very possibly been feeling . . . just a little cranky.

And now I'm thinking, that's all we need for the end of a magical afternoon—to waylay Mary Poppins at her escape car, causing her to lash out . . .

And then bend over double clutching her hamstring, David Hasselhoff–like . . .

"Do I barbecue over the weekend? Fuck you! Leave me alone! And for your family, a spoonful of *shit*!"

"Hannah," I say, "there is a good possibility we . . . won't get to meet Mary Poppins. Today."

Hannah repeats, with slightly less conviction, but still very stubbornly: "I just want to know how she does her magic."

I take a deep breath.

And I tear off the Band-Aid.

I tell her that *Mary Poppins* is just a movie. Julie Andrews is just an actress. An actress who may be kind of tired. "You know when I yell 'Sheise!' or 'Dmitri Sheistakovich!' in traffic and you say, 'Mommy, I'm sorry you're having a bad-traffic day'? It's like that."

At the juxtaposition of Mary Poppins and traffic . . . Suddenly Hannah's face changes into an expression that's less half sickened puppy love and slightly more thoughtful, and knowing.

Mary Poppins and traffic—Hannah can tell that L.A. traffic may well be the one thing that throws Mary Poppins.

What a poor mother I am—essentially powerless, negotiating, apologizing, vacillating . . .

"And the magic Mary Poppins does isn't real. They do it . . . using a movie camera— Hey! Maybe we can have you do her magic on film, with your dad's video camera!"

Hannah's face goes into a subtle "Aha" . . .

And to seal the deal I throw in a three-dollar frozen lemonade and a five-dollar chocolate Popsicle.

She immediately accepts, with surprisingly little fanfair.

Perfectly content with the sugar. Just a bucketful of sugar.

And I realize . . .

We have to make our own inner Julie Andrews. We have to be our own Julie Andrews. Because there's simply not enough Julie to go around.

As we enjoy our treasure trove of frozen sugar, licking delicious ice crystals of lemon off our lips on a hot spring day, I do remember that Hannah later told her school bus story to her little sister, as a tale of grand triumph. In the revisionist history of it, facing the rows of big kids, she was incredibly bold, brave, even cocky!

I remember that when "Pilly" the pill bug died, Hannah cried for about a minute . . . and then excitedly set herself to the task of planning Pilly's funeral. Kids love a pet burial. Complete with the moldy period shoe of an American Girl doll.

And at home, in our tattered bungalow, we do make a Mary Poppins–like video where, when we play it in reverse, all the toys magically jump into Hannah's lap.

The video shows my daughter, in spite of all universal forces to the contrary, irrepressibly hopeful and toothsome and plucky.

She didn't see the research. She didn't peruse the statistics.

She didn't get the memo about giving up, as the world is hopeless.

She still dwells in the neighborhood of Mr. Rogers. She still believes in her dirty pink unicorn, and that a stranger is just a friend you haven't met. Rather than, well, a permanent and eternally unreachable stranger.

I realize I won't be able to protect her from all the world's hurts and disappointments.

But there is a chance she may survive them, anyway.

Like her mother before her, she will do what she will, however I try to control her destiny.

And then Hannah goes into the backyard, in her necklace and in her underpants, covered with mud and marker. In an activity that will definitely *not* get her into Harvard, she makes herself bracelets out of the golden rings that go around the tops of the Mason jars her father uses for canning tomatoes. And then, grinning like a small demon, she does a wild dance in the garden, her gold bracelets catching fire in the heat of the sun.

THE END

M.O.F.

Acknowledgments

I'd like to express thanks for the luxurious and prestigious writer's retreat in which most of this book was written: my brother Eugene's tiny laundry room. I'd like to thank Eugene's sticky-fingered, frequently-dropping-in children for their very interesting literary suggestions, and Elizabeth McCloud for her helpful ones.

Aside from thanking Sloan Harris (ICM) and Kristin Kiser (Crown), who deftly co-merchanted this tome, I believe it is always wise to thank one's friends in journalism up near the top, where they can be readily seen. Pen-wielders who added particular verve during the writing—and even living out—of this book included Caitlin "Stock Liquidatin'" Flanagan, Paul "The Velvet Hammer" Glickman, Al "Very Dry Martinis" Martinez, Allan "Prince Machiavelli" Mayer, Ben "The Puppetmaster" Schwarz, Tina (stet! stet!) Schwarz, Mindy "Getting onto the Next Page" Steinman, Liza Tucker (who has been bookmarked), fellow Hollywood Boulevard slacker Matt

Welch, and motorcycle-booted sisters in time of f&*(&*@#$! Amy Alkon and Emmanuelle Richard. Speaking of f&()@#$@#, those who provided laughs in times of trouble included Leonard Nimoy–angsting Susan Marder and Rich Ruttenberg, the very obscene Neil Gieleghem, the very frank Joe Frank, and KCRW's own (highly nontoxic) Harry Shearer, Wendy Mogel, and Michael Tolkin.

Speaking of possible lawsuits, for the record, apologies to any and all *L.A. Times* editors who have ever edited any Weekend sections involving Matthew McConaughey; Disney Hall does, in fact, offer some reasonably priced tickets; and, while I have not spoken to him recently, I am quite sure Ira Glass is NOT available to fly across the country and give foot baths for one's private-school silent auction. Too, the older I get, the more I become honestly appreciative of real-life figures who are a ready source of narrative color. These include Clive Barnes, Ruth Seymour, and my father and his wife, Alice, Dumpster divers extraordinaire. Good times, people—when all is said and done, good times!

And hey, before any of you crazy-ass type A parents go trying to Google "child development guru Baz Ligiero," know he is an invention, whose marvelous teach-a-five-year-old-square-root technique comes courtesy of CalTech alum Joe Cheng, and his (rights reserved!) "EZ Math." Shout-out too to 9DD Mark Afifi!

But these acknowledgments aren't long enough . . . let me wax on! (I think there are pages that would just otherwise sit blank here at the end of the book!) Anyway—! In all the marvelous wisdom I've accrued by this golden age I call the "back forties," I've come to see the importance—nay, the necessity—of jolly companions. Let me cite them now, so as to secure dinner reservations for the future. On the theatrical journey that was the *Mother on Fire* solo show, hearty pals included Deb Devine and (f&*(&(*kin!) Jay McAdams of 24th St. Theatre; flamboyantly bicoastal directors Bart DeLorenzo and David Schweizer; Frier McCollister (mixologist); Joe Witt (theatrical scarves); Modern Spirits Vodka (inventors of the wonderfully hallucinatory "Mother on Fire" cocktail); flamin' Ann Niemack; for theatrical conviviality in the past, Second Stage in New York and Woolly Mammoth in Washington D.C.; personal-crack-dealer-of-last-minute-house-seats-for-my-dad Ken Werther; Tatjana Loh and the Women's Building (madres inflamar?); and tireless public school mavens in pearls, those I call "the Joans of Pasadena" (Fauvre and Palmer).

Feel free to get up and make yourself a sandwich, if you need to. In the meantime, I will be personally going on to thank the very therapeutic Barbara Ponse, Barbara Campbell (COV), Ronda Berkley and Mel Green for the "stay 'n' dart," the No More Mr. Darcy contingent of Scripps College, Julian "Two Hands" Fleischer, Dan Akst for being himself, Marla Benjamin for pot roast and laughs, Donna Dees for her literary haircut, Vicki Wood for trueness in friendship, Cassandra Clark and Sam Dunn just because, Adrienne Sharp—who has the rare distinction of having given me useful tips on both writing AND breast-feeding, and Beverly and Marc Olevin, who, while they have never provided actual breast-feeding help, have supplied so many other kinds. (PS: Rock on, Suzie Kane.)

And hey—how 'bout a fond shout to friends in public school and Bohemian income Cloggin' Kiffin Lunsford and Kerry Madden, and to friends in Third World humor and Title One glamour (not to mention carpooling): Moira Quirk and Michael Rayner. I must be pretty tired to require all this help, but I do.

Just to cover my bases, I always enjoy thanking Henry Alford. And I think it's never karmically wise not to thank John Rechy.

I know there may be readers now experiencing a sudden, gnawing anxiety that they won't be thanked when everyone else on the planet clearly has. Sadly, though, we are winding to our conclusion, citing friends met in the wild and woolly world of the Los Angeles public schools. Adding, to the fire, their own unique styles of Duraflame Colorlogs have been Steve ("icy beverages") Barr and David Tokovsky, Jefferson Crain, Candy Fernandez-Ghoneim, Suzanne Blake, and Rebecca Kick-Ass Constantino. Those wishing for a true

Acknowledgments

vision of grace should visit the West Valley Special Education School in Van Nuys, and I always light a loving candle for Saturn Elementary. Honorary Mothers on Fire (we forgive them for being men) include Scott Folsom, Bill Ring, Bob Sipchen, and Hylan "Tee" Hubbard (Mother on Fire of color). Hey, even the folks of greatschools.net turned out less scary than feared: a gracious tip of the hat to Marion Wilde, and to greatschools.net founder Bill Jackson, who gamely agreed (in the moment) to come onstage to help me perform *Mother on Fire* in San Francisco.

Finally—and this is a compliment, they will understand—if I were sent to hell, these are the companions I would take with me . . . Keep it flamin', my Mother on Fire sistahs (and brothahs) from the Cool Baby group and beyond . . . Madames Tanya Anton, Dorit Dowler-Guerrero, Martha Little, Christie "Martinis and Magnets" Mellor, Susan Nickerson, Joanne Palmer, the mothers of PART (including Kelly Kane, Forouzan Faridian, Marie Murphy), the parents of PEN (including Chris Brandow and Kristin Maschka), Erika Schickel, Mara and Mark Schoner, Jody Shipper, Maria von Hartz, Spike Dolomite Ward, Ann Wexler, Anji Williams, Angel Zobel-Rodriguez . . . and a last huzzah to LAUSD mom and all-around gem Julia Sweeney (Not afraid to feed us: Jake at Mao's Kitchen)!

And in conclusion (picture very tiny letters now rolling, miniature stagecoach disappearing over the horizon), a big smackeroo to Mike Miller, Man of Steel to my Mother on Fire to my girls, and to my favorite South Dakotan mother-in-law Bernice . . .

And one last bursting-fireworks, raspberry-to-the-man, in loving memory of a true friend and a good writer, she flames forever on the Internet, Cathy Seipp.

The end!

About the Author

Sandra Tsing Loh is a writer/performer whose solo shows include *Mother on Fire* (which ran for seven months in Los Angeles at 24th St. Theatre), *Sugar Plum Fairy, I Worry,* and *Aliens in America* and *Bad Sex with Bud Kemp,* which both premiered off-Broadway at Second Stage.

She has been a regular commentator on NPR's *Morning Edition* and on Ira Glass's *This American Life.* Currently, KPCC (89.3 FM in Los Angeles) broadcasts her daily segment, "The Loh Down on Science," and her weekly segment, "The Loh Life." American Public Media's *Marketplace* broadcasts her monthly segment, "The Loh Down." She is a contributing editor for *The Atlantic Monthly* and was twice a finalist for the National Magazine Award.

Her books include *A Year in Van Nuys; Aliens in America; Depth Takes a Holiday: Essays from Lesser Los Angeles;* and a novel, *If You Lived Here, You'd Be Home by Now.*

Visit her Web site at sandratsingloh.com.